THE
ASIAN
MIND
GAME

THE
ASIAN
MIND
GAME

Chin-ning Chu

UNLOCKING
THE
HIDDEN
AGENDA
OF THE
ASIAN
BUSINESS
CULTURE—
A
WESTERNER'S
SURVIVAL
MANUAL

RAWSON ASSOCIATES
NEW YORK

COLLIER MACMILLAN CANADA
TORONTO

MAXWELL MACMILLAN
INTERNATIONAL
NEW YORK   OXFORD
SINGAPORE   SYDNEY

Rawson Associates
Macmillan Publishing Company
866 Third Avenue
New York, NY 10022

Collier Macmillan Canada, Inc.
1200 Eglinton Avenue East
Suite 200
Don Mills, Ontario M3C 3N1

Library of Congress Cataloging-in-Publication Data

Chu, Chin-ning.
    The Asian mind game : unlocking the hidden agenda of the Asian
  business culture : a westerner's survival manual / Chin-ning Chu.
    Expanded and rev. ed. of: The Chinese mind game. 1st ed. Beaverton, OR:
  AMC Pub., c1988.
    Includes index.
    ISBN 0-89256-352-4
    1. Negotiation in business.   2. Intercultural communication.
  3. National characteristics, Chinese.   4. National characteristics,
  Japanese.   5. National characteristics, Korean.   I. Chu, Chin-ning.
  Chinese mind game.   II. Title.
  HD58.6.C474   1990
  658.8'48'0951—dc20   90-46045
                                                           CIP

A small portion of this book in a different form appeared in *The Chinese Mind Game,* AMC Publishing, Copyright © 1988, by the same author.

Macmillan books are available at special discounts for bulk purchases for sales promotions, premiums, fund-raising, or educational use. For details, contact:

Special Sales Director
Macmillan Publishing Company
866 Third Avenue
New York, NY 10022

DESIGN: Stanley S. Drate / Folio Graphics Co. Inc.
Packaged by Rapid Transcript, a division of March Tenth, Inc.

10

Printed in the United States of America

To

*Gurumayi Chidvilasananda and the memory of
Swami Muktananda, Paramahansa Yogananda,
St. Francis of Assisi, and St. Teresa of Avila*

To the reader:

The orthography used in this book for transcription of Chinese words or names does not adhere to any particular consistent system. Rather, a combination of many different systems has been employed to express the Chinese words and names. In any given instance, the author has chosen the transcription that she considers will best convey meaning to her Western readers.

Contents

Part Two
THE ANT PEOPLE

Part Three
THE MATRIARCH

Part Four
THE SURVIVORS

Part Five
ENDGAME

Acknowledgments

Because of the frankly critical nature of the sections of this book dealing with modern Japan, many of my sources whose livelihoods are dependent on the goodwill of Japanese businesses or the Japanese government have requested anonymity. And because of the uncertainty of the political situation in mainland China, anonymity is always best. My thanks to the many Chinese, Japanese, Taiwanese, Koreans, and Asian-Americans who have shared their experiences with me. Although their names are not written here, I am nevertheless deeply indebted to them.

I am grateful to Eleanor Rawson, my publisher, for her vision and belief in the importance of this book, and her efforts in bringing it to publication.

A thousand thanks to Grace Shaw, my editor at Rawson Associates, for her patient guidance in shaping the final form of this book.

My deepest gratitude to Kurt Survance, my editorial advisor. Without his diligent support, it would not have been possible to complete this book.

My sincerest appreciation to Natasha Kern for her tireless efforts on behalf of this book.

I wish to thank Chen Wun-Yu, Shean-Tzong Tsai, Yong K. Kim, Jay Lee, Ruby Chow, Kyoko Okuno, Gayle Vrla, Lani Searl, James Clauser, and Roger Morgan for generously sharing their time and wisdom with me.

Last, my humblest gratitude to the Power that drives the Universe, for putting me in a time and place where I would be shaped by the many cultures of Asia.

PART  ONE

THE
MIND
GAME

■
———

1

Preparing
for the
Game

The telephone in my Beijing hotel room rang. It was the *Washington Post's* Beijing Bureau Chief, Daniel Southerland, asking if I could meet the following day with him and a Canadian businessman, whom we will call David Buyer. He told me Mr. Buyer had taken a beating on his first business foray into China. Knowing that I was in the city, Dan thought Mr. Buyer might want to talk to me about what had gone wrong. We met in the lounge of the hotel and found a quiet corner where we could speak freely.

David Buyer came from a Canadian family with a long-established reputation in the fur business. Four months earlier, Buyer had flown into China on a custom-fitted Boeing 747 with 3,200 live foxes. In exchange for the foxes and his technical assistance in setting up scientific breeding and feeding programs, he had expected to return to Canada with about a million dollars' profit. But things had not worked out that way.

Mr. Buyer was leaving on the next day's early flight bound for home. He would leave without his million dollars and without his foxes. Once at home he would close the books on a loss of about a half million dollars and would attempt to save his fox farm from foreclosure.

David Buyer's unfortunate adventure started in the summer of 1988. Months passed as he waited impatiently for the arrival of a Chinese delegation that was to inspect the foxes. Buyer thought that perhaps they didn't want to make such a long trip and were putting it off. The real problem, however, was the complicated passport and entry visa procedures they were dealing with.

Buyer was selling breeding stock to the Chinese, and he did not want to miss the fox breeding season. As the season neared, he grew more and more anxious. He was confident that his stock would pass the most rigorous inspection, so he notified the Chinese that he would fly the foxes to China. They could conclude the deal on his arrival. The Chinese voiced no objection to the idea. At the moment the jet lifted off with its noisy cargo, Mr. Buyer's deal was already dead, but he would not find that out for several months.

Shortly after Buyer arrived in China, the price of fox dropped on the world fur market. Since Buyer had 3,200 unsold and hungry foxes 10,000 miles from home, the Chinese used the market fluctuation as a pretext to renegotiate the contract. To put even more pressure on him, the Chinese charged with the care of the foxes deliberately starved them and crowded them into very small cages. Soon disease and mistreatment had killed 150 of Buyer's foxes.

When Buyer found out that the Chinese had started buying quantities of foxes from a breeder in Finland, he was ready to cut his losses. He sought out intermediaries who could break the impasse and put together a deal for him before all his foxes were dead. The intermediaries, of course, insisted on substantial payoffs. After extensive negotiation, the intermediaries managed to convince the original buyers to take 900 of the 3,200 foxes at the original price of $380 each, but these buyers would offer only $30 apiece for the remaining animals.

Eventually, the intermediaries were able to sell the remaining foxes by unofficial means at greatly reduced prices. But, in addition to cutting his prices drastically, to conclude the sale Buyer had to agree to sponsor a dozen children of various Chinese bureaucrats to be educated in Canada. Four years of college tuition and living expenses for each child was to come out of his pocket. But Buyer had learned the ways of the Chinese by now. He told them anything they wanted to hear so that he could unload his foxes and get out of there.

The evening we met, Mr. Buyer was carrying $200,000 in American currency sewn into the lining of his coat. The unofficial nature of the transactions his intermediaries had arranged precluded the usual avenues of transferring money out of China. In addition to the devastating financial loss he had suffered, he was also running a very grave risk of spending the rest of his life in a Chinese prison if airport security detected the cash.

Buyer had made a serious mistake in shipping the foxes without first receiving payment. But this was not his first or most serious mistake. It was not until my return to China in August 1989 that I found out what the real problem had been.

I decided to contact Mr. Zhang, the Chinese official who had originally arranged the deal with David Buyer. It took only a few moments' conversation with Mr. Zhang to find out what had happened. He was eager to express his anger with Mr. Buyer. Buyer's decision to fly the foxes to China instead of waiting for Zhang and his associates to come to him had robbed them of a trip to Canada to which they had looked forward for months. Foreign travel is the most prestigious and sought-after perk available to a Chinese official. They could not forgive Buyer for robbing them of their once-in-a-lifetime opportunity to visit the West. The disappointment completely dampened their enthusiasm for the entire project.

Mr. Buyer's story is an extreme example, but the lack of understanding that it illustrates is all too common. In my professional life as a representative for Western companies doing business in Asia, I am constantly frustrated by the inability of Eastern and Western minds to meet.

The great difference between Western and Asian languages is one obvious barrier to understanding. But language is not only how we express our thoughts, it is also how we create our thoughts. The underlying cause of misunderstanding is not language itself but how we think: Asians and Westerners think as differently as they speak.

I once heard Donald Frisbee, CEO and Chairman of PacifiCorp, say, "If I could just understand how the Asian thinks, I would know how to deal with him." Mr. Frisbee is much more perceptive than most Western businessmen in recognizing the difficulty. Many just assume that they understand, and simply don't want to be told otherwise. I once spent a long afternoon listening to a man who had thirty-five years of successful marketing experience in the United States. "Marketing is marketing," he told me. "I know my business. What could be different about marketing in Asia?"

Books have been written about doing business in Asia. Many are well researched and accurate in their description of how Asians conduct their business affairs, but none I have read has shed much light on why Asians conduct business as they do. Learning about an Asian businessman's actions without understanding his motivation will not greatly help a Westerner to conduct business successfully with him. It is essential to understand the underlying causes of the Asian person's actions. This book is about those underlying causes.

Strategic thinking is deeply ingrained in the Asian mind. Specific strategies to deal with all kinds of life situations have been developed, refined, and studied for thousands of years. If the Westerner does not make an attempt to understand something of the Asian mind, he will find it almost impossible to detect the web of complicated strategies that is woven about him by his Asian counterparts, and he will fall victim to them.

Like David Buyer, too often Westerners have paid dearly for their lack of understanding in dealing with Asians. Mr. Buyer was not a fool. He made an assumption about the Chinese delegation's reasons for delaying their visit to Canada. Within the frame of reference of a Western businessman, it was a good assumption, Mr. Buyer's mistake was that he did not question his belief that what was true for him was also true for the Chinese.

I am a Chinese woman. My family lived for many generations near the Yalu River in Manchuria. As boys, my father and his friends would pay the boatman a few small coins to ferry them across the Yalu to fight mock battles with the Korean boys on the farther shore. At that time, as today, the Yalu was the political boundary between Korea and Manchuria, but over the centuries the border had moved back and forth across the land. The culture of the region was a mixture of Chinese and Korean.

The Japanese had been a presence in Manchuria dating back to the late nineteenth century. In 1931, they officially annexed Manchuria as a Japanese territory. As a colonial power, the Japanese behave very differently from Western colonial powers. They do not simply seek to exploit the wealth and resources of their colonies, they also attempt to replace the native language and culture with Japanese language and culture. They try to instill in the conquered peoples a sense of pride and identity as Japanese subjects.

My parents were educated according to a Japanese curriculum by Japanese teachers in a school where only Japanese was spoken. They learned to speak fluent Japanese and absorbed a great deal of Japanese culture. My mother often passed as a Japanese national in order to obtain better treatment for her family than was accorded to most Chinese under the occupation. In 1949, my family left the mainland for Taiwan, where I was raised.

Taiwan, like Manchuria, had been a Japanese colony for the half-century prior to Japan's defeat in World War II. Throughout my girlhood, the schools retained their Japanese influence. When the teachers would get angry they would curse us in Japanese. It was not until I was an adult and had traveled extensively in Asia and the West that I came to understand how very Japanese my family was—and also how Korean.

The Chinese, Japanese, and Koreans share many common characteristics, but there are also marked differences between them. Westerners tend to see the similarities, but are unfamiliar with the differences. They tend to see them as Asians rather than Chinese, Japanese, and Koreans. It is the purpose of this book to give you an individual and personal sense of what it is to be a Chinese, a Japanese, and a Korean and to show how this affects dealings between Westerners and people of these nationalities. To do this, I must discuss the separate national characteristics.

It is always a little misleading to take traits that are individual in nature and apply them with broad strokes to a whole nation. If it is done at all, it must be done carefully, otherwise we descend into meaningless stereotyping. However, it is a useful way to discuss values and beliefs that are shared widely, if not universally, among the individuals who make up the nation. There is such a thing as a collective consciousness. There are such things as national characteristics. I am going to discuss them without intent to minimize the diversity that exists within each group and without intending to offend anyone.

The important thing about the generalizations I will make is not their literal truth, but that they are commonly accepted to be true by the very people who are being stereotyped. The Chinese especially have a penchant for analyzing the Chinese character in the form of a hypothetical "typical Chinese." The shortcomings of this character are often referred to as the "national disease," the virtues as the "national character."

I am not writing a scholarly study. I do not intend to cite statistics to back up every statement I make. I am dealing in common perceptions. When I state flatly that "Korean businessmen like to drink. They drink heavily and hold their liquor well," I am not going to refer to the latest study on per capita Korean alcohol consumption. Nor do I wish to be taken literally to mean that there are no abstemious or moderate Korean businessmen. What I mean is that if you stop a hundred people at random on the streets of Seoul, Beijing, and Tokyo and ask them, "Do Koreans drink?" eighty of them will laugh and say, "Like fish." In making statements like this, it is not my intent to attack the Korean character, but only to arm my Western readers with the common knowledge that any Asian would have: "If you are going to go glass-for-glass with your Korean host, you had better know what you're doing."

The Asian peoples will all agree that there are discernible

national characteristics that define the Chinese, the Koreans, and the Japanese. They will further agree on what those characteristics are. They differ on whether those accepted characteristics are virtues or vices, and their differences depend largely upon whether the characteristics are applied to them or to someone else.

To some racially sensitive Western readers, discussions of the characteristics of separate ethnic and national groups might seem to border on racism. The Asian concept of racism is very different from the Western concept. Concepts of racial superiority and inferiority have never been questioned as they have been in the West. There are strong feelings among the Chinese, Japanese, and Koreans on the subject of racial superiority, even though the peoples are very closely related from an evolutionary standpoint. In Asia the idea that one people is racially superior to another is almost universally acknowledged.

Asians do not have the same sensitivity to racial issues as do Americans. The issue is not as emotionally charged for them. Asians regard it as natural to feel that their race, their nation, their province, their city, and their family are better than yours. Westerners exhibit most of these same attitudes and refer to them in mildly pejorative terms such as "chauvinistic," "nationalistic," "provincial." But "racist" is a very ugly word in English, even though it often only expresses the common weakness of mankind to believe that "mine is better than yours."

The preoccupation with race is so acute in America that one cannot make reference to race at all for fear of giving offense. Henrietta Anne Klauser, author of *Writing on Both Sides of the Brain* (Harper & Row, 1987), told me of an excited call she got from her editor prior to the book's publication. The editor insisted on a sentence being rewritten because it contained a racially offensive word. This is the sentence: "I have a great respect for paper and I daily bless the Chinaman who invented it." The sentence the editor found acceptable was this: "I have a great respect for paper and I daily bless its Chinese inventor." To this Chinese woman, the first version expressed the personal affection that Mrs. Klauser felt for the Chinese. The sterilized version had lost the sensitive touch. It is very hard for an Asian to understand what the problem was with the original.

Ruby Chow, a retired long-time King County (Washington State) councilwoman, told me the following story:

In the early 1950's, Seattle's Chinatown was renamed "The International District." The reasons for the change are not completely clear. In recent years, there has been a movement to restore the name Chinatown. The restoration has been opposed by some members of the City Council. Norm Rice, when he was serving as a city councilman prior to his election as mayor, opposed the restoration of the name on the grounds that it was an insulting stereotype. Peter Woo, president of the Chong Wa Benevolent Association and a leader of the Chinese community in Seattle, stated publicly that he disagreed with Rice that it was an insulting stereotype.

Asian-born Chinese are proud to be Chinese and, in general, would not have a problem with the name Chinatown. Chinese-Americans who have been brought up with American attitudes about race would be more likely to be offended. Councilman Rice, with all the good intentions in the world, seemed to be bringing his perspective as a black American to bear on a problem that did not have the same seriousness for the people who should have been most offended.

Asians do not feel guilty about thinking in racial terms, but they do understand that Westerners, especially Americans, do. They will often use accusations of racism to disarm their Western opponents. The same Japanese politician who loudly imputes racist motives to American criticism of Japan himself believes implicitly that the Japanese are racially superior to Caucasians, and also to their Korean and Chinese neighbors. He would never admit these beliefs to a Westerner, but among Asians it is so commonplace to think in racial terms that they do not even bother with denial or guilt.

The purpose of this book is to help Westerners understand Asians from the inside out rather than from the outside in. To achieve this understanding, it is necessary for you, the reader, to surrender all preconceptions. While you are reading this book, attempt to transcend your Western heritage and become an Asian. It is only in this manner that you will be able to grasp the essence of being Asian.

2

The Marketplace
Is a Battlefield

■ | USING HISTORY AS A MIRROR

It is not difficult to understand why American business people and politicians often feel frustrated when dealing with Asians. Americans sometimes think of Asian behavior as unprofessional and inconsistent, when in fact Asians study and follow a far more definite set of rules than do their American counterparts. They derive these rules from their study of history and bring them to bear on the events of their day-to-day lives.

The study of history, indeed scholarship in general, is more common in Asia than in the West because the system of examination for many jobs is enormously important to individual advancement in many walks of life. Originating in China, the examination system has been adopted by Japan and Korea to a great degree. In China, the examination system traditionally has been the only avenue of social mobility. Candidates qualify for regional examinations by excelling in local competitions. Success in these regional examinations qualifies them for the national examinations. A high score in the national examinations can instantly elevate a scholar who is poor to a position of wealth and influence. Because the examinations are so important for success, everyone studies for them.

The examinations heavily emphasize history, literature, and philosophy. In the study of these subjects events are less important than people, and the underlying causes of events and actions are more important still. The subject of inquiry is always the human mind. Chinese scholars examine the events of history as illustrations of universal principles at work. They use history so that they can understand those principles and apply them to all the events of life.

In the West, the lessons of history are seldom applied to day-to-day life and are often forgotten entirely after an individual's formal schooling is finished. It is not so in Asia.

All Asians are familiar with this maxim: *Use history as a mirror.* Today's Asian leaders do just that, going back to ancient knowledge gained from the examples of history to seek guidance for their day-to-day business and political affairs. In order to understand today's Asian business philosophies, we need to examine these same sources.

Since the reopening of China in the late 1970's, the Chinese have been criticized in the West for unconventional business and political behavior. But the strategies that underlie the behavior of the mainland Chinese are not very different from those of the people of Japan, Korea, Taiwan, Hong Kong, or Singapore. Because international business has a longer history in those countries, the people there have had an opportunity to adapt their negotiating techniques for use in dealing with the Western world. Their techniques are not really different from the original concepts and strategies the Chinese use, but are simply an updated version.

Regardless of the criticism a Westerner dealing with Chinese counterparts might have of their ways, he must acknowledge that China is the world's oldest civilization. China survived when other civilizations vanished. Now China is once more beginning to assert its position of importance in the international community. Obviously, cultural reasons underlie some of the confusing, unprofessional, and seemingly inappropriate behavior of the Chinese, but perhaps some of their behavior is merely a reflection of the naive and arrogant attitudes of some Western businessmen and politicians who measure the whole universe by Western standards. In the chapters that follow, we will explore the strategies that underlie the actions of Asian business people and provide stories that illustrate their application.

■ THE MARKETPLACE IS A BATTLEFIELD

The Chinese expression, "Shang chang ru zhan chang," translates literally as, "The marketplace is a battlefield." That is how the Asian people view the importance of success in the business world. The success of a nation's economy influences the survival and well-being of a nation as surely as does the course of a battle. Asians understand the true nature of business competition. They see it and call it as it is: "Shang chang ru zhan chang."

The Japanese have always been the greatest disciples of Chinese wisdom. When it comes to the perfect execution of this principle, the pupil has surpassed the master. The limited natural resources of Japan have been cause for much concern among Japanese leaders. Japan's invasions of China and Taiwan in 1874 and during World War II were actions motivated by the need for territorial expansion to ensure the survival of Japan's isolated island civilization. Following World War II, the Japanese remembered the old Chinese saying, "Shang chang ru zhan chang," and began applying it assiduously. Through victory in the marketplace, Japan has overcome military defeat and assured its national survival. It has demonstrated the truth of another Chinese saying: "The highest victory is to win a war without battles."

■ MILITARY STRATEGY AS BUSINESS PRACTICE

Since Asians believe that the marketplace is a battlefield and that life is a series of battles, they also believe that mastering military strategy is essential for success, as well as for survival. Asian rulers have always placed great importance on studying the classical Chinese treatises on military strategy, the Bing-Fa. The common people have also studied them and continue to study them in order to apply their principles to the affairs of daily life.

Asians believe all elements of life are interconnected. The wisdom that guides the general in battle is the same wisdom by which the politician exercises his power. It is this wisdom that guides all of us in our daily lives. Asians find no inconsistency in searching a text devoted to military strategy for the principles to apply to situations of common life, in the family, the workplace, and the world at large.

■ THE ROLE OF BING-FA

The Chinese word *Bing* means soldier. *Fa* means skill or law. *Bing-Fa* has been translated into English as "military strategy" or "the art of war." Neither seems to me a very good translation. Bing-Fa is a form of strategic thinking that was first developed for military purposes and has since been applied to almost all human interactions.

It is especially misleading to translate Bing-Fa as the title of any particular Bing-Fa text. For example, the Bing-Fa of Sun Tzu is not a book called *Bing-Fa* or *The Art of War*. It is Sun Tzu's treatise on the subject of Bing-Fa and, as such, it takes its place among the other treatises on the subject, the Tei Wang Gung Bing-Fa, Wu Tzu Bing-Fa, Sun Bin Bing-Fa, and many, many others.

The first written examples of Bing-Fa were the two books attributed to Tei Wang Gung from the twelfth century B.C. Since that time, hundreds of Bing-Fa texts have been written and many have assumed an important place in classical Chinese literature and in the literature of Asia.

Emperor Chin, in 221 B.C., ordered the burning of all books in China. Scholars risked torture and death to hide their books, and it is recorded that in the early Han Dynasty (206 B.C.), there remained copies of 182 different Bing-Fa texts that had escaped Emperor Chin's fires. During the period 206 B.C. to A.D. 24, a well-known collection of Bing-Fa books was written. This collection, the Yi-Wen Series, contains a total of 596 books. Of these 596 books, fifty-three are on the subject of Bing-Fa. At the time these books were written, there was no printing technology. The books were carved or written on wood or bamboo strips. That the knowledge of Bing-Fa was very important to the Chinese is amply demonstrated by the number of laboriously handwritten and hand-carved books dedicated to the subject and by the dangers to which the Chinese exposed themselves to preserve these books from harm.

In the third century A.D., the Emperor Liu Bei's deathbed admonition to his son was to study well his Bing-Fa. Hearing this, Kung Min, the prime minister and commander-in-chief, put his other duties aside to hand-copy the ancient texts and instruct the young prince personally. This was considered a wise and prudent thing to do. This story is one that every Chinese knows today, and it is still considered wise and prudent to study Bing-Fa well.

■ THE INFLUENCE OF PHILOSOPHY

The Tao gives birth to the one.
One gives birth to two.
Two gives birth to three.
And three gives birth to ten thousand things.
The ten thousand things carry yin and embrace yang.
By combining these forces, harmony is created.

—Lao Tzu, *Tao Te Ching*

The golden age in the development of Bing-Fa was the five hundred years between the beginning of the Spring-Autumn period and the end of the Warring States period of Chinese history (772–221 B.C.). Many of the classic Bing-Fa texts were written during this period. Because this was a time of almost constant warfare, it is not surprising that the study of military strategy gained such importance. But it was also the time of Confucius, Lao Tzu, Zhung Tzu, Han Fei Tzu, and Meng Tzu. The greatest philosophers in Chinese history lived and taught during this period and their teachings influenced the development of Bing-Fa.

Asians do not divide the search for knowledge into separate and rigid categories with a separate set of principles governing in each domain. They search instead for the single unifying principle in diverse manifestations of the universe. There is no contradiction inherent in finding the principles governing military strategy in the words of a holy man. Lao Tzu influenced the development of Bing-Fa perhaps more than any other single man. He taught that universal principles are only one, and the one becomes the many. Bing-Fa masters learned that by identifying and attuning themselves to the universal principle at work in military situations, they could control the outcome of battles and wars.

Almost from the beginning of time, the *I-Ching*, or *Book of Changes*, has influenced all aspects of Chinese thought, including Bing-Fa. From observation of life comes the knowledge of Tao and *I-Ching*. Tao is the essence of Oneness, and the *I-Ching* is the everchangingness of that Oneness. So the combination of these two sources of knowledge allows one to understand the essence of the unchangeable and the everchanging. The ancients embraced the essence of Tao and *I-Ching* and discovered the natural rhythm of military strategy.

■ THE EATING GUEST (SHI KE)

Advisors, both military and diplomatic, have had their place in the history of most nations, but nowhere else have they thrived to the degree that they did in ancient China. The position of strategist was well defined and highly specialized. These advisors were called "Shi Ke," or Eating Guests. The designation of *eating guests* was derived from the fact that the strategists' livelihood was provided by the court in exchange for their wisdom alone. They had no duties other than to provide their advice on the conduct of war or diplomacy. The peak period for these Eating Guests occurred in the third century B.C. when the prime minister Lu Bu Wei assembled 3,000 of them at the court of Chin. Many of the Bing-Fa strategies that have survived to today were formulated by these Eating Guests.

■ THE POWER OF BING-FA THROUGHOUT CONTEMPORARY ASIA

The influence of Bing-Fa is not limited to China, but extends to Japan, Korea, and other oriental countries touched by Chinese culture. Anyone who deals daily with Asian people must master the knowledge and strategies of Bing-Fa.

The most complete of the ancient Bing-Fa texts is the Sun Tzu Bing-Fa (often translated as Sun Tzu's *Art of War*). Written by Sun Tzu in the fourth century B.C., it is one of the most popular Bing-Fa texts among Asian people. It is widely studied by political and business leaders, and in the next chapter we will examine it in some detail. I once interviewed Takashi Yamamura, General Manager for the Japanese conglomerate C. Itoh & Co., Ltd., which has a very large presence in China. I asked Mr. Yamamura whether he studied the Sun Tzu Bing-Fa. He looked at me in utter amazement and answered, "Of course I do." It was a stupid question. Any Chinese should have simply assumed that a successful Japanese businessman would be well acquainted with Sun Tzu. But since the question was for the benefit of Western readers, I had to ask, just for the record.

Japanese students learn the story of Minamoto Yoshiie and the wild geese. While on his way to attack a rival's fortress, Yoshiie, an eleventh-century feudal lord, observed a flock of wild geese rising in disordered flight from a forest through which he must pass. Because he had studied the Chinese Bing-Fa, he knew that these birds had probably been flushed by an army preparing an ambush for him. He was able to lead his army around the ambush and surprise and destroy his enemy.

■ | **LOVE THE GAME**

Formal study of history and the Bing-Fa texts does not entirely account for the prevalence of strategic thinking among Asians. It is practiced even by children and others who have not studied Bing-Fa. Being immersed in Asian culture, one absorbs strategic thinking unconsciously and learns to love the mental thrust-and-parry as a natural part of human interaction.

A personal example will serve to illustrate how deeply strategic thinking influences even everyday transactions among Asians. When I was fifteen years old, I discovered the pleasure of wearing beautiful clothes. In Taiwan at that time, there were no ready-made clothes. One purchased the material for garments and had someone make them up. I had a limited budget and a yearning for lovely dresses. I had not yet studied Bing-Fa, but my intuition revealed to me a vulnerability in the keeper of a small fabric shop that I could exploit.

A local superstition dictated that the shopkeeper must sell something to the first customer of the day. If the customer left without making a purchase, poor sales would result for the remainder of that business day. I spent many rewarding Sunday mornings waiting for his shop door to open so that I might be his first customer. I walked away many times and was called back to renegotiate. Without realizing it, I was applying a sophisticated, classical Bing-Fa strategy. As we bargained back and forth, the shopkeeper served tea and we talked about his children, family affairs, and general gossip. Making friends is another essential element of successful negotiation. Sometimes bargaining took hours but, finally, the shopkeeper would say, "You are such a sweet, nice girl. I will sell this only to you at such a ridiculously low price. Don't tell anyone you bought this fabric at my place at this price." Of course, I know one could not believe what the shopkeeper said, but I bought the material at a good price, and the shopkeeper made a sale to his first customer of the day and also earned a small profit.

Asian people enjoy matching wits with Americans. When they

do business with Americans, they usually control the game since Americans are rarely aware that a game is being played. In a meeting between Henry Kissinger and Zhou Enlai, Secretary Kissinger made a comment that demonstrated an awareness of the strategies that Zhou was employing with him. Zhou complimented him by saying, "You are very smart." Kissinger replied, "You mean, smart for an American." Zhou smiled and said nothing.

But when the Chinese do business with each other, dealings often develop into a sophisticated contest. A Taiwanese diplomat once said, "When I am assigned overseas, life is so much easier and simple. When I am transferred back to Taiwan, it is so complicated. Everyone plays games here."

Sun Tzu said, "Know yourself, know your opponents; one hundred battles, one hundred victories." Anyone dealing with Asian businessmen or political figures must have a thorough understanding of Bing-Fa.

■ ANCIENT TALES OF BING-FA

Bing-Fa texts elucidate the principles of strategic thinking by examples from Chinese history and myth. Sun Bin, who lived during the Period of the Warring States (476–221 B.C.), was a Bing-Fa master. His Bing-Fa had been lost for more than two thousand years when a portion of the manuscript, carved on shafts of bamboo, was discovered in the Silver Peacock Mountain Tomb uncovered by archaeologists in 1972. These two stories of Sun Bin will serve to illustrate the wisdom of this ancient Bing-Fa master.

■ Top Horse, Middle Horse, Weak Horse

Sun Bin's feet had been chopped off and he had been imprisoned by a former schoolmate, Pang Juan, who recognized Sun Bin's genius and feared him as a rival for preferment in the service of the kingdom of Wei. Sun Bin managed to escape prison and return to his homeland, the kingdom of Chi. He was taken into the service of General Tian, where his natural abilities placed him in a position of great influence.

General Tian often raced horses with the king and princes of Chi for entertainment. The wagering often involved large sums of money. One day, General Tian mentioned an upcoming horse race to Sun Bin. Sun Bin guaranteed victory to General Tian if he would follow his advice. He urged the general to bet any amount he desired on the competition. The general was doubtful of Sun Bin's ability to guarantee a win because his horses matched up so evenly with his opponent's horses.

As was customary, the match consisted of three races. According to each man's judgment, he would pit his best, middle, and worst horse against the similar horses of his opponent. Sun Bin told General Tian to instead race his worst horse against his opponent's best horse, to put his middle horse up against his opponent's worst horse, and finally to race his best horse against his opponent's middle horse. General Tian followed Sun Bin's advice and after one loss and two wins, was declared the winner of the match and the wager.

Sun Bin looked at the larger picture. He understood that the objective was to win the war, not all the battles.

■ The Story of the Clay Stoves

Sun Bin was leading the army of Chi in a retreat from the army of Wei. Pang Juan, who had ordered Sun Bin's feet chopped off, led the army of Wei. Wei's army was larger and better equipped than the army of Chi. Sun Bin and General Tian knew from a recent defeat that their army was no match for the forces of Wei and that their own soldiers were fearful. Pang Juan also knew that the army of Chi was afraid. Sun Bin and General Tian looked for a way to turn the situation to their advantage.

When the army of Chi made camp after the first day's retreat, Sun Bin ordered the soldiers to make 100,000 clay stoves (it was standard procedure for an army to construct temporary clay stoves when in the field). The soldiers wondered at the order. They certainly didn't need that many stoves. However, they obeyed and made the specified number. The army moved on. The next evening Sun Bin ordered them to make 50,000 stoves and on the third day he ordered 30,000.

Pang Juan observed that, as each day passed, the army of Chi left behind fewer and fewer stoves. It appeared to him that the soldiers of Chi were deserting. He was convinced that in three day's time two-thirds of the army had fled. He therefore concluded that the army of Chi would never stand to face him. He grew arrogant and less cautious and quickened the pace of his pursuit. Feeling a final victory over Sun Bin within his grasp, Pang Juan finally threw all caution to the wind and led a small mounted sortie in hot pursuit. Riding into the ambush that Sun Bin had laid for him, Pang Juan lost the battle, the war, and his life.

Bing-Fa wisdom has been tested for hundreds of generations. It has been integrated into every fiber of the Asian social, economic, and political structure. Asians play the game of Bing-Fa tirelessly, especially if there is a reward at the end of the contest. A foreigner who thinks Asians are being unprofessional or erratic is simply not recognizing the systematic application of these ancient principles.

3

The Sun Tzu Bing-Fa

The *Sun Tzu Bing-Fa*, written by the master Sun Tzu in the fourth century, is the most complete book of military strategy that has survived to the present. It is also the most widely read Bing-Fa text among modern readers. It consists of thirteen rather short chapters. Because it is customary in Chinese literature to deal with the larger dimensions of a subject before proceeding to specifics, Sun Tzu's first chapter lays the foundation for the chapters that follow. The principles outlined in this chapter can easily be generalized to apply to the world of business and diplomacy as well as to military situations.

Sun Tzu says that the first and most important thing the student of Bing-Fa must understand is its vital importance to the survival of a nation. War is a matter of life and death. The subject cannot be dealt with lightheartedly or carelessly. Every battle determines the future of a nation and its people. No battle should be fought until its strategy has been carefully considered.

In the future, military warfare will likely be supplanted by international economic warfare. Global society has generally recognized that military solutions are impractical and unnecessary, given the destructive capabilities and residual effects of modern weaponry and the fact that economic interdependency and interconnectedness have made the conquest and control of a country possible without the use of military force. Those who shape the economic policies of nations should understand that what they do has the same vital importance as the conduct of war.

■ | **THE HARMONY OF THE FIVE ELEMENTS**

Sun Tzu next discusses the five elements that must be considered in formulating a strategy.

ELEMENT **1** ■ ■ ■ ■ ■ ■ ■ ■ ■ ■ ■ ■ ■ ■ ■ ■

The Moral Cause

> The Tao addresses the morality and righteousness of a battle. This must be thoroughly understood by those who would affect the outcome.

A just cause creates the necessary unity of purpose among the leaders and those led. Japan is a good example of this unity of purpose in today's economic warfare. The Japanese government and people are one in their commitment to the success and survival of the Japanese people, the Japanese economy, and the nation of Japan. The Japanese understand that since Japan is no longer a military state its survival is intimately connected to economic success.

The people of Taiwan are more akin to the Japanese than to the mainland Chinese in feeling a unity of purpose. Taiwan is a small island, whose only asset is its 19 million people. Their survival hinges on Taiwan's economic success. Consequently, Taiwan has created a unity that extends from the highest level of government to the most basic element of the country, the individual, and as a result it has been able to realize a tremendous economic growth.

This kind of unity is less evident in China. China has been unable, or less able, to unite its people and its government. One of the contributing factors is China's immense size. History has proved repeatedly that the Chinese people tend to be more bound to provincial concerns than to the greater good of China.

On April 15, 1989, Hu Yaobang, the former secretary-general of the Chinese Communist Party, passed away. Hu had been recently purged for his failure to deal sternly with the Shanghai student protests of the previous year. His death evoked a unity of purpose among the progressive elements of Chinese society and brought together in Tiananmen Square thousands of people who shared his vision of democratic reform. This rare display of unity occurred because Hu's aspirations were in harmony with the Tao and coincided with the aspirations of the people.

ELEMENT **2** ■ ■ ■ ■ ■ ■ ■ ■ ■ ■ ■ ■ ■ ■ ■ ■ ■

Temporal Conditions

> Heaven is signified by Yin and Yang, manifested as summer and winter and the changing of the four seasons.

One must understand and accept nature's timing. To know Heaven is to understand the timing of nature, the timing of uncontrollable elements. This understanding is knowledge of the soul.

Today, changes and unpredictable political situations dominate the economic environment. Foreign and domestic policies are complex and ever changing, yet they operate within this cycle of natural timing. Understanding and accepting the cyclical nature of events allows you to harmonize your actions with them. It is important to try to figure out which cycle is coming to the fore at a given time.

The events of Tiananmen Square happened largely because of the timing of Hu Yaobang's death. If he had died at any other time of the year, there would have been memorial demonstrations that would have been quickly forgotten. Because Hu died in April, large crowds of liberal students assembled in memorial demonstrations and were still assembled in Tiananmen Square just prior to the historic date of May 4. The proximity to the seventieth anniversary of the May Fourth Movement fueled their enthusiasm and swelled their numbers.

On May 4, 1919, three thousand University of Beijing students demonstrated their discontent with the government's inability to oppose Western imperialism in China. That was the first time in Chinese history that students had ever demonstrated on political issues. Since that time, May 4 has been celebrated, especially among students and scholars, as a symbol of protest and reform.

The events of May 1989 were also energized by the fortuitous timing of Soviet Premier Gorbachev's visit to Beijing on May 16 and the worldwide press coverage that was focused on the city and the students.

The organizers of the Tiananmen Square demonstration understood and benefited from the timing of these incidents in their efforts to draw the attention of China and the world to the need for democratic reform in China. The Shanghai student demonstrations of the previous year were concerned with the same issues, but who now remembers them? The success of one group and the failure of another to spread their message around the world was dependent on timing.

ELEMENT **3** ■ ■ ■ ■ ■ ■ ■ ■ ■ ■ ■ ■ ■ ■ ■ ■ ■ ■

Geographical Conditions

The Earth contains far and near, danger and ease, open ground and narrow passes.

Geography affects matters of life and death in military situations. Each locale has its advantages and disadvantages. Mountains and rivers may aid in an army's defense or hinder its movement. But a general, however great, cannot move a mountain out of his way or cause a river to flow in another direction. He must understand the advantages and disadvantages inherent in the terrain so that he can exploit them.

A similar element is true in business situations. Every business, every nation, has inherent advantages and disadvantages in the marketplace which it must understand and accept. It must also understand the strengths and weaknesses of its adversary's position. Some American firms doing business in Asia do not often search out the weaknesses of their adversary nor do they properly exploit their own strengths.

Taiwan presents us with an example of a nation that has come to terms with its inherent strengths and weaknesses. Two-thirds of this small island are mountainous. Most of Taiwan's population is located in the western coastal region. As previously mentioned, Taiwan has only one significant resource, its 19 million creative and energetic people, but it has used this resource to its best advantage. By providing a good educational system and encouraging a strong work ethic in its citizens, Taiwan has risen to become one of the economic giants of today's world. Japan and Korea have employed the same philosophy and have also made great economic progress.

The United States is envied by the comparatively disadvantaged Asian countries. It is a land of abundant natural resources and a high-quality educational system. It is home to an ingenious and creative people and occupies an unrivaled position of technological and scientific leadership. To the degree the United States does not understand or effectively use these strengths, it has not realized its greater potential; it is much like an army with advantageous terrain that does not properly exploit its position.

The demonstrators during the 1989 Tiananmen incident took full advantage of their geographical position. Beijing is the heart of the Chinese political arena. Tiananmen Square is a symbol of the Chinese People's Revolution. By taking over the square, the demonstrators occupied an important physical and symbolic position that forced the government, the Chinese people, and the world to take notice of their actions. The brutal suppression of the demonstrators took place in front of the cameras of the world press, so that even in defeat the students struck an effective blow for democratic reform. The Shanghai demonstrators of a year before had no real effect on national or world opinion because they lacked this positioning. Consequently, their suppression went largely unnoticed.

ELEMENT **4** ■ ■ ■ ■ ■ ■ ■ ■ ■ ■ ■ ■ ■ ■ ■ ■ ■ ■

Leadership

The commander must be wise, trustful, benevolent, courageous, and strict.

Asian society sees no difference between the qualities required in a military commander and in an industrial leader. Both military and industrial leadership require the same characteristic qualities of wisdom, trust, sincerity, benevolence, courage, and strictness to carry out policies. According to Asian thinking, if business leaders lack these qualities, they will not receive the support of workers; this in turn will lead to low productivity and discontent.

In American companies there is often a great lack of empathy between management and workers. The workers tend to be loyal to their union and to labor in general. Often their objectives are very different from those of management. Significant differences in salary between management and workers add to the problems. In Japan and other Asian countries, these salary differences are much smaller. But the important factor in Japan is the commitment from all levels to the success of the enterprise; this element of commit-ment is often lacking in American industry.

The great weakness of the Tiananmen Square demonstrations was the quality of leadership. Soon after the incident started, the secretary-general of the Communist Party, Zhao Ziyang, was put under house arrest. Zhao was sympathetic to the cause of reform, and had he been able to remain in office he might have provided the moderate leadership that would have allowed the students to make their point and peacefully disperse. But even if Zhao had remained in power, his position would have precluded him from providing any real help or leadership to the demonstrators them-selves. Their only leaders were inexperienced students who could not agree on a specific agenda and mired the demonstrators in factional disputes.

ELEMENT **5** ▪ ▪ ▪ ▪ ▪ ▪ ▪ ▪ ▪ ▪ ▪ ▪ ▪ ▪ ▪ ▪ ▪

Organization and Discipline

Organization and discipline must be thoroughly understood.

Delegation of authority and areas of responsibility within a military or a business organization must be absolutely clear. It is the duty of the leader to communicate these things to those who follow. Sun Tzu makes the point that it is then the duty of the followers to accept the discipline that is imposed on them and carry out their duties to the best of their abilities.

Hearing that King Wu had read and was pleased with his writings, Sun Tzu went to the court of Wu seeking employment. The king first wished a demonstration of his teachings. Sun Tzu organized 180 of the king's courtesans into two military squads. He placed each of the squads under the command of one of the king's two favorite concubines. He armed them and drilled them as if they were common soldiers. After making quite sure that they under-stood what was expected of them, he assembled them on the parade ground in front of the king. Instead of obeying his first command, the women started giggling. He explained to them that it was the duty of the commander to give clear instructions and it was the duty of the rank and file to obey them. He warned that failure to do either would be met with dire punishment. He then reissued his order. The women began to laugh uproariously. Sun Tzu then had the two captains pulled from the ranks and executed in front of their squads. The king pleaded for the lives of his favorites but Sun Tzu was adamant. After the executions, Sun Tzu reissued his order. It was executed with perfect precision and the women performed like professional soldiers for the rest of the drill. This was his way of emphasizing the importance of order and discipline.

Americans tend to have less tightly managed organizations than do the Japanese, and in some cases that looser organization can lead to disorder. On the other hand, American companies encourage much greater individuality, which in turn promotes innovative activity. In any case, Americans in general do not like to take orders. They are discontented in an overly disciplined and restrictive environment.

The Japanese, on the other hand, love discipline and order. The degree of organization in Japanese companies gives the impression that they are running military camps. That impression may be increased by their insistence that everyone, including upper management, wear not only a uniform but the *same* uniform. Some management psychologists say this creates a feeling of equality that facilitates communication vertically within the corporate pyramid. Managers are accessible and they are perceived as working toward a common goal with labor; management and labor are seen to have different but equally important roles to play in achieving that goal.

The Tiananmen Square demonstrators were long on passion but short in the real organization and discipline necessary to win the confrontation. Although part of this was due to the inexperience of their leadership, much of it was the result of the students' inexperience with chains of command and the other necessary apparatus of organized and disciplined action. I discussed this with an American-Chinese scientist whom I am not at liberty to name. He was a guest lecturer at Beijing University at the time of the incident and spent much time in the square sitting in on meetings of the student leaders as well as talking to and observing the rank and file. He described to me a situation of great disorder. The leaders often could not agree among themselves on a unified course of action. The rank and file were intoxicated with a concept of democracy that made it difficult for inexperienced leaders to place themselves in positions of command.

The harmony of the five elements is of great importance to success in any endeavor. The elements have nothing to do with bigger guns, more vehicles, or more soldiers. They are intangible, spiritual, psychological elements. If the Vietnam War taught one thing, it is that military hardware does not win a war; wars are won by people totally committing their hearts and minds to the struggle. Although Sun·Tzu's examples are couched in the terms of medieval warfare, the careful reader can extract from them the fundamental principles that apply to modern life.

■ | **WAR, A GAME OF DECEPTION**

All Chinese Bing-Fa texts agree that the essence of successful warfare is deception. Victory is to be achieved through any means and deception of the opponent plays a vital role in the strategy of war.

Although Western history has abundant examples of deception down through the centuries, the English and Americans especially prize a tradition of openness and fair play. Skill in deception and treachery has never seemed a heroic quality to them, even though they have often used that skill to achieve worthy objectives. When applied to business dealings, the word *deception* has strong connotations of unethical or illegal actions. These attitudes tend to make Westerners naive and vulnerable to Asian strategies of deception. The ability to mislead an adversary has always been seen by Asians as admirable. This does not mean that Asians are without honor, but ethical distinctions are cultural. The differences between East and West are deep and sometimes difficult for the Western mind to grasp.

■ | **If One Is Able and Strong, Then One Should Disguise Oneself in Order to Appear Inept and Weak**

In 200 B.C., Kao-Zu, first emperor of the Han Dynasty, had such difficulties with the northern barbarians that he led 300,000 of his troops northward to put an end to their depredations. The emperor sent a scout to investigate the barbarians' encampment in order to determine their strength so that he could lay his plans accordingly. Knowing that they were being observed, the northern barbarians hid their sleek horses and fresh soldiers so that the scout saw only weak horses and tired soldiers. When the scout returned with his report, an advisor cautioned the emperor. The advisor warned that when two armies are in the field, it is usual for each to exaggerate its strength to intimidate the other. However, when one displays only weak horses and tired soldiers, it is probably a ruse to encourage the other to attack. This meant that the barbarians were prepared and confident of victory. In vain he advised the emperor to withdraw. The emperor attacked and was defeated.

When You Are Ready to Attack, You Must Convey the Impression That You Will Not Attack

Throughout Chinese history this deception has been used repeatedly. In 800 B.C., the king of Zheng wanted to conquer the neighboring kingdom of Hu. He prepared for the conquest by first disarming the suspicions of the king of Hu by giving him his daughter in marriage. A short time after the marriage he contrived a meeting of his advisors so that what happened there would be sure to come to the ear of his new son-in-law. Zheng told his advisors that he felt it was time for a display of his military superiority and asked which of the neighboring countries he should attack. One of his advisors suggested the country of Hu. The king flew into a mock rage and had the advisor beheaded. He said, "The king of Hu is my brother. How can we attack him?" After all of this, the king of Hu felt that his country was under no threat from his powerful father-in-law. His vigilance became lax and military preparedness was neglected. It was then that the king of Zheng marched on Hu and laid waste to the kingdom.

When You Are Close, Pretend You Are Far, but When You Are Far, You Must Give the Illusion That You Are Close

It is of the utmost importance to disguise your intended point of attack in order to prevent your opponent from concentrating his forces. When you are planning a frontal attack, you must make a credible feint at the enemy's flank. When you plan to strike at his rear, you must make it appear that you are attacking his front.

This precept refers to temporal as well as spatial distance. If you plan to attack your enemy in the distant future, you must give the illusion that you are going to attack immediately. The anticipation of attack will keep him on guard and constantly uneasy, thereby dissipating his resources. If, however, you wish to attack immediately, you must give the impression that you will not attack until a later time. This will cause the enemy to relax his guard.

For example, in 205 B.C., a Han general arrayed his forces directly across the river from the enemy camp. The enemy believed that he was preparing to attack across the river and prepared to meet him. Distracted by his movements on the farther shore, they were unaware that he had sent 20,000 of his best soldiers upriver to cross and take up hidden positions behind their camp. While they were occupied with meeting the frontal assault, this hidden force fell on them from behind and routed them.

■ **One Should Bait the Enemy with Small Gains**

The basis of this strategy lies in human greed. The Chinese understand that China has two attractions that are irresistible to Western business interests: a market of one billion consumers and a vast land full of natural resources. These assets are sufficient bait to guarantee that there will always be an adequate number of Western firms competing for a piece of the China market, and thus these firms can be played off against each other.

When the Chinese want to bait Westerners they will call for bids on a lucrative project. They then encourage each bidder by telling him that his bid looks very competitive, but more information is needed before the contract can be awarded, perhaps a training session in Los Angeles arranged and paid for by the Western company. The result is that a number of Western companies end up giving the Chinese lavish vacations and training that they otherwise would have had to pay for. In the end, these perks will have very little to do with the awarding of the contract. The Chinese often have decided to whom they will award the contract well before the bidding process even begins. The whole process has been a long charade to extract the best possible terms from the firm they wish to do business with and to string the others along for whatever they are willing to give away to stay in the bidding.

You must realistically evaluate your company's chances of success by criteria other than the encouragement you receive from your Chinese host. He may be telling your competitors the same things. You need to think about whether your products or services are actually compatible with his needs, and whether you have sufficiently built up a genuine feeling of trust and friendship with him so that his comments to you are not likely to be deceptive.

■ | **If the Enemy Is Well Prepared, Strong, Well Trained, and Secure in All Areas, Avoid a Direct Confrontation**

A wise leader does not oppose his strength to the strength of a powerful enemy. To achieve victory, he identifies his enemy's weakness and brings his strength to bear on it.

A great battle was about to be joined between the armies of the kingdoms of Chi and Lu. As the king of Lu was about to order the sounding of the great battle drum, his advisor bid him wait. "When soldiers are ready for battle and they hear the first drum, their spirits are aroused and they are filled with great courage. When the drum sounds a second time, their spirits are not affected as strongly. The third time the drum sounds, their spirits descend. Let the army of Chi sound their drum three times before you sound yours. Your soldiers will gain their greatest strength at the moment their enemy's is lowest and overcome them." The king heeded this counsel, and he achieved victory just as his advisor had forecast.

A major Japanese port was soliciting bids for the development of computer software to track and control port traffic. In the bidding were a giant Japanese conglomerate and an American firm with eight employees. Asian bureaucrats, like bureaucrats everywhere, prefer to deal with established, financially stable companies with proven track records. The American negotiators would have been foolish to address the issues of size or stability. They instead emphasized their expertise and excellent reputation in this small and extremely specialized field. The port officials saw the wisdom in this argument and awarded them the contract.

■ | **Create Opportunities for Victory by Arousing Your Opponent's Anger and Causing Him to Take Foolish Actions**

In A.D. 618, General Li Yuan conquered the Sui Dynasty and brought the T'ang Dynasty to power. During the campaign, his forces laid siege to a city defended by a famous Sui commander. The city's fortifications were strong and the commander believed the most prudent course of action would be to stay within his walls and let Li Yuan's army spend its strength in costly assaults. Li Yuan's son reminded his father that the commander's reputation was that of a fierce warrior, not a skilled military tactician. He asked that he and his brother be allowed to try to trick the commander into coming out to battle. Li set up troops for ambush outside the walls while his two sons, with a few dozen soldiers, stood before the city gates and hurled abuse at the general within. The old warrior became furious at these two beardless youths. In a fit of rage, he led his army outside the safety of the city walls and was caught in the waiting ambush.

Make Your Enemy Grow Proud and Arrogant by Expressing Humility and Weakness

At the end of the Ch'in Dynasty, around 200 B.C., there were two neighboring barbarian kingdoms: Hu and Mouduen. The king of Mouduen had a horse so extraordinary that it was considered a national treasure. He also had a wife of great beauty. The king of Hu, looking for a pretext for war between the two countries, sent an ambassador to Mouduen demanding the horse as tribute. The king of Mouduen gave up the precious animal, saying that one should live in peace with his neighbors, and it was, after all, just a horse. Not much later, another ambassador arrived demanding that the king's wife also be sent as tribute to the king of Hu. The members of the court were furious, but the king replied that a beautiful woman was a small price to pay for peace, and he sent his queen to the bed of his arrogant neighbor. The king of Hu then demanded a large parcel of fertile land. While the ambassador was waiting for a reply, the supposedly weak king of Mouduen swiftly marched into Hu and routed its astonished king, who, believing by now that his spineless neighbor would give away his kingdom rather than fight, had neglected all preparations for battle.

When Your Opponent Is Inactive, Give Him No Rest

A rebellion occurred during the T'ang Dynasty. The general in charge of suppressing the rebellion adopted this strategy: When the rebels attacked, he would withdraw before them, frustrating their desire to join battle. When the rebels tried to withdraw, he pressed them. All day he sounded his drums and at night he harried their camp with small sorties, giving his opponents no rest. It was not until after he had thoroughly frustrated and exhausted the rebel forces that he met them in full battle and defeated them.

This kind of long tiresome marathon that can go on for a year or even longer, off and on, off and on, is a common Asian negotiating style. The strategy has been proved to be effective in Asians' dealings with the West.

■ | ### Destroy the Enemy's Alliances, Leaving Him Totally Alone

This is a strategy the People's Republic of China has practiced with Taiwan for the last twenty years. The mainland People's Republic has systematically undermined the relations of the Taiwanese government with other governments. The People's Republic will not maintain diplomatic relations with any country that recognizes Taiwan as a legitimate representative of the Chinese people. In this and many ways, they force countries to choose between Taiwan and the People's Republic rather than allowing them to maintain equable relations with both countries. Because the People's Republic is larger, more populous, and more powerful, the leaders of the People's Republic know that the choice will most often be decided in their favor.

■ | ### Victory Is Determined Before the Battle Begins

A superior commander does not fight a battle that he has not already won in his mind. He has foreseen all the possible mischances and calculated a plan for each one. To those unskilled in military strategy, a well-planned battle seems as if it has been won by good fortune rather than by the skill of a commander. A superior commander often does not receive the praise of the ignorant because he seldom places his troops in a situation where there is any question of their losing the battle.

According to the ancient wisdom:

When a victory is seen by all, the victor deserves no praise.
When a warrior succeeds in battle, the warrior deserves no praise.
Lifting thin air is not an indication of one's strength.
Seeing the sun and moon does not indicate sharp vision.
Hearing thunder does not indicate superior hearing.

But the superior commander sees victory where others are doubtful because he has prepared his strategy mentally. It is only through his skillful conduct of the battle that victory seems afterward to have been inevitable.

■ | **The Five Essential Components of Victory**

Sun Tzu says there are five considerations in the preparation for victory:

1. *Know when to fight and when not to fight.*

    One who understands that there is a season for everything will act with forethought and dispassion instead of succumbing to emotion.

    Superiority of numbers or position is not always necessary for victory. One must know when to match a small force against a large force. One who understands the rhythm of the battle and is able to freely utilize other natural advantages can realize victory with a smaller force or inferior position.

2. *Obtain the wholehearted support of your troops.*

    One who understands how to obtain the unconditional support of his troops by creating a common objective will have a great advantage over his opponent.

Japan offers an outstanding example of leaders instilling in their followers the sense of working toward a common objective.

3. *Be well prepared to seize favorable opportunities.*

    One must sharpen his intuition in order to recognize favorable opportunities and be prepared to seize them.

4. *Free yourself from interference from superiors.*

    If an emperor is constantly giving orders to his general, the general cannot fight an effective battle. Freedom from such interference is essential. If a general has been chosen well, he will insist on being given the freedom to win the battle.

5. *When the time is right, act swiftly and decisively.*

> When the victory is long delayed, weapons will grow dull and morale will drop. Do not act precipitously, but do not hesitate when the conditions for victory are present. Delay also has an adverse effect on the productivity of the country. Weakening the country by waging a protracted war may give another adversary an opportunity to attack successfully.

On July 7, 1937, when Japan declared war on China, the Japanese claimed they would conquer China in three months. They clearly understood that the only way to win in China would be to do so quickly. Just maintaining troops in China and holding on to captured areas was an expensive and exhausting undertaking for the Japanese. China, on the other hand, understood that its greatest asset was time. If China could keep fighting, it would ultimately win. Japan conquered the Chinese capital city of Nanjing almost immediately, not knowing that China had secretly moved its capital far into the interior. The Japanese then became engaged in a protracted and exhausting campaign in China that lasted for eight years and ended in their defeat.

■ | **The Highest Form of Victory Is to Conquer by Strategy**

> To win a battle by actually fighting is not the most desirable way. To conquer the enemy without resorting to war, conquering the enemy by strategy, is the highest, most desirable form of generalship. The next best form of generalship is to conquer the enemy by alliance. The next is to conquer the enemy by battle on open ground. The worst form of generalship is to conquer the enemy by besieging walled cities. . . . Those most skilled in warfare are those who conquer the enemy without fighting battles, who capture cities without laying siege to them, and who annex states without prolonged warfare. They can preserve their forces whole and intact while struggling for the mastery of their opponent. They can win a complete victory without as much as wearying their men. All this is due to the use of strategy.

The Japanese in World War II used the worst form of generalship, trying to conquer the enemy by battles and siege. They literally ensured their defeat when they won the first battle. After World War II, the Japanese, partly from necessity and partly from design, took a good look at themselves, their past, and particularly their future. They considered the principles just previously discussed. The result is that they have transferred their efforts to an arena that better suits their capabilities. The *marketplace* is their battlefield. They have consolidated their economic forces into a strong alliance of government and industry; they now compete with America and the world much more successfully than they could by force of arms.

■ The Opportunity for Victory Is Provided by the Enemy

The fruits of action are a gift of the Tao.

Sun Tzu says that an army can only make itself secure against defeat; the opportunity for victory must be provided by the enemy. This is perhaps the clearest example in the Sun Tzu Bing-Fa of the fundamental Taoist principle of nonaction. This principle underlies much of what Sun Tzu teaches. For example, the uncontrollable nature of favorable conditions is central to his concept of proper timing. The wise commander does not create favorable conditions, he awaits them, recognizes them when they occur, and harmonizes his actions to them. It is the same with victory. The wise commander cannot achieve victory unless his enemy presents him with an opportunity.

The Japanese should not get all the credit for their present-day economic success. The Americans have aided the Japanese in their victory by poorly conceived international trade policies and lack of effort in foreign markets. U.S. trade policy has been defensive; a successful effort in foreign markets must be offensive. The Japanese have not caused these errors of judgment; they have simply taken advantage of them.

■ The Combination of Basic Elements into Unique Strategies

In this universe, we can see beauty as beauty,
Because of the contrast of ugliness.
And recognize virtue as virtue,
Because of the contrast of evil.
Have and have not arise together.
Difficult and easy harmonize with one another.

Long and short oppose each other.
High and low balance one another.
Music and sound harmonize with each other.
Front and back follow one after another.
So, the sage is working by nonaction,
Teaching by not speaking.
Ten thousands things evolve ceaselessly.
Create, yet do not possess.
Work, yet do not take credit.
Accomplished, then forgotten;
therefore, it is eternal.

—Lao Tzu, *Tao Te Ching*

Sun Tzu says that all strategies are the combination and recombination of basic elements. In music, there are eight musical notes which, when combined, can produce an endless number of melodies. Three primary colors can produce an infinite number of hues. Five flavors can be detected by the tongue, yet in various combinations these flavors produce numerous palatable sensations. In the same way, a limited number of tactical principles can be combined into an infinite number of strategies.

In order to manipulate these basic elements effectively, the superior commander must understand how they relate to one another. He must especially understand how opposites are contained within each other.

Order gives birth to chaos and disorder, Sun Tzu says. Courage gives birth to fear. Strength gives birth to weakness. Whether order or disorder prevails depends on organization. Whether courage or fear takes possession of the army depends on the manner in which the attack is undertaken. Strength or weakness is a matter of appearance.

Sun Tzu is simply restating Lao Tzu's assertion that there is no difference between goodness and evil, between high and low, long and short, difficulty and ease. The basic elements motivating human beings, such as fear and courage, arise from the same place. They are two sides of the same coin. One can turn fear into courage or courage into fear because they come from the same place in the center of our being.

I had never done any public speaking before deciding a few years ago to organize and conduct a seminar for people interested in doing business in Asia. On the morning of the first seminar, I awoke with a terrible fear: I was going to have to stand up in front of a room full of strangers and speak for six hours. I knew if I did not overcome my fear, the seminar would be six hours of hell for my participants as well as myself.

As I drove toward the hotel where I was to speak, I thought of these teachings of Lao Tzu and Sun Tzu. Instead of trying to fight down the growing fear, I faced my fear directly because I knew if I didn't the alternative was unthinkable—six hours of agony—and I thought of that as more fearful than the fear itself. As I confronted it, my fear transformed itself to enthusiasm and courage. The seminar went so well that at the end of six hours, none of the participants wanted to leave.

■ Use Local Guides

Sun Tzu warns that if one does not use local guides, he will not be able to count on natural advantages. This is true in today's foreign trade. It is vital to use local guides—experts on that particular country or in that particular field—in order to take full advantage of the circumstances. The Chinese distrust and feel distanced from foreigners. They feel at ease with other Chinese with whom they share the bond of a common heritage. This bond encompasses Chinese living overseas as well as in China. Chinese are never bound by passport and nationalities, but by race and common ancestry. This is true of the Japanese and Koreans as well.

A guide interprets the outcome of meetings, considers subtle hints, verbal and nonverbal actions and reactions. He aids in evaluating the negotiating team to determine who is the top man and how the decision-making process is being carried out. The expert guide, or interpreter, can establish very important informal channels of private communication. The guide should have an understanding of American business practices, culture, and sociopolitical structures. He should be able quickly to gather and analyze information on each negotiator's background. He should provide his clients with the proper interpretation of the progress of the meetings and the direction in which matters are going.

■ Keep Plans as Dark and Impenetrable as Night; Move Like a Thunderbolt

One who is skilled in walking leaves no track.
One who is skilled in speaking makes no slip.
A good reckoner needs no tally.
A good door needs no lock, yet cannot be opened.
A good binding requires no knots, yet cannot be loosened.
—Lao Tzu, *Tao Te Ching*

A good plan is dark and impenetrable. It gives no hint of its direction of movement. When it reveals itself, it does so like a thunderbolt, with no previous warning.

If the foreigner does not have the aid of someone expert in language and culture, he will find this an apt description of Asian negotiation. Asians will deliberately obscure their plans and intentions. Sudden surprises will be sprung sometimes just to gauge a reaction or to create frustration for the foreigner engaging in negotiations without expert help.

■ | ## Attack When the Opponent Is Least Prepared and Least Expects It

This strategy is so simple and obvious that it seems as if it cannot be very effective, but that is not the case. Unrelieved vigilance is very difficult to sustain. The superior commander must anticipate lapses in his enemy's vigilance and take advantage of them.

For example: An early end to the Korean War seemed to be in sight in November 1950, when American troops were approaching the Yalu River. But on Thanksgiving Day, more than half a million Chinese troops crossed the river into North Korea and easily established secure positions there because the Americans had allowed holiday festivities to affect their normal preparedness. China's selection of Thanksgiving Day to make a massive attack on the American forces was not an accident; rather, it was a calculated choice.

■ | ## When the Enemy Speaks Peace, He Is Plotting Deception

Sun Tzu says,

> When the enemy's messenger is humble in manner and speech and his troops are simultaneously increasing in number, they are about to attack. When the enemy's messenger is arrogant in manner and speech and the troops' movements appear hasty, they are about to retreat. When the enemy speaks peace, he is plotting deception.

Asians analyze their opponent's every move down to the smallest detail, including the manner of a messenger. The Asian is trained to interpret every nuance of voice or gesture in order to completely understand an opponent. The Westerner, untrained in controlling his outward manner, sends off signals of which he is not aware, signals that expose more of his thinking than is prudent to the scrutiny of an observant Asian.

Many wealthy Asians are now buying homes in the western United States, primarily in California. During the showing of the home, the Asian buyer's attention is fixed not on the property alone, but also on the owner. For example, humility is not a common American trait. If the American owner's manner is humble, it indicates to the buyer that he is eager to sell.

Japan is no longer a second-class nation. It is a world power. But until very recently at least, Japanese diplomats, even the prime minister himself, have always adopted a submissive posture before American politicians. The Japanese pretend to be less than they really are. American politicians, on the other hand, tend to assume a condescending attitude toward the Japanese, even when borrowing money. When a messenger is humble and submissive, advancement is the true intention. The Japanese minister may be bowing and scraping all the way out the door, but his pockets are stuffed with American dollars.

Some American journalists and politicians are taken in by the humble posturing of Asians. In Asia, they should understand, humility is a weapon as well as a virtue.

■ When Facing Death, the Struggle for Survival Will Give New Birth

When an army finds itself in a desperate situation, it will struggle for survival. When an army is facing annihilation, the struggle for survival will give birth to new ideas, new actions. Thus, when an army is completely trapped and in great danger, the imagination and boldness inspired by the crisis may turn defeat into victory.

Japan's recent history provides an example. Immediately after World War II, the Japanese were in a desperate situation. The idea that Japan might cease to exist as a sovereign nation was a very real fear. This fear fueled a fierce determination in the Japanese to rebuild the strength of their nation and once more become the masters of their own destiny.

The Japanese have always believed that the survival of the Japanese race takes precedence over any other cause. Even individual survival is less important to the Japanese than the survival of the race. Through this strong commitment to national survival, Japan has rebounded from its World War II defeat to become the international economic leader and a lender to the U.S. government.

The Sun Tzu Bing-Fa was translated into French in 1772 by the Jesuit missionary J.J.M. Amiot. Whether Napoleon was familiar with the book is an open question, but some military historians feel that he was. But whether he was or not, it is certain that he was familiar with the principles involved. When Napoleon debarked his troops in North Africa, he assembled them on the shore to witness the burning of the ships that had carried them across the Mediterranean. At the beginning of a difficult campaign, far from home, he wished to instill in his army the fierce determination for victory that is only born out of desperation.

■ **The Necessity for Espionage**

Sun Tzu discusses the use of spies:

> An army may be forced to fight for years, yet victory may be decided in one day. Unless a leader is willing to pay handsomely to employ spies, he will remain ignorant of his enemy's condition. This shows extreme lack of consideration for his troops. Such a man cannot be a good leader. He cannot be a useful servant to his sovereign if he is unable to achieve victory. To obtain information one cannot depend on gods and spirits, nor simply logic and calculation. One must obtain information from those who have a thorough knowledge of the enemy's condition.

The ancient Chinese believed that the person able to use spies properly and subsequently interpret the information possessed certain uncommon qualities. Only the wise and holy could successfully use spies, they thought; only the benevolent and righteous could find the right men for espionage and use clear and correct judgment in handling them. The ancient Chinese believed that in order to be put to effective use, the information obtained by espionage needed to be analyzed and interpreted by one of real discernment. To understand the use of spies was considered the most mysterious display of a leader's ability.

Today, in California's Silicon Valley, the high-tech center of the world, many Japanese companies have offices among the hundreds of U.S. companies located there. The American engineers often joke about the Japanese companies being "spy stations." It is not a joke to the Japanese.

Military, political, and industrial forms of espionage are realities in today's world, as are entirely ethical techniques for obtaining information about your adversaries. In the West, however, there does not seem to be adequate concern with the qualifications of the person who must direct these intelligence operations and interpret the information obtained. Some Western firms have elaborate and expensive networks for gathering information about competitors and clients in the Far Eastern market. Often we find, however, that the man charged with interpreting the information gathered has so little understanding of the working of the Asian mind that he is incapable of properly interpreting the data he is given.

The Sun Tzu Bing-Fa emphasizes that it is important to present spies with the highest rewards because of their vital importance. Similarly, in the modern business world it is important to allocate adequate resources for gathering information about your markets, your clients, and your competitors, if not to espionage itself. It is also important to realize that this information must be put into the hands of someone capable of properly interpreting it.

Sun Tzu also gives a complete definition of the five types of spies. The local spies use the enemy's local people to gather information. The inside spies bribe the enemy's officials to gather information. The converted spies, or counterspies, use enemy spies to provide information and return propaganda to the enemy. Doomed spies are those who enter into a situation knowing that death is the only way to get their information out. The missionary spies enter the enemy camp and return with information. The manipulation of each type of spy was totally worked out in ancient China.

It is clear that the ancient Chinese regarded the use of spies as vitally important. The ultimate goal, then as now, was to obtain information that would provide a thorough understanding of enemy conditions.

A battle is fought by men, and the essence of a man is the human spirit. The essence of the human spirit includes determination and emotion. The ultimate objective in conquering is to defeat the opponent's determination and emotion—his spirit. The highest form of victory is to conquer by strategy, triumphing over the opponent's spirit, making the use of weapons unnecessary. The use of weapons to defeat the physical form ultimately defeats the spirit, but if one can subdue the spirit first, there is no need for laboring in expensive battles.

Believing this, the Japanese have made Japan a walled city of regulations that prohibit the free flow of American goods into their market. When they meet with resistance from the American public due to the trade imbalance, they then apply the strategy of alliance by building manufacturing plants in the United States.

Sun Tzu said that when one is skilled in the tactics of *defense*, he can hide *beneath* the Ninth Level of the Earth—the deepest, darkest, most inaccessible place in the universe. When one is skilled at the tactics of *offense*, he can maneuver his force to an advantageous position *above* the Ninth Level of Heaven. Here, he can assure his safety as well as complete victory.

One does not have to be fearful or courageous, strong or weak. One can be all things at all times depending on the circumstances. One can freely use all human elements for maximum advantage.

These methods of deception are the essence of military victory. It must be determined when to use each strategy. An appropriate decision must incorporate the peculiarities of each situation.

4

The 36 Strategies

The 36 Strategies is an ancient Chinese collection of strategies for dealing with all manner of situations. It is a well known part of the folk literature of China, and is believed to be about 1,500 years old. It is traditionally composed of six sections, each containing six related strategies. There are different versions of *The 36 Strategies*, but the arrangement of six sections of six strategies is always the same because of the significance of the number six in the *I Ching* and also the common perception among Chinese that the number six is associated with deceit.

Most examples of Chinese wisdom relate themselves in some way to the *I Ching*. Bing-Fa masters such as Sun Tzu, Sun Bin, Han Xin, and Li Chin all relied on the wisdom of the *I Ching* and utilized the theory of "I" (Change) in their military philosophy and strategy. Using the *I Ching*'s fundamental principle of ever-changing Yin and Yang, *The 36 Strategies* describes methods for manipulating specific manifestations of the universal duality to one's advantage.

The Chinese language is composed of three- and four-character idioms which derive an extended meaning from the history, philosophy, or myth with which they are associated. The study of literally thousands of these idioms and their extended meanings is an integral part of Chinese education. Thus, with only a few characters, an idea can be expressed with a subtlety or complexity far beyond the literal meaning of the characters that make up the idiom. *The 36 Strategies* is a special set of such idioms, along with commentary and examples of each. Over the centuries, different authors have offered differing commentaries and examples, but there has been only one minor variation in the set of thirty-six idioms that make up *The 36 Strategies*.

It is my intention to draw examples of the strategies from the Bing-Fa, which we discussed in the preceding chapter. The original orientation of *The 36 Strategies* was military. The six sections into which the strategies are always grouped are defined by six different military situations to which the strategies are most applicable. There has always been a strong connection between the folk wisdom of *The 36 Strategies* and the ancient classical Bing-Fa texts, but never before have the examples been drawn directly from Bing-Fa.

The phrase "thirty-six strategies" is a common Chinese expression used to describe someone's actions as deceitful. Even Chinese children are aware of its meaning. The Chinese maintain that their study of these strategies is not motivated by a desire to deceive others, but rather to recognize and prevent these strategies from being used against *them*.

STRATEGY **1** ■ ■ ■ ■ ■ ■ ■ ■ ■ ■ ■ ■ ■ ■ ■ ■ ■

Deceive the Sky and Cross the Ocean

To accomplish one's objective, it is sometimes necessary that a falsehood be openly displayed and the truth hidden. An opponent's attention is thereby focused on the false situation, allowing the true objective to be accomplished easily without detection. This is similar to the distraction a magician creates to divert his audience's attention from his sleight-of-hand. Chinese history includes a number of occasions on which this strategy was utilized.

In A.D. 589, for example, it was the intention of the country of Sui to conquer the neighboring country of Chen. Sui's general marched his troops back and forth along the Yangtze River. After each march, they encamped directly across the river from Chen, displaying a great array of banners and tents. Alarmed at first by these troop movements, Chen gathered all its military strength to oppose any attempt to cross the river. But, after these marches were repeated many times with no attempt to cross, the Chen commanders concluded that the Sui were simply patrolling their side of the river for defensive purposes. When Chen's forces relaxed their vigilance, the army of Sui swiftly crossed over and defeated Chen. The Sui Dynasty was established in that year and China was united once again, bringing to an end nearly three hundred years of division.

During the Spring-Autumn period (770–476 B.C.), two princes, Xiao Bai and Jiao, escaped from the country of Chi to avoid assassination by their brother, Chi's newly established ruler. Two loyal advisors named Guan Zueng and Bao Su each accompanied one of the princes into their separate countries of exile to wait for the right moment to overthrow the despotic ruler. Guan and Bao promised each other that no matter which of their princes then succeeded to the throne, one would assist the other to rule the country.

Prince Xiao Bai managed to be crowned king and sought to have his brother's advisor, Guan Zueng, returned to him from the country of Lu, where he was living in exile. If the ruler of Lu had known Xiao Bai's true intention, which was to have Guan become prime minister and assist him in ruling the country of Chi, he would never have released Guan. In order to avoid any suspicion in Lu, Xiao Bai downplayed the situation by requesting that Guan be returned as a prisoner for punishment, offering to exchange him for a bounty of a mere five lamb skins. To further display to the ruler of Lu that he really did not care about Guan, he sent a common jail cart to transport the prisoner back to Chi. In this way, Xiao Bai fooled the ruler of Lu by treating the exchange of Guan as he would a transaction involving an ordinary prisoner.

These historical incidents demonstrate that if we see a situation as a usual event, it arouses no suspicion. The darkest of secrets are often hidden in the open. Yin exists in Yang, Yang exists in Yin; light in darkness, darkness in light.

STRATEGY **2** ■ ■ ■ ■ ■ ■ ■ ■ ■ ■ ■ ■ ■ ■ ■ ■

Surrounding Wei to Rescue Zao

Instead of taking a strong enemy head-on, one should divert the enemy's strength, attack vital points, and avoid direct confrontation. This strategy was used in 354 B.C., the period of the Warring States, when Zao was under siege by the country of Wei. Zao requested assistance from the country of Chi. Chi sent General Tian and his forces as well as Sun Bin, the master strategist. General Tian wanted to lift the siege of Zao by direct attack but Sun Bin counseled otherwise: "The entire army of Wei is presently besieging Zao; Wei itself is unprotected. If we attack Wei, the army will naturally return to defend its own land." General Tian saw the wisdom in Sun Bin's plan and marched on the undefended Wei. As Sun Bin had predicted, the army of Wei immediately lifted the siege of Zao. As they hastened homeward, the army of Wei marched into the ambush that Sun Bin had laid and was destroyed.

> When attacks are aimed directly toward an enemy's weak points, the advance becomes irresistible.
>
> —Sun Tsu Bing-Fa

> "Is there a strategy that can use one to attack ten?" asked the king.
> Sun Bin replied, "Yes. Attack the enemy's weak point; attack the enemy where he least expects it."
>
> —Sun Bin Bing-Fa

STRATEGY **3** ■ ■ ■ ■ ■ ■ ■ ■ ■ ■ ■ ■ ■ ■ ■ ■ ■

Borrow Another's Hand to Kill

This strategy is used to destroy an opponent without bloodying one's own hands. It is accomplished by introducing a third element into the struggle between you and your opponent. It may mean creating or intensifying an existing enmity between your opponent and the party you wish to use. This will cause the third party to do the injury you wish done to your enemy. It may also mean simply introducing this third party into the conflict in such a way as to justify doing your enemy the injury with your own hand without receiving the censure you might otherwise receive. In either case your hands remain clean.

In the Warring States period (476–221 B.C.), King Zu had a prime minister, Nang, and three assistants. Among the three assistants, Fei was very jealous of his colleague Buo, because Buo was the king's favorite. One day Fei went to Prime Minister Nang and told him that Buo requested that Nang attend a party at Buo's home. Prime Minister Nang graciously accepted the invitation. Fei then went to Buo's house and informed him that the prime minister was coming to dine. Of course, Buo had no reason to refuse. Fei asked Buo what kind of gift he would prepare for the prime minister, since in China, it is imperative, during a visit by distinguished guests, that a gift is given to express pleasure at the guests' acceptance of the invitation. When Buo was unable to think of an appropriate gift, Fei reminded him of the prime minister's love of weapons and suggested that Buo select his gift from the arms recently captured from the country of Wu. Fei told Buo to arrange the arms inside the gate so that when the prime minister entered, Buo could ask him to inspect the arms and could present them to him. When the day of the party arrived, Fei went to the prime minister's house in great distress. He told the prime minister not to attend the party because there were armed soldiers in Buo's house waiting for his arrival. The prime minister did not believe this so he sent his confidant to examine the situation. The confidant came back and verified there were arms ready at the gate. In great anger, the prime minister arrested Buo. Buo realized he had been set up, so he took his own life.

Another story in the Spring and Autumn Annals (770–476 B.C.) tells of King Zhang's clever plan to conquer the country of Kuei. Before he marched to attack, he ordered spies to prepare him a list of all the most capable advisors who served the king of Kuei. He then publicly made a solemn vow sanctified by the sacrifice of animals and priests offering prayers to Heaven. King Zhang read out the list and vowed that, upon the conquest of Kuei, he would divide the land among those men. Heaven and Earth were to be his witness. When the king of Kuei heard this, he was so certain that he had been betrayed by his advisors that he had them all killed. Left without the benefit of their counsel, he was easily conquered by Zhang.

During the Tiananmen Square incident in 1989, Communist Party conservatives effectively utilized the hands of the protesters to eliminate the party's secretary-general, Zhao Ziyang, a liberal who was apparently being groomed by Deng Xiaoping for the succession to supreme power. A similar incident occurred a year earlier in Shanghai when students protested for better school conditions. The conservatives used that protest to eliminate another sympathetic liberal, Hu Yaobang, the previous secretary-general. In both incidents the students gave the conservatives the excuse they had been looking for to eliminate the liberal leadership within the party, the very people most sympathetic to the protesters' cause. The radical and disruptive nature of the students' actions rendered Deng Xiaoping powerless to intervene on behalf of his protégés.

When destiny is subtle and formless, intangible and mysterious, the strong-minded one is able to hold the fortunes of the enemy in his hands by creating a third element to insure victory.

—*Sun Tzu Bing-Fa*

STRATEGY **4** ▪ ▪ ▪ ▪ ▪ ▪ ▪ ▪ ▪ ▪ ▪ ▪ ▪ ▪ ▪ ▪ ▪ ▪

Make Your Enemy Work While You Wait at Leisure

There are only twenty-four hours in the day. If the day is long, the night must be short.

—*Chinese aphorism*

If you are in a weak position and engaged with a strong enemy, delay the confrontation and continue to delay. The enemy will tire and lose his enthusiastic spirit. While you delay, rest and wait for a change of fortune. If one can cause an enemy's position to worsen when one's own position remains unchanged, one moves from an inferior to a superior position.

This strategy is the basic element of current Chinese negotiating techniques. The Chinese badly need certain things from the West, notably capital and technology. In negotiations for these items, the Chinese are in a weak position because of their need. But the Chinese, understanding the fundamental disadvantages of waging a protracted negotiation in a foreign land, always place that burden on their adversaries. Important negotiations rarely occur outside of China.

When a foreigner has to live in Beijing for an indefinite period, he is at a distinct disadvantage in comparison to his Chinese counterparts. He is under a great deal of pressure, both financial and psychological, to strike a deal, any deal, in order to get back home in a timely fashion. For the foreigner, Beijing is one of the most expensive cities in the world. He must also cope with foreign food and a culture that is completely different from his own. Eventually, the strength of his negotiating position will be eroded and the Chinese position correspondingly strengthened. The Chinese might come to visit a foreign company on a short-term basis, especially if the foreign company is willing to pay for the trip, but when it comes to bottom-line negotiations, the Chinese insist on the home court advantage.

Those who arrive on the battlefield early will have time to be rested as they wait for the enemy. Those who arrive late rush into battle when they are already exhausted. The one who is skilled in warfare forces the enemy to encounter hardship in coming to him while he waits in ease.

—*Sun Tzu Bing-Fa*

STRATEGY **5** ■ ■ ■ ■ ■ ■ ■ ■ ■ ■ ■ ■ ■ ■ ■ ■ ■ ■

Use the Opportunity Offered by a Fire to Rob Others

Victory is gained by benefiting from the misfortunes of your opponent. When someone's house is on fire, utilize the resulting chaotic situation to steal their possessions. There are two kinds of fire. The first is set deliberately as a diversion by one who wishes to rob another. The second is the result of unknown or accidental causes and one merely takes advantage of it. In ancient China, when a country was in distress from natural calamities such as flood or drought, its neighbors often took advantage of its weakened condition to attack the country and conquer it.

There is a well-known story about the overthrow of the Ming Dynasty (A.D. 1368–1644). The bandit Li's army had entered Beijing's Forbidden Palace after his army had swept almost the whole of China. The defense force had been demolished and the emperor had hung himself from a plum tree on the hill behind the palace. Li had declared himself the Emperor of China.

As General Wu, stationed at Shanhaiguan ("Sea Mountain Gate," the beginning of the Great Wall), was preparing to surrender, he heard that his most beloved concubine had been captured by the bandit Li. In his fury and thirst for revenge, he turned to the northeastern Manchurian people for help. The Manchurians were the barbarian neighbors of China and were considered the Chinese emperor's subjects. They were often mistreated by the Ming court. Manchuria, like a hungry tiger, had long awaited this opportunity. General Wu, leading the Manchurian army, charged into China, and in just a few short days, Li was destroyed. This brought about the end of the Ming Dynasty and established the Ching Dynasty. The Manchurians took advantage of the internal dissension and Wu's rage at Li to enter China and remain as conquerors.

When the enemy is thrown into disorder, crush him.

—*Sun Tzu Bing-Fa*

STRATEGY ▪ ▪ ▪ ▪ ▪ ▪ ▪ ▪ ▪ ▪ ▪ ▪ ▪ ▪ ▪ ▪ ▪ ▪

Display Your Forces in the East and Attack in the West

Disguise the intended point of your attack by feigning preparations to attack at another point. Your enemy will be expecting you to employ some sort of feint, so it requires the greatest creativity to devise a feint that will fool him. The most important element of this deception is the ability to correctly anticipate the enemy's reaction.

At the end of the Han Dynasty and the beginning of the Three Kingdoms (A.D. 198), Cao Cao was the strongest leader in the north of China. He was emperor in all but name. In the literature and folk tales of China, there are many stories about Cao Cao and his cleverness.

On one campaign, Cao Cao attacked the southern city of Nanyong. Commander Zhang of Nanyong retreated behind the city wall and prepared to defend the city to the death. Cao Cao circled the city for three days. He discovered that the wall at the southeastern corner was constructed of both new and old stones. Cao Cao knew from his experience in building fortifications that this mixture of materials meant that the southeastern corner would be the weaker part of the city wall. As a ruse, he gathered all of his troops at the northwestern corner and feigned preparation for an attack there. Commander Zhang's advisor had been watching Cao Cao circling the wall and was also aware that the weakest point of the city's fortifications was the southeastern corner. Knowing Cao Cao's strategic ability, he was certain that Cao Cao had discovered this weakness and was setting a trap. He convinced Commander Zhang to accommodate Cao Cao's strategy. Zhang ordered all his soldiers to exchange clothing with the civilians. He sent the civilians to the northwestern corner to make Cao Cao believe he had fallen for the ruse. Meanwhile, his professional soldiers lay in ambush at the southeastern corner. When Cao Cao's troops stealthily approached the city that night they were surprised and routed by Zhang's waiting army.

It is somewhat ironic that when Cao Cao attempted this strategy his feint was not convincing enough to fool his enemy. He then fell victim to Zhang's employment of the same strategy.

Modern Western military history includes a classic example of this strategy. During World War II, the allies allowed to fall into

German hands very convincing evidence that the imminent invasion of Europe was to come far to the north of Normandy. Hitler and the German High Command were fooled so completely by the cleverly manufactured evidence that they pulled troops away from the defense of the Normandy beaches, where the invasion actually took place, and sent them north to await the Allied invasion.

STRATEGY 7 ■ ■ ■ ■ ■ ■ ■ ■ ■ ■ ■ ■ ■ ■ ■ ■ ■

Create Something from Nothing

The objective of this strategy is to make the unreal seem real; the empty, full. If there is no wind, there are no waves. Wind must be created if waves are desired.

In A.D. 755, An Lu San rose against the emperor and surrounded a city in Henan Province. An Lu San's forces outside the city wall were superior in number to the emperor's forces, but the commander of the city, Zhang Xuen, decided to defend his city to the last man. Zhang ordered the making of many thousands of straw men. The straw men were dressed like soldiers and lowered over the city walls by rope. An Lu San's soldiers thought the straw men were real soldiers preparing to attack so they shot hundreds of thousands of arrows at them. Zhang's soldiers hoisted up the straw men while taunting An Lu San's archers, thanking them for the arrows. Zhang later ordered five hundred real soldiers to be lowered over the city walls. This time, An Lu San's soldiers did not shoot because they thought that it was another ploy to make them waste arrows. They laughed and ignored the whole thing. Zhang's five hundred real soldiers then charged into the enemy camp, surprising and defeating them.

During the Korean war in the 1950's, the opposing forces often faced each other from fixed positions for long periods of time. The Chinese used empty cans to make noises at night to disturb the Americans. At first the Americans got nervous and stayed very alert, but after many nights of this, the American soldiers became accustomed to the noise and relaxed. The Chinese then attacked under the cover of thousands of rattling cans.

The good warrior imposes his will on the enemy, but he does not allow the enemy to impose his will on him.

—Sun Tzu Bing-Fa

STRATEGY **8** ▪ ▪ ▪ ▪ ▪ ▪ ▪ ▪ ▪ ▪ ▪ ▪ ▪ ▪ ▪ ▪ ▪

Secretly Utilize the Chen Chang Passage

During the battle between Liu Bang and Xiang Yu, at the end of the Ch'in Dynasty (208 B.C.), Liu was forced to retreat to Sichuan Province. Liu wanted to allay Xiang's suspicions of immediate counterattack, so he destroyed the only road to Sichuan. Later, when Liu was ready to march back into central China, he openly began to repair the destroyed road. This led Xiang to believe Liu would not be attacking him until he finished the road. Instead, Liu used the previously unknown Chen Chang passage and took Xiang by total surprise, thus defeating him and establishing the Han Dynasty.

> One should vary his plans according to the situation of the enemy in order to obtain victory. In the beginning, when enticing the enemy to battle, one may appear to be as shy as a young maiden. Then, when the enemy shows an opening, one must move as fast as a fleeing hare and catch the enemy by surprise . . .
>
> . . . one should attack the enemy where he is least prepared and when he is least expecting it; and one must feign weakness to make the enemy grow arrogant.
>
> —Sun Tzu Bing-Fa

STRATEGY **9** ▪ ▪ ▪ ▪ ▪ ▪ ▪ ▪ ▪ ▪ ▪ ▪ ▪ ▪ ▪ ▪ ▪

Watch the Fire Burning Across the River

Watching the fire burning across the river is the act of exercising the proper patience and allowing favorable events to progress. A good strategist understands the best time for action and inaction. Internal struggles weaken the enemy's strength and make for an easy victory. An attack from without may very likely become a unifying force. When an enemy has conflicts within, it is best to watch from across the river and let the fire do its work.

Chinese children know the story of the clam and oyster. A clam and an oyster were fighting on the beach. Each caught the other in a tenacious grip, and neither would loosen its hold even when a fisherman happened upon the struggle. The fisherman scooped the two up and took them home for dinner. The clam and oyster were oblivious to their mortal danger because of their own petty conflict. Death came to them both by the hand of a third party.

Cao Cao applied this strategy again against the two Yuan brothers. Following their defeat at his hands, the two brothers managed to escape north to Laodong with several thousand of their troops. Cao Cao did not give chase. He knew that the lord of Laodong had always been afraid of General Yuan, the father of the two brothers, and had developed a deep hatred for the Yuan family.

But Cao Cao knew also that the lord of Laodong would accept the two brothers with their troops because he feared an attack by Cao Cao. When no threat developed, the lord of Laodong relaxed and saw no further reason to give the two Yuan brothers sanctuary. Just as Cao Cao predicted, messengers from Laodong brought Cao Cao the heads of the two brothers a few days later.

Cao Cao watched the fire burning across the river. By allowing the situation to develop on its own, a fire was allowed to consume his enemies and Cao Cao prevailed without expending any of his strength in battle. It is important to know when to simply watch the fire and when to intervene actively. Timing is all important.

The only winner of the confrontation between the students and the government troops in Tiananmen Square was the government of Taiwan. The Chinese believe that there is only one Chinese people. Whether living on the mainland, in Taiwan, London, or Los Angeles, a Chinese person is regarded as part of that single enormous family. Both governments claim to be the legitimate voice of the Chinese people. The claim of the People's Republic was weakened by world press coverage of the massacre in the square. It seemed hardly the actions of a legitimate government to crush the bodies of unarmed citizens beneath the treads of tanks. Taiwan lost no opportunity in capitalizing on the internal strife in the People's Republic. Immediately after the massacre, the Taiwanese government took out a full-page ad in *The Washington Post* among other newspapers, restating its claim to be the legitimate voice of the Chinese. The student leaders who managed to escape the mainland are now traveling on passports issued them by the Taiwanese government. The government of Taiwan is underwriting the living expenses for the most influential of the student leaders now residing in the United States and Europe. In short, the government of Taiwan is sparing no expense to keep the student protest movement alive so that Taiwan may continue to benefit from future confrontations.

When one is skillful in warfare, he must first place himself in an invincible position and then seize any favorable opportunity to defeat the enemy. To secure oneself against defeat depends on one's own efforts, while the opportunity for victory must be afforded by the enemy.

—*Sun Tzu Bing-Fa*

STRATEGY **10** ■ ■ ■ ■ ■ ■ ■ ■ ■ ■ ■ ■ ■ ■ ■ ■

Knife Hidden Under the Smiling Face

This strategy is used to gain an advantage over an opponent by inspiring trust in him so that he lets down his guard.

In modern history, the Japanese attack on Pearl Harbor serves as an example of this tactic. Japan prepared for years to attack the United States while Japanese diplomats used every means at their disposal to assure the United States that they wished to maintain peace. They wanted the U.S. to be totally unprepared for attack. Negotiations continued right up until December 7, 1941, when Japan wiped the smile off its face and revealed the knife hidden in its hand with an attack on Hawaii's Pearl Harbor.

Today, this strategy is more commonly used in economic warfare than for military advantage. Beware of smiling faces and effusive displays of friendship at the negotiation table.

When the enemy speaks peace, he is plotting deception.

—*Sun Tzu Bing-Fa*

STRATEGY **11** ■ ■ ■ ■ ■ ■ ■ ■ ■ ■ ■ ■ ■ ■ ■ ■

The Plum Tree Sacrifices for the Peach Tree

According to an old Chinese fable, there was a plum tree with a peach tree growing next to it. Insects attacked the roots of the peach tree. Because the peach tree was the more valuable of the two, the plum tree volunteered to take the place of the peach tree and sacrifice itself to the insects.

The forces of Chi, under General Tian and Sun Bin, marched toward Wei's capital while the Wei army was fighting elsewhere.

The Wei commander ordered his troops to return to defend the capital as quickly as possible. Sun Bin's spies reported that they were hastening to Wei in three groups of unequal strength. General Tian wished to use the strategy of the three horses against Wei's three armies but Sun Bin did not. He said the objective here was not to have two wins, but rather to destroy the greatest number of enemy troops. Sun Bin then divided Chi's troops into three units, using his weakest force to fight the enemy's strongest; the middle force was sent to fight Wei's middle force, and the strongest group sent to fight the weakest. The first two groups needed to pick their ground carefully to be able to prolong the battle. Chi's strong group quickly destroyed the enemy's weak force and joined the middle force to create a unit strong enough to overwhelm Wei's middle force. These two groups then hastened to assist the weakest group, which had been suffering fearful losses while holding off the strongest of Wei's army. Together they crushed the last of Wei's forces and achieved a complete victory.

Victory was dependent on two factors: the soldiers of the weakest force being willing to fight valiantly in an unequal contest, enabling the other forces to achieve quick and easy victories; and Sun Bin's ingenious ability to identify the primary objective of the encounter.

A recent vivid example of this strategy was the Tiananmen Square incident. The demonstrators realized that there was great personal danger in opposing themselves to the will of the Communist Party hard-liners. But like the plum tree, they were willing to sacrifice themselves for the greater good, the cause of democratic reform in China.

In the business world, negotiators must always keep the primary objective in sight and be willing to sacrifice the less important parts to preserve the more important elements of their agenda. This is the principle of giving the insignificant and in return gaining what is significant.

STRATEGY **12** ∎ ∎ ∎ ∎ ∎ ∎ ∎ ∎ ∎ ∎ ∎ ∎ ∎ ∎ ∎

Walk the Sheep Home, Just Because It Is There

If you see a sheep beside the road without anyone tending it, take the sheep home and make it yours. This means that when you come across an opportunity for a small advantage, you should act upon it swiftly, turning the carelessness of your enemy to your benefit.

While Liu Bang was secretly using the Chen Chang passage to reenter central China during his war with Xiang, he discovered three territories nominally under the control of his enemy. Tucked into this out-of-the-way corner of China, the principalities were completely undefended. Liu simply took them for his own. This opportunity was unexpected and unplanned, but Liu seized it swiftly. These territories later proved to be of great strategic value to him.

Recall the story of General Wu, who invited the northeastern Manchurian people into China. From the Manchurians' viewpoint, they merely took advantage of an enemy and profited from their vulnerability. In this case, the untended sheep was China.

> The opportunity for victory is provided to you by the enemy.
> —*Sun Tzu Bing-Fa*

STRATEGY **13** ■ ■ ■ ■ ■ ■ ■ ■ ■ ■ ■ ■ ■ ■

Disturb the Snake by Hitting the Grass

To disturb the snake by hitting the grass can be, according to circumstances, either a desirable or an undesirable action. When the intention is to catch the snake by surprise, disturbing the grass would be a mistake. If, however, a direct confrontation with the snake is wanted, then hitting the grass is recommended so that the snake will make itself visible.

Most often it is better to refrain from disturbing the snake so that one can gain the advantage of surprise. If you know the snake is in the grass, you have a considerable advantage as long as the snake is not aware it has been discovered. When one knows the enemy's intent, it may be best to feign ignorance. The enemy will not become suspicious if he believes his intent is not known. When it is to your advantage to flush the snake out, hit the grass. See how the situation develops and work it to your advantage.

George "Sparky" Anderson, manager of the Detroit Tigers, told me of an incident that occurred when he was manager of the Cincinnati Reds. During his time with them, the Reds won five division championships, four National League pennants, and two World Series. These successes were followed by two disappointing seasons. Shortly after the close of the season, the Reds went on a good-will tour of Japan. Upon his return to the U.S., Sparky received word from the team's new president that he was fired. Anderson told me that getting fired was not the part that really bothered him but the way it was done. They let him go to Japan even though they planned to fire him. He wondered, if they were going to fire him, why they hadn't done it at the end of the season. The owners apparently did not want to hit the grass to disturb the snake because they wanted to exploit Sparky's publicity value in Japan before they let him go.

> The best strategy to overcome an enemy is to stand as still as a forest on a windless day, to be as immobile as a mountain, to be as impenetrable as darkness.
>
> —Sun Tzu Bing-Fa

STRATEGY **14** ▪ ▪ ▪ ▪ ▪ ▪ ▪ ▪ ▪ ▪ ▪ ▪ ▪ ▪ ▪

Borrow Another's Body to Return the Soul

According to Chinese mythology, Li was a meditation master. One day, he told one of his students that he would be traveling in spirit to visit Heaven and that he would be back in seven days. The student promised to guard Li's body during those seven days and to look after it with great care. On the sixth day following Li's departure, the student received an urgent request to come home because his mother was gravely ill. The student wanted to see his mother again before she died. Li had been gone for six days, and the student wondered if he might remain in Heaven, never returning to reclaim his body. So, the student burned Li's body and left to see his mother. When Li returned on the seventh day, he was unable to find his body so his soul entered the body of a beggar who had just died on the roadside. Thus the beggar's corpse was given new life.

When a Chinese company is on the brink of failure, through some stroke of luck it may run into an uninformed Western company that will enter into a joint venture with the dying company, thereby breathing new life into it.

STRATEGY **15** ■ ■ ■ ■ ■ ■ ■ ■ ■ ■ ■ ■ ■ ■

Entice the Tiger to Leave the Mountain

The tiger is powerful only when it is in its natural environment—the mountain. Examine your adversary's source of power, and if the source is an individual, remove that individual. If an individual's source of power comes from his advisor, then remove the advisor. Entice the tiger to leave the mountain. The key word is *entice*. It may not be easy to entice a wary tiger from the mountain. The nature of the tiger must be understood so that appropriate bait can be used.

When the CEO of a large U.S. company visits Asia on a business venture, it is like the tiger leaving the mountain. He leaves behind his impressive office building, factories, and his luxury car, replacing them with a hotel room, a taxicab, and the handful of aides traveling with him. He is left struggling with a foreign language and the customs of a foreign land.

The 1989 student demonstration in China was focused on Beijing's Tiananmen Square because the square is a symbol of the People's Revolution. Possession of the square placed the students' struggle in a historical perspective and associated it with the struggle of the Chinese people. The government repeatedly tried to entice the students to leave the square before they began negotiations. The students, however, understood the powerful symbolic significance of the square and refused to leave.

In January 1990, for obvious reasons, the Chinese government enacted a new law that prohibits any demonstration around or in Tiananmen Square.

STRATEGY **16** ■ ■ ■ ■ ■ ■ ■ ■ ■ ■ ■ ■ ■ ■

In Order to Capture, One Must Let Loose

If the enemy has no way to retreat, desperation will increase his valor. The enemy should be given room to retreat. Retreat will sap his strength and his spirit. When the enemy's resolution is completely gone, then he can be captured with minimal effort, and will be a passive prisoner.

While Kung Min, the prime minister of Su, during the time of the Three Kingdoms, was battling with his eastern and northern neighbors, his barbarian neighbor to the south continually harried Su's southern border. Kung Min finally decided it was time to take care of the problem. During the ensuing campaign, Kung Min quickly captured the southern chief. Then he released him. Seven times he captured and released the barbarian chief. Finally, the southern chief realized he was powerless before this great king and swore loyalty to Kung Min. Without peace in the south, he would have been unable to deal with his enemies to the east and north, and Kung Min knew that to have real peace on his southern border, he needed to have the loyalty of the barbarians, not simply victories over them.

During the 1989 Tiananmen Square demonstration, the weather was unseasonably hot. The government troops assembled in the blazing sun on the perimeter of the square were very uncomfortable. The demonstrators brought Popsicles to the soldiers to show them respect and friendship. When the order was given to attack the demonstrators, the soldiers refused. The Chinese government had to bring in troops from the outer provinces who had no knowledge of recent events in Beijing to attack the demonstrators.

This strategy demonstrates a soft approach, showing that kindness can be effective. In business management, for example, instead of severely punishing an erring employee, a dose of compassion and a light punishment might result in a more loyal staff.

> When you surround an enemy, you must leave an outlet for him to go free. Do not press a desperate enemy too hard.
>
> —*Sun Tzu Bing-Fa*

STRATEGY **17** ∎ ∎ ∎ ∎ ∎ ∎ ∎ ∎ ∎ ∎ ∎ ∎ ∎ ∎ ∎

Trade a Brick for a Piece of Jade

Exchanging a common brick for a valuable piece of jade would be an advantageous transaction. But how would you convince someone to take your brick in exchange for their jade? You must convince him that your brick is of greater value than his piece of jade. If you are to convince him, an understanding of his character is essential. The bait must be tempting enough for him to react to it.

Each year, many Asian countries send delegations to the United States to purchase grain. These high-profile delegations travel from state to state finalizing purchases in each one. In fact, they have already purchased the grain from a single major broker. They travel to each state in which the broker has offices to shake hands, pose for pictures with local politicians who will take credit for bringing in all this business, and in general create the impression that they have bought all the grain locally. Since they have already bought the grain, what they actually are buying on their junket is political clout. They are making sure that the governor and senators of each state see them as major players in their state's economy and use their influence accordingly. They are exchanging something of lesser value, the price of the grain, not only for the grain but for political influence in the United States that prevents the federal government from enacting a realistic trade policy toward them.

It is certainly possible for the West to receive full value in its commerce with the East, but it is necessary to examine carefully what is given and what is received. Things are not always as they seem.

STRATEGY **18** ▪ ▪ ▪ ▪ ▪ ▪ ▪ ▪ ▪ ▪ ▪ ▪ ▪ ▪ ▪ ▪

Defeat the Enemy by Capturing Their Chief

Defeat through capture of the enemy's chief is a principle everyone can understand. Throughout history, there are thousands of proofs of the effectiveness of this strategy.

Not long ago an article in a well-known U.S. business magazine analyzed the top four network anchorwomen. The article attributed the success of one of these women in a large measure to her ability to capture the hearts of network executives. It is common for her, the article stated, to receive phone calls from the president or CEO of the network in the middle of a production conference. The news director and producer are awed by her ability to capture the chief.

In the world of business, the chief, the decision-maker, must first be identified, then he must be captured. You must obtain a thorough understanding of exactly what the chief is looking for, then put yourself in a position to give it to him. If you cannot provide what the chief wants, you will not be able to capture him. In a socialist or communist country, identifying and satisfying the chief's need is much more complicated than in a capitalistic society. The chief's ultimate goal may not always be money. It may be his desire to obtain a position of power in the party or advancement in the bureaucracy or an educational opportunity for his son in the United States. The ability to capture the chief is dependent upon one's ability to understand the chief.

> Know yourself, know your opponents; one hundred battles, one hundred victories.
>
> —*Sun Tzu Bing-Fa*

STRATEGY **19** ■ ■ ■ ■ ■ ■ ■ ■ ■ ■ ■ ■ ■ ■ ■ ■

Remove the Firewood Under the Cooking Pot

The strength of the fire determines whether the water will boil. The strength of the fire comes from the burning wood. If the force of the boiling water is great and dangerous, one may not wish to confront it directly. By removing the firewood from under the cooking pot, one can cool the water and remove the danger. In other words, do not confront your opponent's strong points. Rather, avoid his strong points and remove the source of his strength.

In the Warring States period (476–221 B.C.), General Le, leading the army of Yan, captured more than seventy Chi cities. Chi was left with only two cities, one of which was defended by Tian Dan. Tian Dan realized that the enemy's success was a result of the great competence of General Le. His first priority was to remove the general. Tian Dan planted a rumor that the general was dragging his feet in conquering the two remaining cities because he was planning to establish himself as the king of Chi. When this new reached the king of Yan, he immediately replaced General Le. With the formidable General Le out of the way, Tian Dan was able not only to defeat the army besieging his city, but to go on and liberate all the seventy cities Le had captured.

In today's political and business negotiations, difficulties can often be traced to a single individual whose function seems to be continually to stir up unnecessary difficulties. Rather than dealing with the problems he creates, efforts should be made to remove or discredit this individual.

STRATEGY **20** ■ ■ ■ ■ ■ ■ ■ ■ ■ ■ ■ ■ ■ ■ ■

The Guest Becomes the Host

The host has a great advantage in controlling the outcome of meetings. In preparing the meeting place and controlling the agenda, he can create conditions favorable to his own interests. It is possible for a clever guest to assume some of the perquisites of the host and turn the advantage to himself or herself.

In 1985, the U.S.–Japan Mayor and Chamber of Commerce Conference was held in Portland, Oregon. The trade imbalance was of great concern to the American delegates and should have been a major item on the agenda. The Japanese would have preferred not to discuss it at all, but a staff member of the Tokyo Chamber of Commerce told me his group had worked very hard to prepare for the unavoidable and possibly heated discussion on the subject. As it turned out, the trade imbalance was not even mentioned during the week-long conference. The Japanese had very skillfully manipulated the agenda by playing on their American hosts' sense of hospitality. The Americans were reluctant to cause their guests discomfort by discussing a subject that was obviously unpleasant to them. The aide happily left his material on the subject with me because he felt he wouldn't need it any more and he didn't want to carry the heavy baggage home.

STRATEGY **21** ■ ■ ■ ■ ■ ■ ■ ■ ■ ■ ■ ■ ■ ■ ■

The Golden Cricket Sheds Its Shell

When a cricket has grown to a certain stage, it sheds its outer shell. The cricket then flies away, leaving the empty shell behind. But after it has been abandoned, the empty shell is often mistaken for the real cricket.

In ancient Chinese tales, often an army would cover its retreat by leaving its camp behind. A small number of men were left to beat the drums and keep the cookfires burning. This strategy was not employed exclusively as a means of escape. It was also put into practice in preparation for a sneak attack behind enemy lines. While you are displaying the empty shell, your actual force comes from behind the enemy lines for an unsuspected attack.

Wong Yong-min was a great scholar and politician of the Ming Dynasty. His political enemy, the powerful eunuch Liu, brought false charges against him, and Wong was exiled to a remote area in southeastern China. Liu was not content with Wong Yong-min's exile, however; he wanted Wong dead. On his journey into exile, Wong discovered he was being followed by Liu's assassin. He knew that while he might escape this attempt on his life, Liu would not be satisfied until he was dead. To permanently escape the threat, Wong left a suicide note, threw his clothing into the river, and ordered his servant to cry his heart out on the river bank. The assassin reported Wong's suicide to Liu and the matter was closed.

STRATEGY **22** ■ ■ ■ ■ ■ ■ ■ ■ ■ ■ ■ ■ ■ ■ ■ ■

Accuse Others of Murder by Moving the Corpse

During the T'ang Dynasty, a concubine named Wou gained the favor of the emperor. Not content to be the first among his concubines, Wou asked the emperor to dismiss his empress and make her his wife. But, without proof of some great wrongdoing, even the emperor could not dismiss the empress. Such an action also required the approval of council and ministers of state.

Unable to achieve her ambition immediately, Wou set out to gain the confidence and affection of the empress herself. The lavish gifts that the emperor showered on her, she, in turn, gave to the empress. The empress was warned by loyal and perceptive members of her staff that Wou was not to be trusted, but she did not listen.

When Wou delivered her first child, the empress visited Wou's chamber. She held the infant daughter and praised the baby's beauty. When the empress left, Wou strangled her own child and claimed the empress had done the despicable deed out of jealousy because she herself was childless. The possibility that Wou had killed her own daughter was unthinkable to most of the court since Wou had always feigned a gentle and kind nature. The empress's motivation was clear: She had failed to provide an heir and was in danger of being put aside. The empress was executed and Wou was put in her place.

Few play as viciously as Wou, but this strategy can easily be applied with less extreme measures. Even children commonly point a finger at another to cover their mischief. In the complex world of corporate politics, laying the blame on someone else is a common game.

STRATEGY **23** ■ ■ ■ ■ ■ ■ ■ ■ ■ ■ ■ ■ ■ ■ ■ ■ ■

Kill the Rooster to Frighten the Monkey

Monkeys are very intelligent animals. Although they can easily be trained, they are often disobedient. Years ago in China, when a monkey did not obey, the trainer would kill a rooster in front of the disobedient monkey. Witnessing the poor rooster's death agony in the hands of the trainer, the monkey immediately gave up any resistance to control and became totally submissive.

During the 1989 demonstrations in Tiananmen Square, the Chinese government used this strategy on the Chinese press. Through the early part of May, the government tolerated the sympathetic coverage that the Chinese press gave to the student demonstrators. But in late May, after some elements of the Chinese press actually joined the demonstrators, the Chinese government decided to take a tougher stand. They ordered CNN to unplug its transmitter and silenced Dan Rather of CBS in the middle of a broadcast. It is well known how much the Chinese government cares about its international image. If the government was prepared to pull the plug on the most influential of the world media, it was abundantly clear to the Chinese that it would not scruple at much more extreme measures in dealing with the domestic press. The Chinese government used the Western press as the rooster.

On June 4, the government again employed the strategy. This time it was the students slaughtered in Tiananmen Square who served as the rooster, and the people of China as the monkey the government wished to control.

STRATEGY **24** ■ ■ ■ ■ ■ ■ ■ ■ ■ ■ ■ ■ ■ ■ ■ ■ ■

Steal the Dragon and Replace It with the Phoenix

During the Sung Dynasty, Emperor Zhen Zhoung (who reigned from A.D. 997 to 1022) had a beloved concubine who threatened the position of the empress by giving birth to a prince. The empress paid the doctor who delivered the baby to switch the baby prince with a dead fox. The empress then took the newborn prince and claimed she had given birth to the baby boy. Because the concubine had apparently given birth to a fox, she was branded a witch. The concubine was sent from the palace and the empress secured her position by becoming the mother of the next emperor.

In another example, Emperor Chin fell gravely ill while he was out inspecting troops. Knowing he would not live, he immediately wrote a will deciding the succession in favor of Prince Fu. On his deathbed, he gave the will and the royal seal to the prime minister, Li, who returned immediately to the court. Li was concerned about the succession and asked the advice of the eunuch Zhou. "Who is closer to Prince Fu, Yiou or yourself?" Zhou asked. "I think that when Prince Fu becomes Emperor, he will use Yiou as prime minister and at that time your life will be in danger. I suggest you change the will, condemn Prince Fu to death and make Prince Hu the heir." Although Li was confused and fearful he decided to follow Zhou's advice. He ordered Prince Fu to drink poison and Prince Hu became emperor. Emperor Hu named his mentor, the eunuch Zhou, as prime minister and Zhou killed both Li and Yiou.

You often see plastic food displayed in the windows of Japanese restaurants. Since the plastic food all comes from the same factory, it really has nothing to do with the quality of the food offered by the specific restaurant. Why it serves as an inducement is a mystery of human nature. We often see this strategy being used in advertising. The representation of the product often has nothing to do with the reality. For example, breakfast food that has been concocted specifically to satisfy an unhealthy craving for sugar is presented as wholesome nutrition. Market the dragon, but deliver the phoenix.

STRATEGY **25** ▪ ▪ ▪ ▪ ▪ ▪ ▪ ▪ ▪ ▪ ▪ ▪ ▪ ▪ ▪ ▪

Attack When Near, Befriend When Distant

It is prudent military policy to advance in an orderly fashion, keeping lines of supply open and secure. You should never engage a distant enemy because of the uncertainty of conducting operations across some intervening territory not under your complete control. Rather, it is advisable to form alliances with those at a distance, and engage adversaries who border on your territories.

During the five-hundred-year Warring States period, China was divided into seven states, each ruled by an independent monarch. In 221 B.C., the strongest of the seven accomplished the conquest of the others and brought the whole of China under his dominion. This was Chin, the first emperor. To eliminate his six opponents, Chin adopted this strategy: He formed alliances with his distant neighbors and provoked a quarrel with the nearest. Chin's adversary was caught between enemies and destroyed. After Chin had annexed the conquered territory, one of his allies was now his nearest neighbor. Chin provoked war with this new neighbor while preserving the alliances with his distant neighbors. Soon, this new enemy was overcome and Chin repeated the process until there was none left. The other monarchs should have realized Chin's intentions and met him with a united front, but such is human nature that each thought his relationship with Chin was special and that his treaty with Chin would be honored.

Hitler attempted this same strategy in Europe in the months leading to the outbreak of World War II. In exchange for promises that the fury of the Nazi blitzkrieg would not be turned on them, nations were induced to abandon traditional allies to German aggression. England thought they were buying "peace in our time" at the cost of betraying the Czechs. The Russians purchased a few months of peace by allowing German tanks to roll across Poland. Each thought that Hitler, although he had lied to everyone else, would keep his word to them.

In the business world, when you see an ally betray his other allies, do not assume that your relationship is so special that he will not eventually betray you too.

STRATEGY **26** ▪ ▪ ▪ ▪ ▪ ▪ ▪ ▪ ▪ ▪ ▪ ▪ ▪ ▪ ▪

The Hidden Message

The Asian peoples do not always say things directly, especially if what they have to say is unpleasant. It is common for them to criticize someone who is not present, but through subtle hints indicate that the criticism is meant to apply to someone present. It is a way of saying what needs to be said without provoking a confrontation. This strategy can be very effective in a sensitive situation if employed tactfully. Asians are trained to understand these hints, but foreigners often do not. I was present once when a group of Chinese were trying to impart some subtle criticisms to an American diplomat. The American did not understand that he was actually the one being criticized.

In ancient China, one day, Yu, a favorite advisor of King Chu, met the son of the late prime minister gathering firewood to eke out a meager living for his widowed mother and himself. Yu was shocked to realize how poorly the king was taking care of the family of his loyal minister, Sun. The following day, Yu entered the court dressed like the late prime minister. This pleased King Chu, who said, "Even the false one pleases me. I certainly miss Sun and because you dress and act like him, I would like to appoint you as the new prime minister." Yu told King Chu that he would like to discuss the matter with his wife before accepting the appointment. The next day, Yu told the king that his wife would not let him accept the post of prime minister because the family of the late minister was so poor that his son had to gather firewood to keep them from starvation. Yu said that his wife was afraid that if he accepted the post, when he died she would starve to death. King Chu realized then that he had been remiss in not caring for the late prime minister Sun's family and rectified the situation by providing them with a generous pension.

When dealing with the Chinese and other Asian peoples, one must listen carefully. The dropping of hints is a Chinese national pastime. In a business transaction, if you miss a hint, it could turn out to be very costly.

STRATEGY **27** ■ ■ ■ ■ ■ ■ ■ ■ ■ ■ ■ ■ ■ ■ ■ ■

Pretend to Be a Pig in Order to Eat the Tiger

When a hunter goes to the mountain to hunt the tiger, he can lure the tiger by dressing as a pig. When the tiger draws near, he can be killed. When a strong enemy appears, pretend to be weak and servile to put the enemy off guard. Wait until the right moment to spring your trap.

Sun Bin understood the value of pretending to be a pig in order to eat the tiger. When Pang Juan chopped off Sun Bin's feet and imprisoned him, Sun Bin pretended that the mistreatment had caused his mind to snap. He acted like an idiot to make Pang Juan think that he had nothing more to fear from him. When Chi's ambassador visited Wei, Sun Bin used him to make a clever escape. Sun Bin later destroyed Wei and put Pang Juan to death.

This strategy is especially popular in Asian literature and heroic folk tales. The making of a hero lies not in the moment of victory when he is eating the tiger, but rather in his period of endurance, his apparent acceptance of disgrace by acting like a pig. To Asians, endurance beyond any normal human's capacity is the true proof of manhood.

> When the enemy is strong, one must be careful in making preparations. One should avoid strength and attack weakness. When one is capable, he must feign being incapable.
>
> —*Sun Tzu Bing-Fa*

STRATEGY **28** ■ ■ ■ ■ ■ ■ ■ ■ ■ ■ ■ ■ ■ ■ ■ ■

Cross the River and Destroy the Bridge

A bridge is useful for crossing a river. Once the river is crossed, if there is no need for return, the bridge can become a liability. In Chinese history, the people who suffered hardships and sacrificed greatly for new rulers, and supported and contributed the most to a new regime, often ended up dead. Like the bridge, these supporters were no longer useful and could be destroyed.

The king of Yue had two loyal and able aides, without whom he could not have conquered the country of Wu. In peacetime however, he saw these able men as liabilities. One was sent into exile and the other was killed.

In another example, after Liu Bang united China, one of his three valuable aides wisely chose to leave the court and retire. Of the remaining two, Liu Bang imprisoned one and had the other chopped into meat sauce. All were effectively removed from the possibility of becoming competition for Liu.

A leader needs strong supporters when he is fighting to achieve a goal. Once the goal is achieved, these same adherents, because of their superior abilities and talents, may be considered liabilities. Smart Asians learn the importance of timing, and leave before the party is over.

STRATEGY **29** ■ ■ ■ ■ ■ ■ ■ ■ ■ ■ ■ ■ ■ ■ ■

Be Wise but Play the Fool

When one faces strong opposition, it is best not to take premature action that may lead to defeat. One should instead play the fool, posing no threat, arousing no suspicion.

In the third century, Shi Ma was the commander of the army of Wei. The king chose a successor who greatly displeased Shi Ma, so he resolved to prevent his successor's access to power by deposing the king.

To avert suspicion, Shi Ma pretended to be growing old and feeble. He demonstrated little concern or attention for the affairs of state and no interest in military events. As a result, the king and court considered him senile and totally ignored the old warrior. One day when the king and his successor were off hunting, Shi Ma took control of the palace and captured the king and his designated successor upon their return.

After Japan's defeat in World War II, the country humbled itself to the West while quietly rebuilding its industries. Japanese industry gained a position of world leadership by maintaining a nonthreatening posture. "Made in Japan" signified third-rate merchandise to American consumers and politicians throughout the 1950's and

60's. Few Americans could envision any threat to American industry from these makers of shoddy trinkets. Few people saw the powerful industrial base that was being created in Japan.

> The essence of war is deception. The capable must display incompetence. When ready to attack, demonstrate subservience. When close, pretend to be far, but when very far, give the illusion of being near.
>
> —*Sun Tzu Bing-Fa*

STRATEGY **30** ■ ■ ■ ■ ■ ■ ■ ■ ■ ■ ■ ■ ■ ■

Provoke Strong Emotion

Provoking strong emotion within others is the key to controlling their actions. Anger is an especially powerful emotion. Anger can conquer the world, but more commonly it blinds one's judgment and causes fatal mistakes. Anger has caused generals to lose battles and kings to lose kingdoms. Properly channeled, the energy in anger can enable one even to face death without fear. When a country enters a war, the first order of business for the commander-in-chief is to kindle anger in both the military and civilian personnel. A soldier's willingness to die for his country is dependent in large part upon how well his anger and hatred are aroused. The same principle applies in times of peace. The more a worker's emotions are stimulated to work toward company objectives, the more successful the company will be.

It is important to cultivate the ability to provoke strong emotions in others, but it is just as important that others are unable to stir up strong emotions in you. To remain untouched by another's provocation prevents another from weakening your judgment and controlling your actions. The wise man practices a detachment from his emotions. He is indifferent to praise or abuse. He will not succumb to provocation and become the victim of his own emotions.

STRATEGY **31** ■ ■ ■ ■ ■ ■ ■ ■ ■ ■ ■ ■ ■ ■ ■

The Beauty Trap

From the earliest times, sex has been used as a weapon of espionage and intrigue. The story of the king of Yue's revenge, as told in the Spring and Autumn Annals (770–476 B.C.), contains the earliest recorded instance of the use of a beautiful woman as a spy. The king of Yue sent Xi Si, one of the most beautiful women in the history of China, to Wu's king ostensibly as a gift. Her true purpose was to capture the king's affection and divert him from matters of state as well as to gather information for the king of Yue. She was successful in both and, as a consequence, the king of Yue was able to destroy his enemy.

Even in today's business world, the gift of women is not uncommon in Asian societies. It is the host's duty to understand tacitly and provide for the desires of the guests. It is felt that the barrier between host and guest, buyer and seller, may be removed in an atmosphere of wine, women, and song, and a closer business relationship achieved.

In every period of history, in the East and West, there are instances of sex being used as an effective tool when employed with care. But it can also have adverse results. There is a Chinese proverb that says, "You can lose your maiden as well as your troops." In general, Asian society feels that the seductive power of a woman can be a very effective tool in manipulating an adversary. Thus, the saying: "Woman is water, and man is mud. They mix well together."

STRATEGY **32** ■ ■ ■ ■ ■ ■ ■ ■ ■ ■ ■ ■ ■ ■ ■

The Empty City

During the Three Kingdoms period (A.D. 220–265), Kung Min sent his troops off to battle. His city was left without good protection. His greatest enemy, Si Ma, the commander of the army of Wei, made an unexpected approach while Kung Min was in this vulnerable position. But Kung Min used the empty-city strategy to defend the city. He sent an old man to open the city's front gate and sweep the entrance way. Kung Min then went to his tower to prepare food and wine. He played a musical instrument and sang poetry as if he had not a care in the world. Commander Si Ma approached the city gates, but hesitated to enter. He was wary of tricks and feared a trap was waiting because of this obvious lack of security. Si Ma ordered his troops to retreat and wait so he might discover the true situation. While Si Ma waited and wondered, Kung Min's soldiers returned from their campaign and the city was once more defended.

A deliberate display of weakness can conceal true vulnerability and confuse the enemy. Creating a mystery by hiding your real strength is an effective weapon.

STRATEGY **33** ■ ■ ■ ■ ■ ■ ■ ■ ■ ■ ■ ■ ■ ■ ■ ■

Espionage and Counterespionage

The history of espionage and counterespionage is nearly as long as history itself. Information on the condition of an enemy is vital to the survival of a nation. It is also vital to the survival of a business.

Because the investment of time and money in research and development can be very high, Asian businesses often prefer to obtain technological information through covert means rather than develop their own. They feel it is much more efficient and cost-effective for them to acquire and refine another's technology. This is often accomplished simply by purchasing a piece of equipment, disassembling it, and analyzing the parts. Asians may request training courses to accompany a purchase of new equipment. The Asian buyer does this not simply to learn the usage of the product, but rather to learn how to reproduce it. Seemingly harmless questions will be asked in order that a missing piece to the puzzle may be passed to them by an unwary engineer.

After introduction of the IBM Personal Computer, IBM contracted with some Taiwan manufacturers to produce some of its components. Shortly thereafter, Taiwan became the world leader in the manufacture of IBM PC compatibles.

The Japanese would like the world to view their country today as an innovator rather than a copycat, but it is still widely accepted that Japan achieved its present economic success largely by adopting technology developed mostly in the West. Since the Japanese know how easily valuable information can be passed on, they also understand the importance of withholding information. The Chinese know that Japanese mouths are shut tight. They share nothing.

The Japanese often refuse to answer even the most general questions about their technology. This does not, however, discourage the Chinese from asking. Attempting to gain valuable information simply by asking is common practice in Asia, but the Americans are the only ones who answer every time they are asked.

American companies rarely protect themselves against industrial espionage. American executives often do not understand the seriousness of their losses, and it is a well-known failing in American engineers that they cannot resist showing off how much they know.

Asians know the value of another's knowledge. It is not that they do not recognize the intellectual property rights of others, it is just that they sometimes choose to ignore them.

STRATEGY **34** ▪ ▪ ▪ ▪ ▪ ▪ ▪ ▪ ▪ ▪ ▪ ▪ ▪ ▪

Mutilate One's Body

This strategy is very persuasive when one wishes to make a convincing demonstration of commitment or loyalty. During feudal times, a spy preparing to enter a neighboring country would often volunteer to cut off a body part or pluck out an eye to convince the lord of the neighboring country that he had been mistreated and as evidence of his sincere desire to serve his new lord.

The Bing-Fa master Wu Tzu lived during the Spring-Autumn period. As a young man, he traveled through China from the court of one feudal lord to another, trying to convince them of his brilliance so that he would receive a worthy post. After countless rejections and personal tragedies, he finally obtained a minor position in the court of Lu. The king of Lu noticed Wu Tzu's talents and appointed him commander of the army in the face of an imminent attack by their neighbor, Chi. Advisors to the king, jealous of Wu's ability, put his loyalty in question by noting that Wu Tzu's wife was a native of Chi. To demonstrate his unquestionable devotion to the king, Wu Tzu killed his wife.

One of the objectives of the students in Tiananmen Square was to make China and the world aware that many Chinese people wanted democracy and greater freedom. Because of the intense press coverage, this objective was realized to a great extent before the massacre. But another objective was to bring about immediate democratic reforms. In order to induce the students to end the demonstration, the government promised certain concessions, but the students knew that these could not be relied upon. They knew that blood must and would be shed. They used their bodies and blood to communicate their message of liberty and democracy for China across the world.

STRATEGY **35** ■ ■ ■ ■ ■ ■ ■ ■ ■ ■ ■ ■ ■ ■ ■

Chain Links

Chain-link strategies are the combining of all tricks, devices, and schemes into one interconnected arrangement, like the links of a chain.

Dong Zou held the power in China during the Han Dynasty. He was an excessively cruel person. After inviting members of the court to a party, he would display captured enemy soldiers, behead them, chop off their hands or feet, or poke out their eyes. Bloodshed did not move him. He would go about the party as if nothing out of the ordinary were happening. Court members felt that sooner or later they would all become victims of Dong Zou. He was too strong to plot against. He had total control over the emperor and the protection of his stepson, Lu Bu, one of China's legendary military heroes. There seemed no way to remove the tyrant.

Wong Yuen, a man of little wealth or power, was determined to find a way to overthrow Dong Zou. He knew both Dong and Lu Bu had a weakness for beautiful women, and Wong designed a strategy to make use of this weakness. Diao Chan was Wong's beautiful stepdaughter. Wong invited Lu Bu to his house and had his beautiful stepdaughter Diao Chan serve tea. Wong Yuen gave Lu Bu and Diao Chan time alone. Very taken by Diao Chan's beauty, Lu Bu asked for her hand in marriage. Wong Yuen agreed. Wong Yuen then invited Dong Zou to his home. When Dong met Wong's beautiful stepdaughter, he also was attracted to her and wanted to take Diao Chan as one of his wives. Wong Yuen agreed to this also. Each of the men thought he was the only one who had the hand of Diao Chan.

Dong Zou immediately married Diao Chan. Lu Bu could not protest her marriage to his stepfather because Chinese ways required that Lu Bu respect the elder's wishes. But Lu Bu could not resist seeing Diao Chan secretly. She told Lu Bu that she was in hell every day living with this old man. She taunted Lu Bu, telling him that, although he was a great hero of China, he couldn't save her from this misery and suffering. Finally, Lu Bu arranged the murder of his stepfather, ending the tyrant's grip on China.

This plan utilized the Beauty Trap, and the Fire Burning Across the River. A conflict of interest arose between the two men when they fell in love with the same woman. The conflict was a fire burning between Dong and Lu Bu. Then, Wong Yuen borrowed Lu Bu's hand to kill. In this case Wong used not just one but a set of strategies to accomplish his goal.

STRATEGY **36** ■ ■ ■ ■ ■ ■ ■ ■ ■ ■ ■ ■ ■ ■ ■ ■ ■

Escape Is the Best Policy

Retreat is another form of advance. A good man does not fight a losing battle.

—Chinese maxim

When faced with unfavorable conditions, retreat. Attack when conditions are more favorable. In order to attain the ultimate victory, it is sometimes necessary to accept a temporary defeat and, by escaping, to preserve one's strength. For some, though, it may be more difficult to accept the shame of retreat than to die with glory.

Chinese history holds many examples of escape. The founders of many of the Chinese dynasties were masters of escape. The founder of the Han Dynasty, Liu Bang, for example, escaped repeatedly throughout his life as a commander. Before Liu united China by defeating Xiang Yu, he spent four unsuccessful years warring against Xiang. Each time Liu was defeated, he retreated and awaited a more favorable time to attack anew. Xiang, on the other hand, was only defeated by Liu once. But once was enough for one who did not understand the art of escape. To save face, Xiang took his own life on the banks of the Wu River.

Escape may not be heroic, but it does ensure that one can fight another day. In such a large place as China, if one cannot win a battle immediately, escape is usually easy. China has many places in which to hide. Escape became an important element of military strategy. The Chinese have learned to accept temporary disgrace in order to achieve ultimate victory. Chinese battles tend to drag on for years, with each defeat followed by a successful retreat.

In Japan, there is no room to escape and regroup. Once something is started, it must be finished because on this island nation there is no place else to go. Therefore the Japanese developed quite different battle strategies. When faced with the possibility of defeat, the Chinese use ingenious means to live to fight another day, while the Japanese have developed a philosophy of death before dishonor. While the Japanese and Chinese share many attitudes, they differ in this.

This last strategy of the thirty-six is the most popular in China. All Chinese school children know it. The Chinese feel, "If I can fight and win, I will fight. If I cannot win, I will escape."

5

Thick Face, Black Heart

In 1911, *The Chengdu City Daily* ran the first installment of an article entitled *Thick Black Theory* by S. W. Lee. The article was to be published in three installments, but the furor created by the first installment was so overwhelming that the paper did not publish the others. Soon thereafter, the entire text of the essay was published privately in Beijing as a booklet entitled *Thick Face, Black Heart*. The book went through several printings between 1934 and 1936. Each edition sold out immediately. The original article was scarcely two thousand words long, yet its influence has been very great. For many years it was banned in both Taiwan and mainland China, although it is once again available in Taiwan.

Mr. Lee put a name to the obsessive and ruthless quality of those who pursue their own ends without regard to the effect of their actions on others: "thick face, black heart." The concept of a black heart is easy for a Westerner to understand, while that of a thick face might be a bit more obscure. Recall the Asian concept of *face*, then consider the Western idea of a person having a thick skin; in other words, such a person is one beyond shame or guilt who does not care what others think. So, a person with a thick face is not bound by the conventional thinking of others and thereby can

achieve things unachievable by someone worried about the appearance of his actions to others. The only concern a thick-faced person
has about his actions is whether or not they are effective.

Thick Face, Black Heart is a very natural principle of action in
a world where a great many people are competing for too few of the
necessities of life. Only the strongest, smartest, or most ruthless
will survive in such a world. Although the practice of Thick Face,
Black Heart is common, most practitioners wish to gloss over their
actions with a veneer of ethical rationalization. Lee's frank statement of the principles of selfish action shocked even the most
selfish and ruthless people.

In the storm of protest and criticism that followed the publication of *Thick Face, Black Heart,* a well-known official published a
sanctimonious and self-righteous rebuttal titled *Thin Face, White
Heart,* in which he attacked Lee as if Lee himself had invented the
things of which he wrote. Some time later, this same official was
proven guilty of extreme corruption in the discharge of his official
duties and was executed.

Lee described three levels in the practice of Thick Face, Black
Heart. The first—"Thick as a castle wall, black as charcoal"—is the
level of the cheap hustler, the crook and con man. Men like these
do not truly understand what they are doing. Their blackness is
apparent to all who see them. Though they are given to evil pursuits,
they do not understand and embrace the blackness of their hearts.
They are still capable of guilt.

The second level—"Thick and hard, black and shimmering"—
is the stage of those confirmed in their evil actions. They are
unconstrained by feelings of guilt or shame, and their blackness
remains for all to see.

The third stage—"So thick it is formless, so black it is color-
less"—is the highest level. This is the level of seemingly virtuous
men. They can ruthlessly pursue their own ends while being extolled by their victims for their virtue.

Although Lee put a name to it, the concept is an ancient one.
The lust for personal power has been the single most important
influence on the destiny of the Chinese empire. It has been the force
behind the rise and fall of dynasties. Sons have killed fathers and
brothers have set their swords against brothers in the quest for
power. The lust for power kept China in a state of constant war for
hundreds of years.

Today, battles are joined across the negotiating table. Armor has
been replaced by Brooks Brothers suits, but the lust for power has
not changed, nor have the principles for satisfying that lust. Over
the course of centuries, those who have acquired great power have

always been those who understood the principles of Thick Face, Black Heart and ruthlessly, singlemindedly adhered to them.

Han Fei Tzu wrote the first exposition of the principles underlying Thick Face, Black Heart during the Warring States period. Han's work was read by Emperor Chin during the period when he was gathering all of China under his dominion. He is said to have remarked, "If I could but meet this man and speak a while with him, I would not regret it, if it cost me my life." Han was summoned to the court of the great emperor, but before he could establish himself there, he was poisoned by another of the emperor's advisors who was afraid that Han would supplant him.

Han had studied under a Confucian scholar who disagreed with the classical Confucian notion that the human soul comes into being in a pure state and that experience of the world creates the evil tendencies that later creep in. Han's master taught that the soul is born in an impure state and struggles constantly against the tendency to evil.

Han's philosophy was stern and pragmatic. He believed in a world where it was every man for himself and every nation for itself. Han advocated strict discipline and severe punishment for wrongdoing. He taught that the superior leader should be above human emotion. Although guided by a benevolent regard for the good of the state, he should be a strict and heavy-handed enforcer of justice. He should be beyond the reach of praise or criticism, motivated only by a desire to make his country and himself strong enough to overcome their enemies. Han disdained the formation of alliances as a national policy either for conquest or defense. He believed that a nation's power must lie within itself, that there is no truly common interest among allies. The only interest is self-interest. In this he foretold Chin's success in the conquest of China by the betrayal of one ally after another.

Han's writings described a method of action that was beyond everyday concepts of good and evil. Actions were judged solely on whether they helped one survive in a hostile, dog-eat-dog world.

Throughout Chinese history there have been figures who embodied the principles of Thick Face, Black Heart. Their stories have been put down in many histories and are read and studied today throughout Asia.

Cao Cao, the dominant figure of the Three Kingdoms period, was a man of very black heart. To him, no deed was evil if it advanced his interests. He said, "It's better to wrong others than to let others wrong me." Cao Cao's counterpart, Liu Bei, had an extremely thick face. On several occasions when he was in the grasp of his enemies, he went down on his knees, cried, and shamelessly begged for his life. But when his enemies fell into his hands, he had no mercy for them at all.

After the end of the Ch'in Dynasty (207 B.C.), Liu Bang and Xiang Yu battled for control of China. Xiang Yu had every advantage: He had the best troops, he already controlled most of China, and he was a great warrior. Yet he lost China because he had not as thick a face nor as black a heart as Liu Bang. Liu Bang repeatedly lost battles and returned home for new recruits. When Xiang Yu lost only one important battle, he felt so full of shame that, instead of returning to his homeland to regroup and recruit, he took his life.

In their last battle, Xiang Yu was unable to withstand Liu Bang's force. For just such a situation, Xiang Yu had long been holding Liu Bang's father as hostage. Xiang Yu ordered him to be brought out and tied in front of a pot of boiling oil. Liu Bang was ordered to retreat with all his forces or see his father boiled alive. Liu rode to the front of his troops and shouted, "You and I were blood brothers at one time, General Xiang. My father is also yours. If you wish to cook our father, please share a cup of the broth with me."

We all practice Thick Face, Black Heart. When practiced in the small matters of our daily lives, small gains are realized; when used in great matters, as they were by Cao Cao and Liu Bang, empires tumble.

In Lee's collection of writings, he describes two characteristically Chinese ways of getting by at the expense of those we deal with: Sawing Off the Arrow, and Patching Up the Wok.

■ | **Saw Off the Arrow**

In China, the practice of medicine is divided into two domains: Outer Practice and Inner Practice. There is a story of a man who had been hit with an arrow and went to see a doctor of Outer Practice. The doctor sawed off the arrow's shaft but did not remove the arrowhead. Nevertheless, he told the patient that he was done. The startled patient asked the doctor, "Why don't you remove the arrowhead inside my body?" and the doctor replied, "Because that is a job for a doctor of Inner Practice."

Asians often take care of business by sawing off the arrow. In Asia, you will find that your proposals are often met with some form of agreement that is contingent on someone else's approval. You will often hear, "Regarding this matter, I really agree with you, however, I must discuss it with Mr. Chen." You will also hear: "I

will take care of this part of the job. The rest can be left for later."
The Chinese use these methods to defer accountability. They do not
care if something goes wrong, so long as the blame can be laid on
whoever gave the final approval or finished the job.

■ | **Patch Up the Wok**

This technique also derives its name from an old tale: A housewife
discovered that her wok had developed a crack and was leaking.
She summoned a wok craftsman to repair it. The craftsman asked
the woman to go build a hot fire so that he could burn off the soot
and examine the wok more closely. Left alone with the wok for a
moment, the craftsman tapped it lightly to enlarge the crack. When
the soot had been burned off, the repairman showed the crack to
the owner, saying, "The crack is worse than it first appeared. It will
be a difficult job. You're lucky that you called me when you did."
The owner looked at the crack with great surprise: "You are right,
you are right! It probably would have been impossible to repair it if
it had got any worse."

Both of these methods involve looking after your own interests
with total disregard of the effects of your actions on the other party.
Although the principles of Thick Face, Black Heart may never
be mentioned in today's Asian business and political worlds, they
are certainly the principles on which much effective action is based.
While it is considered that using them for self-gain is a lowly deed,
to use them for the good of all is a virtuous deed. When dealing
with foreigners, the practice is used for the good of one's country,
and, therefore, it is a noble action.

■ | **DENG XIAOPING'S STRATEGY**

In the early morning hours of June 4, 1989, tanks rolled across
Tiananmen Square, crushing the bodies of scores of protesting
students beneath their treads. The Chinese people knew that this
massacre had occurred by the will of Li Peng, the hard-line con-
servative prime minister of the People's Republic. But the shocking
and puzzling thing was that they also knew that it could not have

taken place without the consent of Deng Xiaoping. This brutal action seemed completely out of character for Deng and out of step with his known agenda for the political and economic future of China.

During the occupation of Tiananmen Square, the moderate Zhao Ziyang had been purged from his position of secretary-general of the Chinese Communist Party. After the incident, it appeared to have been a showdown and complete victory for Li Peng. It remained only for Li Peng to be named to Zhao's office to ensure his succession to the leadership upon the eighty-six-year-old Deng's demise. But in a surprising move, Deng appointed Jiang Zemin, a relative moderate to fill Zhao's post. Deng also protected Zhao from further persecution.

What was Deng's purpose in sending these mixed signals? He had been in the party since he was a teenage boy. He had fought as a common soldier in the civil war and followed Mao on the Long March in the darkest days of their struggle. His entire political life had been dedicated to reforming China politically and economically. Why, in the last days of his life, would he throw all his work away and put China in the hands of the backward-thinking conservatives?

Each time in the past that he had marked a man for the succession, it was a moderate reformer that he picked, and each time, the hard-liners were able to undermine his choice. I believe Deng recognized and seized his last opportunity to strengthen the liberal wing of the party at the expense of the hard-liners. It is no secret to Deng that China will go through a tremendous power struggle after his death, and despite his best efforts, it had appeared that the liberals were going to be no match for the conservatives. He recognized that by allowing Li Peng and his hard-line colleagues to carry out such a brutal action, he would mark them as enemies in the eyes of the people. When the day of the power struggle at last arrives, the liberals will realize that Deng has forged for them a powerful alliance with the Chinese people.

In its noblest manifestation, the art of Thick Face, Black Heart is the strength of a surgeon to amputate a limb while disregarding the agonized entreaties of the patient. It is the strength of a general to order beloved troops to their deaths. It is the strength of a leader to do what must be done.

PART  TWO

THE
ANT
PEOPLE

■
_____

The following four chapters describe a plan of national development formulated by the Japanese more than one hundred years ago. They have carried it out by utilizing the principles of deception that we have discussed in the previous section.

6

Japan Says No
for 300 Years

When the new book *The Japan That Can Say No* reached the United States in the fall of 1989, many Americans were deeply offended by the attitudes toward America expressed by Sony chairman Akio Morita and his co-author, Shintaro Ishihara, the former minister of transportation and possibly the future prime minister of Japan. But these men are merely expressing an attitude that is common to most Japanese and has its roots far back in Japanese history. The only thing new about this book was the open expression of these thoughts.

To understand current Japanese political and economic objectives and, most important, why the Japanese behave the way they do, one must know something of Japanese history.

The history of Japan as a unified nation begins in the sixteenth century. Until that time, Japan was a diffuse collection of feudal states without a strong central government. In the sixteenth century, the shogunate of Toyotomi Hideyoshi began the centralization of Japan's ruling power. After Hideyoshi's death, Tokugawa Ieyasu murdered Hideyoshi's young heir and proclaimed himself shogun. He established Edo castle, on the site of present-day Tokyo, as the seat of Japanese government.

Tokugawa Ieyasu's contribution to the development of the Japanese state was the establishment of an orderly succession of leadership. He had seen the shogun Nobunage's powerful heir overthrown by Toyotomi Hideyoshi, and had himself overthrown Hideyoshi's heir. To avoid the vacuum of power created when a shogun dies and an untried youth steps into his position, Tokugawa Ieyasu resigned in 1605, two years after assuming the title of shogun, in favor of his elder son, Hidetada. Thus he allowed Hidetada to consolidate his power while the formidable Ieyasu was still alive and standing behind the throne. Following his father's death in 1616, Hidetada did the same thing by resigning the shogun's post in 1623 to his son. This tradition firmly established the Tokugawa shogunate. Japan, for the first time, enjoyed more than two hundred years of political stability and domestic peace.

■ JAPAN'S EARLY ISOLATION

In the sixteenth century, Christian missionaries and Western traders began to appear in Japan. Because there was no genuine national government, there was no national policy regarding these Westerners and for a time they flourished. But when Ieyasu acceded to power, he established a policy to rid Japan of all foreign influence. He wished to keep Japanese thought purely Japanese and he believed that the true intent of Westerners was to colonize Japan. The Tokugawa court promoted the reestablishment of Confucianism and Buddhism, not so much for their philosophical or spiritual values, but as effective tools and doctrines to support the unchallenged authority of the shogunate's central governing power, and as a means to counteract Christianity.

In 1606, the shogunate issued anti-Christian decrees. Over the next sixty years, Japan expelled missionaries and killed or exiled anyone who would not renounce the Christian faith. All Japanese were forced to register at local temples so that their religious affiliations could be confirmed.

In addition to uprooting Christianity from the culture, control of foreign trade was tightened as another way to isolate the people from foreign influence. European trading ships were limited to two ports. The English voluntarily gave up trading with Japan because it was not profitable for them. The Spanish were expelled for their missionary activities, and Portuguese envoys were executed in 1640.

By 1635, all Japanese were prohibited from overseas travel, and those already in foreign countries were not allowed to return to Japan for fear they might bring with them foreign thoughts. By 1641, Japan's only contact with the Western world was through the isolated port of Nagasaki where the Dutch were allowed to remain on the island of Deshima. As that island measured only some two hundred yards long and eight yards wide, the Dutch were actually no better off than prisoners.

Japan's few outside contacts consisted of tributary trips to China and occasional trading expeditions to Okinawa and Korea. China was Japan's only significant outside contact, and Chinese books contained no Western thoughts.

The Japanese went about isolating themselves in typical Japanese fashion. As is still true today, everything they chose to do was carried out as if it were a sacred mission. They restricted the building of large ships, so that their vessels could travel only in and around the Japanese islands. They banned the use of Western guns during this time and returned to using traditional Japanese swords. Japan thus successfully kept her doors closed to the rest of the world for more than two hundred years.

■ THE WEST BEGINS ITS ENCROACHMENT

During Japan's two-hundred-year seclusion, technology in the Western world was developing at an extraordinary rate. At the end of the eighteenth century, the industrialized West was ready to give Japan another try. The chronology that follows lists the events that ultimately led to the opening of Japan to the West.

1791   Two American ships manage to enter Japanese waters.

1792   Adam Laxman, commander of the Russian ship *Ekaterina*, arrives in Hokkaido to negotiate an official trade agreement and is rebuffed by the shogunate in Edo.

1797   An American ship chartered by the Dutch visits Nagasaki. British vessels visit Hokkaido.

1804   The head of the Russian-American Company visits Nagasaki seeking a trade agreement, and is rebuffed.

1806–7 The Russians establish trading posts north of Hokkaido without the permission of the Japanese government.

1806   The shogunate issues instructions to Hokkaido officials to close the port to all foreign ships.

1808   British vessels visit Nagasaki in search of Dutch ships under the control of Napoleon.

1811   Japan imprisons Russian traders at posts established in 1806 and holds them captive for more than two years.

1818   British vessels visit Edo Bay.

1824   Armed British sailors clash with local Japanese on the southern island of Kyushu.

1830   Tokugawa Nariaka, a young noble, calls for administrative reform and for greater national unity. He urges the acquisition of Western military technologies to strengthen the Japanese military.

1837   America's interest in opening Japan increases, due to the large number of ships that are sailing from New England to China. Americans are interested in obtaining supplies in Japanese ports, and in establishing an official agreement with the Japanese government to protect American sailors against the brutal treatment of foreigners mandated by the shogunate. An American businessman in Canton sends the *Morrison*, an unarmed merchant ship, to show goodwill, but the Japanese fire on the ship.

1838   The liberal scholar Takano Choei urges the opening of Japan to foreign contact. He is imprisoned and is later forced to commit suicide.

1846   Commodore Biddle of the U.S. East India Fleet visits Japan in a vain effort to open trading.

1849   Commander Glynn visits Nagasaki and, despite a new note of firmness in the American demands, gets nowhere with his proposal for a trade agreement. He is able to pick up fifteen stranded American sailors.

1853   American Commodore Matthew Perry enters Edo Bay with three steam frigates and five other warships, one-quarter of the entire American navy. He forces the Japanese to accept a list of demands from President Fillmore to the Japanese emperor. Perry promises to return the following spring for an answer.

1854   Perry returns from Japan with the Treaty of Kanagawa, signed on March 31. The Japanese agree to open two ports to American vessels, to allow an American consul to reside in Shimoda, to provide for proper treatment of ship-wrecked American sailors, and to grant the United States most-favored-nation status. This treaty opens the door to the Western nations and is quickly followed by similar treaties with the British, Dutch, and Russians.

■ | ## JAPAN TAKES REVENGE

The Japanese bowed to American demands in 1854 under the implied threat of military reprisals if they did not. They had witnessed the ineffectiveness of the Chinese against the British in the Opium War and were under no illusions about the outcome of a military confrontation with the West. The harsh terms of the 1842 Treaty of Nanking (Nanjing) that were imposed on the Chinese after their defeat caused the shogunate to feel that a voluntarily signed treaty was more desirable than one imposed by a conqueror. Japan's two hundred years of isolation and national tranquility ended under the shadow of Western guns.

There followed an influx of what the Japanese saw as ill-mannered, offensive, and unclean foreign creatures. In the Shinto religion, cleanliness is godliness. The Japanese held the "un-washed" foreigners in great contempt and they felt anger and shame for their inability to rid themselves of these alien people. The common slogans of the time came to be "Honor the emperor" and "Expel the barbarians." Since the emperor had been for two hundred years a powerless figurehead under the shogunate, and since the shogunate was manifestly unable to expel the barbarians, both these slogans were expressions of popular discontent with the government.

In 1863, the samurai in the domain of Choshu, frustrated by the shogun's reluctance to use force against the foreign barbarians, independently undertook the task of expelling them. But American warships immediately sank their two newly purchased gunboats. French soldiers destroyed their fortress and ammunition depot. The samurai of Choshu reconstructed their fortifications and doggedly resumed the unequal contest, but in the following year, a combined fleet of seventeen French, Dutch, British, and American warships again leveled their fortifications.

The samurai of Choshu were not alone in their humiliation. Following the assassination of an Englishman by a samurai of the domain of Satsuma, a British squadron reduced the Satsuma fortifications to rubble and extorted 100,000 pounds in reparations from Satsuma.

Samurai of the Satsuma and Choshu clans also shared another grievance; more than 250 years earlier, they had been defeated by Tokugawa Ieyasu's forces in his rise to power. Armed with the common goals of removing the ancient shame of their defeat by the Tokugawa shogunate and the present disgrace of losing one battle after another to Western troops, the two joined forces in a civil war against the shogunate. While the ultimate goal of both sides was the expulsion of the foreign barbarians, neither side scrupled to use these same barbarians to further their immediate aims. The French supported the shogun; the British supported the Satsuma and Choshu samurai in their attempt to eliminate the shogunate and restore the emperor to power.

■ THE RESTORATION OF THE EMPEROR

The Satsuma and Choshu clans prevailed in their battle with the shogunate. In 1868, Emperor Meiji (Emperor Hirohito's grandfather) acceded to the throne at the age of fifteen. He ruled Japan until 1912.

The repeated military defeats of the former shogunate at the hands of the Western powers had clearly demonstrated to the new leadership the inadequacy of medieval weaponry against that of the industrialized West. In 1868, the new emperor announced a profoundly important document, the "Five Articles Imperial Oath," which has served as the focus of Japanese economic and political objectives since that time.

The Five Articles Oath set forth the basic plan for Japan to regain her national pride and control of her own destiny. The first four articles addressed the need for domestic unification. The fifth and final article addressed the problem of Japan's relations with the outside world. The document recalled the proposal of Tokugawa Nariaka in 1830 regarding the need for national unity and the adoption of Western technology.

Article One: All matters were to be decided by public discussion.

Article Two: The Japanese people, from the emperor down to his least subject, would share one heart and would unite in an effort to achieve common objectives.

Article Three: The central government and local warlords would share the same path. The court and commoners were equal.

Article Four: Japan would eliminate outdated customs.

Article Five: Japan would be receptive to knowledge and technology from whatever source it came. Japan would send students to the United States and Europe, and would invite foreign experts to come to Japan and disseminate their knowledge to the Japanese.

With this document, Japan set herself on a deliberate course to become a world power. Japan's commitment to modernization and her will to power grew out of her humiliation at the hands of the Western powers and a determination to be rid of the foreign barbarians.

Japanese culture did not develop through evolution, but rather through revolution and adaptation. The Japanese transformed themselves from a primitive society to a highly civilized society more than two thousand years ago by adopting what they admired or found useful in Chinese culture. The adoption of Western ways was much easier for the Japanese than for the Chinese because much of Japan's culture was borrowed already. Except for the two hundred years of xenophobia discussed earlier, Japan has never been reluctant to adopt customs or ideas from the outside world.

Japan also learned from the West the advantages of establishing colonies in the interest of the motherland. Japan's victory over China in 1894 resulted in Japanese colonies in Korea, Taiwan, and Okinawa. By the early part of this century, only forty years after resolving to become a dominant player in the global arena, Japan was established as one of the major colonial powers in the world.

■ THE NEW SAMURAI

As the Meiji government gradually eliminated the expensive anachronism of the samurai class, some samurai turned to a new battlefield—commerce. Since many of the same qualities that made a good samurai also made a good businessman, many samurai were highly successful at commerce. Today's huge Mitsui, Mitsubishi, and Sumitomo conglomerates all have samurai origins.

In former times, the rulers paid little notice to commerce. After the Meiji restoration and the emperor's mandate to modernize Japan, the government began to provide financial assistance to individuals who demonstrated the ability to further the objectives of Japanese industry. The government took a hands-on position to eliminate obstacles for selected business leaders by creating laws and regulations favorable to them. The government also forced small businesses to merge with large and profitable businesses for greater industrial efficiency. When government-operated industries proved to be unprofitable, the government sold the concern at a fraction of its value to Japanese individuals who were close to the court; no public announcements of these transactions were made. The government's objectives were to contribute to the security and development of imperial Japan.

Business goals and objectives were set by the divinely inspired pronouncements of the Meiji court. The government decided what industries were in need of development and helped generate the necessary working capital for the ventures. A company could go from shipping to mining, from textiles to finance and banking, depending on the perceived need in furthering the economic development of the nation.

In the court of Meiji, many leaders had dual responsibilities— one political and one commercial. Even Inoue, the foreign minister of the Meiji court, acted as mediator between the court and the house of Mitsui.

■ BREATHING THROUGH THE SAME NOSTRIL

The cozy relationship existing between the present Japanese government and Japanese industries is based on a tradition that goes back more than a hundred years. The ancestors of Mitsui, Mitsubishi, and Sumitomo drank tea and sake at the court of the Meiji emperor. They supported the imperial court in times of war. Through business mergers and intermarriages, the bonds have tightened over time between the largest businesses and the government policymakers.

Big business provided major financial support in the formation of the party movement in the 1880s. Mitsubishi's founder, Iwasaki, was the primary sponsor of the founding of Japan's first political party, the Constitutional Progressive Party. In the same period, the Mitsui family played a similar role in the formation of the Liberty Party. Historically, government and big business in Japan are members of one big family. As the Chinese say, they breathe out of the same nostril.

■ | **THE KEIRETSU**

A *keiretsu* can best be described as a cartel. It is a family of businesses, banks, and government agencies that work closely together to achieve common objectives. In the United States, similar relationships were outlawed by antitrust legislation, but in Japan they evolved naturally out of the complex personal, political, family, and feudal relationships of the Meiji court. The *keiretsu* are not an incidental phenomenon in the industrialization of Japan, they are the fundamental units of the Japanese industrial economy.

■ | **T. BOONE PICKENS' ASIAN ADVENTURE**

In 1989, T. Boone Pickens, the Texas oil magnate, spent $1.2 billion to acquire 26.2 percent of the stock of Koito, a leading auto parts manufacturer in Japan. Despite his position as the major stockholder, Mr. Pickens can get neither financial information nor board representation. Although the Toyota Motor Corporation has only 19 percent of Koito stock, it maintains three seats on the board and participates in the appointment of key management personnel. To Pickens' mind, this constitutes a conflict of interest, since Toyota is one of Koito's biggest customers.

Pickens accused Toyota and Koito of hiding something. And of course he is right. Among the many things that they are hiding is that Toyota controls the profits of Koito by setting the prices for the components it purchases. The Japanese are not going to dismantle the *keiretsu* system simply because the Americans think it is unfair. As the Japanese see it, the *keiretsu* system works exceptionally well and the American economic system is teetering on the brink of collapse. They might pay lip service to the ideas of free trade and fair and open competition, but they have no intention of seriously tinkering with a system that has wrought such economic miracles.

Along with Toyota, Pickens also has Nissan, Matsushita, and many Japanese banks as partners in the Koito Company. None of these Japanese insiders intends to open their hearts and minds to Mr. Pickens or open up the books to him either. Nor is it likely that they will be compelled to. Mr. Pickens' reluctant associates will have a little chat with their old political friends just to remind them that while they might have to pay lip service to free trade and open economies, they must not forget the importance of discouraging foreign "interference" in the Japanese economy.

On June 28, 1990, Pickens and his entourage went to the Koito annual shareholders meeting to make their displeasure felt. After three hours of chaos, they retreated with none of the seven proposals they had brought with them adopted and no board representation. During Pickens' speech to the shareholders, taunts were hurled at him from the floor: "Go ahead, suit yourself in the U.S. Congress. See if we care. We are not afraid of the U.S. Congress." "Japan has already defeated America in the economic war!" "Yankee go home!" "Remember Pearl Harbor!" "Damn you, . . . F**k you!"

Pickens vowed to continue his fight. He filed suit in the Japanese courts to obtain financial information, and he promised to raise the subject at the upcoming Houston economic summit. But Pickens' most credible threat was to make a case before the U.S. Congress that since a cartel system like *keiretsu* would be illegal under U.S. law, the importation of goods produced under such a system should be restricted. If he succeeds in making his case over the objections of the powerful Japanese lobby in Washington, it is likely that the Japanese will accommodate Pickens in some way, but it is unlikely that they will make the alterations in their economic system that would be necessary to truly address the fundamental issues.

■ ATTITUDES AND ROOTS

The single most important document in recent Japanese history is the Five Articles Imperial Oath of 1868. The first four articles set the tone for the transformation of Japanese internal attitudes. The fifth article deals with the Japanese attitude toward the West and has served as Japan's guidepost in formulating foreign and economic policies for the past hundred years.

Many of the unique aspects of Japanese society that are endlessly extolled by Western observers can be traced to one or more of the Five Articles. Certainly the overall success of the Japanese economy is a result of rigid adherence to this document. Although we noted its provisions earlier, an analysis of their content will cast considerable light on how they affect Japan's contemporary behavior.

Article One: All matters should be decided by public discussion.

The effect is to create common objectives through group decision-making. American managers who work in Japan invariably are impressed by the Japanese group decision-making process. Although it takes more time to reach a decision than by allowing an individual or small group to make a decision and impose it on those under them, once the decision is made it is much more effective in implementation.

Article Two: The Japanese people, from the emperor down to his least subject, should unite in an effort to achieve common objectives.

This article enjoins the Japanese people to present a unified front. Following the invasion by foreign powers, a common enemy was identified. Articles Two and Three called for the unification of the Japanese people for a common cause. This is the cornerstone of the unified front within Japanese corporations.

Article Three: The central government and local warlords should walk the same path. The court and commoners are equal.

The traditional bond of loyalty between samurai and master was based on a lifetime commitment. The samurai's life and the lives of his family members were the property of the master. The bond between employer and employee in today's Japan is of the same nature. Japanese workers are willing and often expected to work twelve or more hours per day.

For the Japanese individual, this fierce bond of loyalty does not stop with the employer, it extends to the Japanese nation and culture as a whole. Even Japanese nationals living overseas express their loyalty in every way they can. In Los Angeles, Japanese housewives told me they would rather pay more in a Japanese-owned grocery store for the same products than shop in an American-owned supermarket.

This article is a major reason for the minimal distinction between management and labor in Japanese industry. Article Three stressed the equality of the court and commoners. There is less distinction in Japan between high-level management and low-level laborers than in the United States. Salaries are not as disparate between the two classes as in this country. Management and labor can often be found wearing the same uniforms in the work place, singing the company anthem, doing exercises, and saluting the company flags together in the morning.

Article Four: Cast off and eliminate outdated customs and follow the laws of nature.

The most dramatic application of this article was the deliberate elimination of the samurai class after the announcement of the Five Articles Oath in 1868. For a thousand years the samurai had been the defenders of the nation, but in the face of Western military technology these medieval swordsmen had proven to be an expensive and ineffectual anachronism. It is clear that a nation that undertakes to remove the livelihood and the privileges of rank from the only armed members of its population is very serious about casting off that which it believes is no longer necessary. The elimination of the samurai demonstrates the depth of commitment the Japanese have made to implementing the Imperial Oath.

Article Five: New knowledge should be sought throughout the universe, thereby strengthening the imperial power.

After three hundred years of rebuffing the overtures of the West, the Five Articles Oath exhorts the Japanese people to adopt what is useful from Western science and technology. Over the past forty years, Japan has developed its formidable economy by taking Western technological innovation, perfecting it, manufacturing it, and exporting it back to its nations of origin. Although Japan is known as the world leader in consumer electronics, in the production of microchips, and in countless high-technology industries, very little of that technology was developed in Japan initially. It is a particularly Japanese genius to be able to graft Western knowledge onto Japanese habits of mind. The result is that they refine the technological innovation that they import, seek new uses for it, and create, manufacture, and market these products better than any other people in the world. The fifth article does not enjoin the Japanese to think like Westerners but rather to be able to incorporate Western knowledge into Japanese thought, all for the greater good of the state.

■ THE HUNDRED-YEAR PLAN

Japanese companies love to brag about their ten-year or fifty-year plan, but no one ever mentions to the Westerner the national objectives Japan has pursued over the past hundred years. These objectives were set down in 1868 by the Emperor Meiji, who swore that Japan would be a rich country, strong in the military power required for the survival of the Japanese race. In pursuit of these objectives, the Japanese decided to make use of Western technology and to beat the West at its own game.

Everything the Japanese have done since the mid-nineteenth century has been done in pursuit of these objectives. Out of their desire to be *fukoko-kyohei* (a rich country), the Japanese embarked on a policy of colonial expansion to acquire sources of natural resources for their industry. This expansionism eventually led them into World War II. After Japan's devastating military defeat, Western experts predicted that Japan could not recover to a point of self-sufficiency in less than fifty years. These experts were obviously not taking into consideration the fierce determination of the Japanese people. The reconstruction and industrialization of Japan in the postwar era is a miracle wrought by the willpower of a nation clear in its objectives and determined in its resolve, from the emperor down to the least citizen. Japan rose out of the ashes of its cities to become one of the world's greatest industrial powers in just over forty years.

The restriction against the buildup of a Japanese military capability after World War II allowed the Japanese to concentrate solely on their country's economic and industrial development. They were able to ride on the back of Uncle Sam to achieve economic supremacy quickly. Perhaps Japan would have taken fifty years to get on its feet if it had not been for the millions of dollars it received in U.S. aid.

Today's Japanese business leaders are being much too humble by citing examples of Japanese corporate wisdom in looking ten years ahead. Actually, Japanese corporations are much wiser than they care to acknowledge to the Westerner. Japan's objectives have been the same for one hundred years, and they follow the same blueprint set forth by Emperor Meiji, with government and private enterprise marching hand in hand.

■ JAPAN REARMED

While Western nations do not give much thought to the consequences of Japanese rearmament, the governments of China, Taiwan, and Korea, who perhaps have a better understanding of the Japanese than Westerners do, are seriously concerned about a resurgence of Japanese militarism.

Madam Chiang Kai-shek gave a speech during the 1987 centennial celebration of her late husband's birth. She mentioned with concern the increasing nationalism in Japanese attitudes. This could be a dangerous sign, she warned, if it were coupled with a military capability.

Robert Neff wrote an article in *Business Week* (September 25, 1989) in which he said that Japan's recent passion is *kokusan*, that is, products "made in Japan." But Neff was not writing about consumer goods. He was writing about military hardware: jet fighters, tanks, helicopters, and missiles. "Military self-reliance is suddenly enjoying a new cachet in Japan. Flush with a growing sense of economic and technological superiority, the Japanese increasingly want to strut their own stuff in defense."

The Pentagon is watching nervously where the Japanese are heading and is waiting for them to make clear their intent. Of course, that intent will never be clear to the Pentagon, because the Japanese are not going to spell it out, and the Pentagon has seldom been able to see through Japanese subterfuge.

7

Virtue and
Hypocrisy

Often, when reading yet another book about modern Japan written by a Western scholar, I am amazed at the uncritical attitude the author manifests toward all things Japanese. Western orientophiles in general often are blinded by their enthusiasm for the lofty and mysterious qualities of Asian cultures. They tend to find exotic explanations for actions and events of which they might be more critical if encountered in a Western context. Asians, on the whole, are much more honest about their faults and shortcomings than are the Western experts who study them. The Japanese national character, like that of all peoples, is a mixture of good and bad, virtue and vice. The special characteristics that are unique to the Japanese people, the very qualities that make them Japanese, are not comprised of virtue alone.

The most remarkable characteristic of the Japanese is their ability to place the interests of the state, the interests of the company, the interests of the family above their personal self-interest. Like all Asian people, they are hardworking and able to endure hardship beyond the experience of most Westerners. But much more so than other Asian peoples, the Japanese are willing to sacrifice their self-interest for the common interest. It is a degree of self-

99

denial that Chinese and Korean corporate and political leaders can only envy.

Even though Japan has tremendous economic power in the world today, the majority of her people still live a life of personal privation. A common city apartment in Japan consists of a single 700-square-foot room in which a family of five will cook, eat, sleep, and conduct the daily business of their lives. The prices of consumer goods and food are outrageously disproportionate to the average income. The burden of Japan's industrialization was borne on the backs of her workers and, as yet, the workers have not shared in the financial rewards. Their pay is low and their hours are long. Even stockholders often do not receive the dividends to which they might seem entitled. Earnings are retained within the company so that it might expand its operations and its markets. Workers and investors understand and agree with that policy.

The economy of Japan revolves around huge industrial conglomerates, and this has tended to produce a very few very wealthy people and a great many wage earners. In comparison, the economies of Taiwan, Singapore, and Hong Kong are dominated by large numbers of small- and medium-sized enterprises; this has created a large middle class and caused wealth to be distributed among a much larger number of people.

The work ethic of the Japanese people puts all of her Asian neighbors to great shame. Each worker pursues excellence as if the quality of work achieved is a statement of the individual's moral worth. An individual's character will be judged to a large degree by the quality of his work. An individual who does sloppy work, besides not having a job for long, will also be a joke among his peers.

In feudal times, a ruling lord demanded absolute obedience and loyalty of his samurai. Tests of obedience and loyalty sometimes required a samurai to sacrifice his wife and children with no explanation ever offered or asked for. Such virtue was highly regarded in the old Japan. Obedience and loyalty were more highly regarded than human life. The devastating effectiveness of the Japanese military during World War II had a great deal to do with this tradition of complete, unquestioning obedience and loyalty.

■ | OUTWARD VIRTUE

The Japanese regard themselves as an especially virtuous people. Much of their conception of virtue has come from their adaptation of the moral principles of Chinese Confucianism and Zen Buddhism. These religions both stress proper conduct as an essential element in the attainment of spiritual fulfillment. In many cases, however, the means have been mistaken for the end, and the outward form of proper conduct has become more important than the attainment of true virtue. In a culture where a great deal of lip service is paid to virtue, the appearance of virtue is of great social importance. A person who ignores the outward forms risks great censure.

■ | Cleanliness

A central concern of the Shinto religion is the question of purity and impurity. Shintoism places a heavy emphasis on the cleansing ritual because it is believed that the purity of one's physical environment and one's physical body plays a vital role in one's spiritual advancement. It is also believed that an impure environment will inhibit the development of a pure state of mind and will cause one to perform unworthy deeds.

Cleanliness is a public virtue as well as a private one. Although Japanese cities and towns are extremely crowded, the streets are always clean. This truly puts the Chinese and all their ancestors to shame. In spite of the street signs imploring "Do not spit, do not litter," the Chinese people have their own idea of what a street should look like.

■ | A Networking Society

Japanese society is a highly networked society. Everybody has to be introduced through the proper social rituals. To get anywhere in Japanese society, you must be introduced by the right people. It is important to go to a prestigious university as much for the contacts one might make as for the quality of the education.

■ | **Politeness**

The Japanese people by tradition are submissive and polite. They have difficulty saying no directly. When they mean no, they often express themselves by circumlocution. Instead of saying no, they say, "I'll get back to you later on that," or "I must refer that matter to my superior." But just because the Japanese do not often say no, it does not mean they are always agreeable and easy to deal with. Misunderstanding a silent or implied no in a business negotiation can prove to be more costly than receiving an unambiguous no.

■ | **Racial Purity**

Unlike Americans, who take pride in being a nation of mixed races and ethnic groups, the Japanese consider the "pure blood" of the Japanese people to be the wellspring of their superiority. They believe that genetic purity is the source of their unique ability to unite all elements of their society in a single will.

Prior to World War II, some Japanese leaders used theories of racial superiority to justify Japan's military and imperial ambitions. They believed that the Japanese and the Germans were genetically superior to the other peoples of the world. It followed in their thinking that these two nations should rightfully dominate the world.

There is still a strong racial prejudice toward the non-Japanese races living in Japan. This is normally not visible to Western eyes. Of their own volition, American and European residents of Japan seldom attempt to integrate themselves into the mainstream of Japanese society. As a consequence, they seldom confront the prejudice against those who do.

Over the years, I have had frank discussions with many Japanese friends and associates about these matters. There has not been much disagreement. They freely admit, at least in private, that the Japanese have a racial bias against Westerners—white, black, and Jewish. They consider themselves unquestionably superior to the Chinese, the Koreans, and the rest of the Asians as well.

After the Sino-Japanese War and the Russian-Japanese War in the early 1900's, Korea fell under Japan's control. In order to ensure a measure of cooperation from the Korean people, the Japanese uprooted the ruling families and moved them to Japan so that they would not be in a position to organize or participate in resistance to the Japanese occupation. This was the first influx of Koreans into modern Japan. During World War II, when Japan experienced severe manpower shortages, they drafted Koreans to serve as virtual slave labor. After the war, these people settled in Japan. It was not until 1985, however, that the Japanese government granted citizenship to these Koreans and their Japanese-born descendants. Previously, they could only obtain citizenship by marriage to a male Japanese citizen. Such marriages were extremely rare. No Japanese family with any sense of propriety would permit the marriage of one of its members to a Korean.

In any situation where there might be doubt, a Japanese will go out of his way to make it clear that he is not Korean. For the Koreans living in Japan, there are few prospects of a good job or improvement in their social status. Many change their names, but often their physical appearance will not allow them to pass as ethnic Japanese.

A few years ago in San Francisco, an American friend of mine married a Korean girl. Just before the wedding, a young Japanese friend of his took him aside. With the greatest sincerity the friend advised him not to go through with the ceremony. When pressed for some reason that the marriage should not take place, the Japanese told my friend, "The Korean people are lower than the nigger in Japan."

Racial purity is a farfetched concept to begin with, but it takes on almost comic dimensions when the Japanese talk about "pure blood." It is well documented that the present-day Japanese are the product of Chinese and Korean immigrations as well as periodic influxes of people from all over Southeast Asia, starting as early as the second century B.C. These immigrants mixed with the aboriginal inhabitants of the Japanese islands. According to anthropological evidence, these aboriginal inhabitants had certain traits in common with Caucasoid man, particularly in their hairiness of face and body, a characteristic notably lacking in most Mongols. There is corroborating evidence in the ancient Chinese records to indicate that Japan was a nation of hairy men. If claims of racial purity are based on the previous three hundred years of isolation, such a span seems insignificant in the time scale of human evolution.

■ | ## Castes and Outcasts

During the Tokugawa shogunate in the seventeenth century, Japan officially adopted a class system similar to that of the Chinese. It divided society into four social classes: samurai, farmers, artisans, and merchants.

The samurai class was the highest and most privileged. It included the shogun and all of the ruling lords as well as their military retainers. The farmers occupied the second echelon of the social hierarchy as the producers of food. Artisans included tradesmen and craftsmen of all kinds. Merchants were considered nonproductive and relegated to the bottom rung of the ladder.

There was another, unnamed class—the Japanese untouchables. They were called *eta*, meaning people who touch dead animals or unclean objects. They were known also by the euphemism *burakumin*, which literally means "the hamlet dwellers," which referred to the poor people living in the ghettos.

After his restoration in 1868, Emperor Meiji eliminated the samurai class and, along with it, officially eliminated all other class distinctions. But, however much the common people delighted to see the revocation of privileges of the samurai class, they entirely ignored the order of nondiscrimination against the *eta*.

Since the early seventeenth century, these people had been outcasts because of the work they did. They were butchers, leather craftsmen, shoemakers. The occupations of prostitute, beggar, gravedigger, and carnival entertainer were later added to the list of those proscribed.

The rejection of the untouchables can be understood as a result of the misinterpretation of certain doctrines of Zen Buddhism. It is very similar to the Hindu attitude toward the Indian untouchable class.

In Zen Buddhist doctrine, from which Shintoism has derived many of its principles, there are three states of being through which the human spirit expresses itself. These are: *Sattva*, the principle of being, light, and harmony; *Rajas*, the principle of motion, activity, and disharmony; and *Tamas*, the principle of inertia and delusion. Although none but the enlightened possess any one of these principles unmixed with the others, each being is characterized by whichever of these principles dominates their spirit. Zen Buddhism considers that these inborn tendencies guide one toward the proper station in life. One will, by each individual's particular mixture of these qualities, become a wise and great leader, a skilled butcher, or a prostitute.

In Japanese society, anyone who happens to be a butcher or prostitute, or to pursue any of those occupations considered to be unclean, is harshly judged by the society at large. This is the secular misapplication of a spiritual principle. In present-day Japan, a man is not an *eta* because he is a gravedigger; he is a gravedigger because he is an *eta*. The CEO's position at Sony is not open to him. The Zen Buddhist doctrine was not meant to apply to a situation where the individual's natural inclination was constrained by social restrictions that forced him into certain occupations and excluded him from others. But often in Japan, an individual's occupation is determined by the conditions of his birth. Access to occupations of power and privilege has been protected by custom and usage. Jobs considered unclean have been relegated to the *eta* and the children of *eta*. In this way the *eta* have become a hereditary caste, exactly like the untouchables of India.

One may wonder why the butcher, who slaughters and dresses animals for the table of the samurai, should be considered more unclean than the samurai whose occupation it is to slay his fellow human beings. But it is so. The word *eta* is not even spoken in polite society. It is considered to be an obscenity. Even today, Japanese families and employers routinely investigate suitors and job applicants to make sure that no *eta* will be married into their family or work in their company.

■ | **The Bond of Amae**

The Japanese word *amae* means indulgent love and interdependency. It describes a relationship similar to that between a mother and child. It is a condition of absolute trust and love. The bond of *amae* can pervade every relationship in Japanese society—with family, friends, employer, state. In business, two people who share this bond will look out for each other's interest. The buyer will not take advantage of the seller and vice versa. In contrast, a Chinese businessman will sometimes jeopardize a ten-year business relationship to make a quick profit when a stranger comes along who can sell him something cut-rate. The *amae* relationship seems an enlightened way for people to interact. In practice, however, it is not all sunshine and roses.

The *amae* relationship is almost never extended to Westerners, but I have seen it exist between Japanese and Taiwanese. The Taiwanese people have fifty years of history as subjects of the Japanese empire. One Taiwanese friend of mine who served in the Japanese army during World War II said that some of his Japanese comrades in arms had such sentiments toward him. Another who took his Ph.D. in Japan said that he and a few of his professors developed such a relationship. But such relationships are almost never extended to any Western-looking people.

The bond of *amae* gained importance under the Tokugawa shogunate. Wracked by internal strife and political instability for centuries, in the sixteenth century Japan entered into a period of peace. The Tokugawa shogunate strongly stressed the importance of social stability and glorified the bond of *amae*. Eventually, *amae* came to be seen as an important expression of individual virtue.

Among business associates, the *amae* relationship is built, to some extent, on self-interest. To be successful, it is necessary to be perceived as one who has virtue. One is not going to lightly discard a long-term business relationship for a short-term profit; one would gain such a poor reputation among his business associates that any momentary advantage would be trivial in comparison to the long-term damage to one's career. If the business world expects there to be such a bond in relationships between employee and employer, customer and supplier, then one had better make it happen and disregard any personal feelings in the matter.

A Japanese friend of mine, after graduation from the university, obtained a job with a prestigious Japanese firm. After he had worked for the firm for seven years, he had an opportunity to be considered for an excellent position in a U.S. company in Tokyo. He decided to do an initial interview with the American firm. Somehow the word got out and reached his superiors. Because he had broken the bond of *amae* with his original company, he was fired. His breach of faith, once it became known, made it next to impossible for him to find employment with another Japanese firm. In this context, *amae* is an effective tool with which to control Japanese workers.

On the other hand, it is important not to be too cynical about the bond of *amae*. In many cases the bond is real and heartfelt, and as such it can truly work miracles among those who share it.

■ SUPERIORITY AND INFERIORITY

The Japanese are deeply preoccupied with questions of superiority and inferiority. Relations between nations and between individuals are always analyzed in terms of which is the superior party. Although Japan does have a strong sense of national superiority, it is mixed with the unarticulated sense of inferiority of a people whose culture is borrowed from the very nations it professes to disdain. Many Japanese with whom I have spoken privately agree about this ambiguity.

No national culture evolves in a vacuum, but the Japanese culture is especially derivative. As I noted earlier, it has been derived in great measure from the Chinese. The Japanese written language is based on Chinese characters. The philosophies and religions are built on Chinese models. The governmental bureaucracy and the highly structured social order are adapted from ancient Chinese forms. The first written histories and all the early developments of natural science came to Japan from the Chinese mainland. The Japanese absorbed these influences and modified them to suit the Japanese character.

In the nineteenth century, Japan was exposed to an entirely different kind of influence, that of the industrialized West. Once the decision was made to have anything at all to do with the foreign barbarians, it became an explicit article of national policy to absorb all that Japan found useful from these technological societies and to integrate that information into Japanese society.

While Japanese thought was molded by Chinese Confucianism and Zen Buddhism, Japan's scientific knowledge came from the West. This has caused the Japanese to feel the lack of a true national identity forged from totally Japanese ideas; it has contributed to the Japanese people's vague feeling of inferiority. Witness their sensitivity to charges that they do not innovate, that they only copy.

Japan has adopted and refined already proven concepts and ideas, the best the world has had to offer. She has not wasted much time working through her own dead ends and misdirections. This has often made the Japanese system work better than those of the countries from which the Japanese have borrowed. That the Japanese culture works so well is the source of the Japanese sense of superiority; that it is not truly Japanese has given them an ambiguous sense of identity.

Feelings of inferiority and superiority ebb and flow with the fortunes of the Japanese nation. The first time Japan felt a sense of total superiority came at the height of her colonial conquests, prior to taking on China and the West in World War II. As we are approaching the twenty-first century, Japan has again regained her unalloyed sense of superiority. The world is beginning to see the Japanese nation drop its air of diffidence and gradually assert its will in the global arena once again.

In both their personal and political interactions the Japanese are obsessed with relative rank. When Japanese meet a new acquaintance, they first settle who is the superior and who is the inferior so that they will know how to act. Until the late 1970's, when Japanese met a Westerner they would automatically defer to him because of Japan's international status. At the same time, they also felt superior because they were of the Japanese race.

A few Japanese writers have undertaken to examine the ambiguity of Japanese attitudes. Of these social critics, the most widely known is the late writer Yukio Mishima. In a sense, Mishima's whole career consisted of confronting the dark side of the Japanese character.

Since his death, Mishima has become the most acclaimed Japanese author of the twentieth century, but during his lifetime, his eccentric ways and blunt honesty put many Japanese readers off. The Japanese prize conformity, not rebellion. Mishima encouraged the Japanese people to examine themselves honestly as individuals and as a nation. Among his forty novels, thirty-three plays, and eighty-odd short stories, there is a collection of essays entitled *The Unvirtuous Educational Seminar;* these essays were published originally as weekly newspaper columns and produced later as a television special in Japan. In this collection Mishima makes a series of sharp, honest observations that created a storm of controversy among the Japanese people and a deluge of hate mail.

In writing about his countrymen's mixed sense of superiority and inferiority, he described an incident that took place when he was in the United States in 1957. He had been invited to a dinner party at an American professor's home. To his delight and surprise, he found that a famous Japanese university president was also invited to attend. This man was well known for his flamboyant manner and Mishima looked forward to an entertaining evening. During dinner, this famous raconteur said little. He responded deferentially when spoken to and acted with abject humility toward his American host. Yet the man saw Mishima as his inferior and treated him as such. All evening long the president alternated between humility before the American and arrogance toward his countryman.

Mishima himself was obsessed by the Japanese belief in the superiority of the Japanese race. He was enraged by this craven vacillation between humility and arrogance before foreigners. On one hand, the Japanese shout slogans among themselves ("Japan is a country of divine origins and cannot be defeated"). On the other hand, they humble themselves before the Westerner. These ambiguous feelings arose, Mishima said, out of a strong desire to cover up a sense of inferiority and to gain a false sense of self-respect.

■ | **The Civilized Savage**

Mishima said, "Man's transcendental emotional state can often only be invoked by the sight of blood. Not only do we see it in the bullfight but we also see that Japanese rituals often cannot proceed to a climax without a frenzied group of people struggling together until blood is shed." He maintained that the hypocrisy in modern Japanese attitudes arises from the inability to satisfy this blood lust directly. Since the end of the samurai era, Mishima stated, this urge to violence could only be satisfied vicariously. "Until the end of the Tokugawa shogunate, Japan, although a civilized nation, was able to indulge its primitive blood lust. Blood pervades everything the Japanese enjoy: literature, theater, or cinema. The Japanese never shun scenes of violence or mutilation." He suggested that the Japanese could relieve much of their frustration by wearing a samurai sword to work.

Mishima accepted that there is a dark and savage side to the Japanese as there is to many peoples. This urge to violence is frustrated by the constraints of modern civilized society. Mishima's observations touched a raw nerve. The subject is one that few Japanese wish to confront.

The excessive cruelty of the Japanese during World War II is known throughout the world. On February 15, 1989, United Press International in Australia distributed a story about a sixty-nine-year-old Australian war veteran named George Stevenson who charged that Australian prisoners of war were fed human meat by their Japanese captors.

In February 1942, as a prisoner of war in forced labor as a truck driver, Stevenson says he delivered three hundred cases of meat to a POW camp in Cambodia. The meat was pickled with sugar and ginger and covered with maggots. Mr. Stevenson thought he was delivering horsemeat or pork. The smell was so bad that he asked an Oxford-educated Japanese officer what kind of meat it was. The answer was extremely candid. "We Japanese know what is good nutritious food," the officer told him. "We have the Chinese butchers kill the Chinese civilians and then package and pickle the meat; the majority is for the consumption of the Japanese troops."

The Japanese slaughtered a half-million Chinese in chemical warfare testing. They also revived in the twentieth century some of the cruelties practiced in the feudal era. One of the particularly grotesque practices was that of skinning people alive. The Japanese would force one Chinese to skin another. If, out of mercy, the Chinese would kill the person before skinning him, the Japanese conqueror would then have another Chinese skin the merciful one alive. These acts of barbarity are difficult to write about and difficult to read. Nevertheless, this is reported to have been a rather common practice during the Japanese occupation of China, a mere fifty years ago. The cruelty practiced in Japanese concentration camps equaled the barbarity of the Nazis.

■ │ **A Nation in Denial**

Unlike Germany, Japan has barely confronted the national guilt stemming from its actions during World War II. Little contrition has ever been expressed. As a matter of policy, the educational system glosses over the whole subject. Most young Japanese have no idea what really happened. If you ask a Japanese teenager about Japan's involvement in the war, you will most likely hear an answer like, "We did not have any choice. All of the other countries cut off our supplies of natural resources. We had to fight for our survival."

Of older people who experienced the war, I asked this question: "The Japanese treat each other so politely, so why, as conquerors in Korea, Taiwan, and China, were they so barbaric?"

The interesting thing is the uniformity of the answers I received from some thirty Japanese. They all said something like, "It was war. People go crazy in war." They all spoke matter-of-factly as if that were sufficient explanation. I got the same response from one of my closest friends, a woman, half Japanese, half Chinese. This feeling of having done no particular wrong seems to be shared by most Japanese.

In December 1937 the Japanese captured the Chinese capital of Nanjing (Nanking). For three days after the city fell into their hands, the Japanese soldiers went on an unrestrained rampage of torture, murder, and rape. They shot or bayoneted every Chinese they encountered. They gang raped and then murdered women and girls from the age of seven to seventy. They disembowelled pregnant women to settle bets about whether the fetus was male or female. Then they took photographs to capture these bloody and glorious moments. When they had finished, 350,000 Chinese were dead. The Yangtze River, which flows by the city, literally ran red with human blood.

I have heard the Rape of Nanjing justified by comparison to everything from the My Lai massacre to the Spanish Inquisition. One Japanese told me, "The American soldiers during the postwar occupation raped many Japanese girls. So what is the big deal with the Rape of Nanjing?"

The Japanese have created their own history of World War II and suppress any attempt to contradict it. On a flight from Tokyo to Beijing, I met a former Japanese soldier who participated in the Nanjing massacre. He said that as a sort of expiation of the guilt he felt, he had often wanted to publish the diary he had kept during the war. All his attempts to do so were greeted with rejection and anger at his unpatriotic urge to revive such an incident. He told me sadly, "There is a great danger in a nation refusing to acknowledge its past evil."

My own attempt to document the Rape of Nanjing met the same resistance. A few years ago, I was looking for a sponsor for a docudrama about the massacre that I wished to produce for public television. I thought there might be a few enlightened Japanese who would want to underwrite such an effort to help ensure that such a thing could never happen again. Westerners are well acquainted with the atrocities of Nazi Germany but they have not been well informed about the horrors of Japan's occupation of China.

I asked a distinguished American friend, a man who had been decorated by Emperor Hirohito for his outstanding contribution to Japan, to request the funding for me from a Japanese organization dedicated to world peace. The response he brought back to me was that unless I wish to start World War III, I should drop the idea totally.

On January 18, 1990, Hitoshi Motoshima, the mayor of Nagasaki, was shot and critically wounded by a member of the ultranationalist group Seiki Juku. The assassination attempt resulted from some remarks that Motoshima had made in December 1988. As the Emperor Hirohito lay dying, Motoshima, in answer to a question put to him in a public forum, suggested that the emperor might bear some responsibility for the outbreak of World War II. Motoshima received many death threats after refusing to retract his remarks and had been under heavy guard, but no overt attempt was made on his life until the end of the mourning period for the emperor. Although many Japanese share Motoshima's views privately, voicing those opinions in public is still a serious indiscretion in Japan.

■ | **The Victim Syndrome**

To some extent, the feeling of being victimized by outsiders is shared by most Asian peoples. In Japan, however, it is a national fixation. All Japanese bitterly resent Hiroshima and Nagasaki and the humiliation of the postwar U.S. occupation. For those who remember their history lessons, the feeling of humiliation at American hands extends back to the time of Commodore Perry.

By no means do the Japanese see this alleged victimization as being in the past. They view U.S. demands to open Japanese markets to American goods as another attempt by Uncle Sam to victimize them. The threat of American trade restrictions is seen as an attempt to force on the Japanese people products so shoddy that not even Americans will buy them. They do not acknowledge that Japanese prosperity has come about largely because of America's postwar assistance and a lenient trade policy toward them.

Traditional Japanese art inevitably is concerned with tragedy. The themes of theater, music, and painting most often center around sadness. The Japanese like to view themselves in a bleak light. When the tragic element is lacking in day-to-day life, some Japanese feel a need to create it. A friend, the CEO of a Japanese agricultural concern, once told me, "Every day in my diary, I write very sad things." I asked, "Why don't you write something nice? Just look at your life; you have so much to be thankful for. I am sure you can find one thing pleasant to write about in your diary." He replied, "But I really enjoy the sad feeling."

■ | **The Watchdog Society**

Recently on U.S. television, I saw a program about a group of American police chiefs who went to Japan to study the reasons underlying Japan's low crime rate. But what the American chiefs of police learned on their whirlwind tour had little or nothing to do with the low crime rate. The most important factors were not visible to them. The reasons lie deep in the social fabric.

Almost everyone in Japan keeps an eye on everyone else, not necessarily to ferret out criminal activity but just to see what their neighbors are up to. There is a rigid, if unwritten, code to which respectable Japanese must conform. They live under the constant scrutiny of neighbors and acquaintances. For example, a respectable, hard-working husband must go to work each day and return home late each evening. If he comes home early, he will bring great shame to his family. A man with a future is supposed to work late and then get invited to accompany his boss to entertain clients. His wife will be the subject of neighborhood gossip if he returns early each evening.

Japanese people really care about the opinions of the others. They mold their lives according to the opinions of others and they are extremely generous about giving unsolicited opinions to each other. These characteristics are not unique to the Japanese, but to understand how deeply they pervade the society, one must look at their origins.

In feudal times, families were grouped into units of five families. These family units were responsible to their lord for the actions of all individuals within the group. If anyone, including children, committed a transgression against the lord, every member of the group would be punished equally. Quite understandably, everyone came to be concerned about everyone else's private business.

In today's Japan, it is common to receive anonymous letters concerning personal matters—for example, that your son's fiancée comes from an *eta* family. Mishima's fiancée received anonymous letters warning her not to marry a man like Mishima.

■ **Label Me Gucci**

Because Japanese society is so status-conscious, it is important to wear the right clothes and do the right things. The best way to make sure not only that you are wearing the right thing, but that everyone knows it, is to wear designer-label products. Designer clothes and accessories have become the supreme symbols of status. The exorbitant duty on designer imports just makes them more desirable. They make the statement that you not only have expensive tastes, but that you can afford them.

A young Japanese executive often will wear a Gucci belt, a Chanel handbag, and a key ring with another notable name. A well-to-do young woman will carry a Gucci or Chanel handbag and wrap around her neck a signature scarf. I have seen, on occasion, a person's body entirely clothed with European signatures. Pictured in a recent Japanese fashion magazine was a woman wearing a T-shirt with the name "Chanel" printed across the chest; over the right shoulder she carried a Gucci handbag; in her left hand she carried a Vuitton travel bag. On her head she wore a Fendi cap. The caption on the picture read, "This woman has an identity problem."

■ **The Sky Is Falling**

There is a famous Chinese tale from the Shang Dynasty about a man who sat around and worried about the sky falling. "What will happen if the sky falls down?" he would fret. "I will be crushed by all the stars." The Japanese use this tale as a parable in which the Japanese nation is likened to the Chinaman, sitting around worrying about an unlikely catastrophe. The Japanese seem obsessed with the survival of the Japanese nation and the Japanese race in the face of some ill-defined but clearly felt menace. But the Japanese are not sitting around whining; they are working at fever pitch to maintain and increase their nation's strength.

■ **There Is No Concept of Guilt**

Japanese people feel they are much better off than Christian Westerners who are accountable for every action on Judgment Day. The Japanese are predominantly Shinto or Zen Buddhist, neither of which includes the equivalents of the Western concepts of guilt, hell, or heaven.

Those Japanese who truly understand the Zen Buddhist law of cause and effect (Karma) will always live clean and pure lives. But the law of Karma is very subtle. For the majority of the Japanese, religion is simply a set of ceremonious events.

■ Suicide—A Way to Clear Everything Up

In Japan, if all else fails, one can always commit suicide. Suicide makes everything right. The suicide, of course, will be past caring, and respect will be restored to those he has dishonored by his failures. If a man has committed a dishonorable deed, his family shares in his dishonor. His son will not be able to find decent employment, his daughters will not marry well. In order to remove this burden from his family, a man often chooses to commit suicide. Suicide restores honor to the dead as well as the living. People forgive one who chooses to restore honor at the cost of life itself. To the Japanese, honor is far more important than the value of individual life.

■ Never Forget, Never Forgive

Most Asian peoples are vengeful. The Japanese have no monopoly on this trait. If you watch samurai and Kung Fu movies, you will notice that most of the stories center on revenge. There aren't many different plots; most of them go something like this: The hero's whole family is killed by the evil lord. The hero dedicates his youth to studying the martial arts and his young manhood to hunting down and killing the lord and several dozen of his retainers. Never for a minute does he forget that his duty requires revenge.

In the mid 1800's, when Satsuma and Choshu joined forces to overthrow the shogun's power and reestablish the emperor, their only common bond was that their ancestors were defeated by the Tokugawa shogun two hundred years earlier. Satsuma and Choshu had been rivals but they put aside their enmity toward one another in the face of their duty to avenge their ancestors' defeat.

A popular Japanese tale concerns a seventeenth-century samurai named Oishi. Oishi's lord was forced to commit *seppuku*— suicide by disembowelling oneself—after having been falsely accused by a high-ranking lord of the shogun. Oishi vowed to avenge his lord's death. First, he pretended to be a drunkard for seven years in order to allay the suspicions of his powerful enemy. He secretly recruited forty-six of the lord's samurai who shared his determination for revenge. Ultimately, they were able to behead the man responsible for their master's death. They then took his head to the shrine where their master's ashes were kept. After their duty was done, all forty-seven warriors committed suicide.

That this story was the basis for a very popular novel, a Kabuki theatrical presentation, and later a popular film, says a great deal about the Japanese attitude toward implacable vengeance. The difference between the way that Japanese and Chinese achieve revenge is that Chinese revenge is generally carried out by a single person while the Japanese carry it out in groups.

■ | **The Ant People**

Japanese society is something like an anthill. Each member has a post and specific duties to be performed in service to the colony. In the same sense that a colony of ants is much more powerful than a swarm of crawling insects, so Japanese society is more efficient than societies in which the individual does not so readily subjugate himself to the will of the whole.

The greatest virtue as well as the greatest curse of the Japanese is their ability to sacrifice personally for the objectives of the nation. In many cases, after graduating from college and entering a large corporation, a young Japanese knows exactly what his life is going to be like for his remaining years. When an entire people are willing to sacrifice their individualism and become faceless and nameless entities laboring for the common weal, happy are their employers and political leaders.

The difference between people and the ants is that ants can only be ants. They are incapable of individuality. Some Japanese have absorbed enough of the influence of the Western world to understand the joy of coming home immediately after work, the joy of taking vacations, and the joy of expressing their individuality and personal ambitions. But these feelings are hard to express in a highly regimented anthill.

It is impossible not to admire the Japanese for their sense of purpose, their ability to subjugate their individual interests to the larger good, and their industry. They take the simplest of everyday activities and turn them into art forms out of their drive for perfection in all they do. Yet it is wise to keep in mind that while these qualities in a friend are laudable, in an adversary, they are formidable.

The Chinese and other Asian nations believe that Japanese individuals manifest these characteristics in the most positive way. However, we also know that the Japanese people as a collective entity with a common purpose have often constituted a danger to their neighbors.

8

The Corporate Samurai

■ | **THE ORIGIN OF THE SAMURAI**

On the surface, Japan is a modern industrial society. Beneath the surface, however, lies a society deeply rooted in its feudal past. The Japanese people are still bound to the samurai tradition. To understand the Japanese, one must examine both the history and myth surrounding that tradition.

According to the oldest written records extant—the *Kojiki* (Record of Ancient Matters) compiled in A.D. 712, and the *Nihon Shoki* or *Nihongi* (History of Japan) compiled in A.D. 720—when Heaven and Earth were made, a mysterious power separated them one from another. Kunitokotachi, the Deity Master, created Izanagi and Izanami, the first pair of male and female deities. He ordered them to create Japan. Izanagi and Izanami stood together in Heaven and stirred the sea with their jewel-encrusted coral spear. When they lifted the spear, the droplets that fell back into the sea formed the islands of Japan. They descended and made their home on these islands. The coral spear became the center pole of their house. Thus, in both myth and history, a weapon of war was the foundation upon which Japan was built.

118

In A.D. 200, Emperor Sujin ordered four generals to lead armies to conquer the four corners of the country. Sujin gave these generals the rank of shogun (commander). This was the first time the word *shogun* appeared in Japanese history.

Sujin's successor, Emperor Keiko, had a son named Yamato. Prince Yamato was courageous, skilled with weapons, and capable of killing without hesitation or remorse. His was a solitary, romantic, and tragic nature. Prince Yamato was regarded as the first human incarnation of the divine warrior, the model for all samurai to follow.

Prince Yamato gave an early indication of the path his life was to follow when he killed his elder brother for being late to an evening meal. His astonished and angry father sent Yamato off to war, hoping that his son would expend all his violent energy battling the enemies of the empire. Armed with Cloud Cluster, a sacred sword given to him by his aunt, a high priestess, Yamato went to battle.

His first victories were achieved through guile rather than valor. On one occasion, he disguised himself as a girl in order to kill the enemy captain during a banquet in the enemy camp. Passing through Izumo Province on his return from this campaign, he again found an opportunity to employ deception to dispatch an adversary.

For some reason unrecorded in history, he resolved to kill a certain village leader. First he befriended the man in order to establish a strong bond of trust between them. Meanwhile, he planned a way to kill him with little effort or danger to himself. He made a wooden sword that he wore every day in an elaborate scabbard on his belt. No one suspected that within this ornate scabbard was a useless wooden sword.

One day he invited the village leader to bathe with him in the river. As they were dressing after their bath, Yamato suggested that they should exchange swords as a pledge of their friendship. The man agreed and Yamoto then proposed that they try their new swords in a friendly duel there on the banks of the river. The village leader drew the useless wooden sword and Yamoto slew the surprised and helpless man with the man's own sword.

This story points to a great difference between the Western and the Japanese conceptions of heroism. By Western standards, Yamoto was treacherous and cowardly. By Japanese standards he was a wise and skillful strategist.

On a journey to Mount Fuji, a great dragon barred Yamoto's way. The dragon claimed Cloud Cluster and demanded its return. Yamato simply made a mighty leap over the serpent demon and went on his way. Later, Yamato met the beautiful Iwotohime and fell deeply in love with her. His heart struggled between the impact of human love and his solitary devotion to his divine calling. Eventually, he forced himself to leave Lady Iwotohime and continue his journey. On the slopes of Fujiyama, Yamato was set upon and surrounded by his enemies. They attempted to burn him alive by setting fire to the field he was in, but Yamato used Cloud Cluster to cut a path through the grass to safety.

Burning with desire to see Iwotohime again, Yamoto retraced his steps to her. Once again he was confronted by the dragon, but this time when Yamoto jumped, his foot brushed against the serpent. The touch of this magical beast infected the prince with a fierce fever. As he lay dying, the prince's only wish was to see the Lady Iwotohime once more. Unknown to him, Lady Iwotohime had followed him on his journey and had come upon the dying prince in his final hour. Yamoto, drifting in and out of consciousness, briefly opened his eyes. He beheld the form of his beloved and died.

Both in the circumstances of his life and the romance of his death, Yamoto came to be thought of as the first samurai. The story of his life defined the essential elements of all Japanese samurai stories to follow: The hero is a skilled warrior unrivaled for prowess in arms. He is also a skilled tactician who does not always scruple to use treachery and deceit to accomplish his victories. Though solitary by nature, the hero is drawn to a tender maiden's love and torn between that love and his devotion to duty. Always in the tales of samurai, love and duty are mutually exclusive. The story ends in tragedy, with the lady's heartbreak and the hero's death. These stories still have a powerful emotional impact on the Japanese. At one time or another, every Japanese man feels the samurai within him.

Samurai, a word that for centuries referred to the social class to which the emperor, the shogun, and all the nobility belonged, means "those who serve." It is represented by a Chinese character that in Chinese has the offensive connotation of a mean and lowly person. In Japanese, the connotation is one of faithfulness and adherence to duty. That probably says as much as anything can about the difference between Chinese and Japanese attitudes toward being in service to another. As a reference to military retainers, the word came into common usage during the tenth century. In the twelfth century, the Japanese War Department instituted the official title of *samurai dokuro* to refer to the military retainers of the great lords.

The samurai as a class evolved out of the feudal relations between the large landholders and their tenants during the eighth and ninth centuries. These landlords dispensed justice, maintained order, and organized the defense of the villages in time of peril. In such times, it was the duty of the tenants and small landholders to serve under the great lord for the common defense. In their capacity as soldiers, these men came to be called "samurai."

As the samurai evolved into a specialized military class, a code of behavior was established: the way of the warrior, or *bushi-do*, codified the relationship between master and man-at-arms. Both became members of the same social class, differing only in degree, not in kind.

From the tenth century to the present day, the samurai has been the ideal of manhood toward which every Japanese male has striven. Although the samurai class was officially abolished over a century ago, the influence of the samurai tradition still permeates Japanese society. To a great extent, the Japanese worker sees himself as a faithful and valorous samurai serving his employer as his ancestors served their feudal masters.

■ THE CODE OF THE SAMURAI

The Code of Samurai is a book written in the sixteenth century by the samurai and scholar Daidoji Yuzan. It is one of the most complete statements of what it meant to be a samurai. It shows that the samurai code was deeply influenced by the teachings of Confucius, the principles of Zen Buddhism, and the Shinto religion. The ultimate purpose of the samurai was to attain enlightenment by way of the sword.

Since courage, loyalty, duty, and skill at arms are easier concepts to grasp than enlightenment, these outward expressions of the samurai spirit have always received more emphasis in the popular mind than the profound and subtle inner state to which they are but paths.

The code of the samurai has played a vital role in forming the Japanese national character. It has at times made Japan strong, but at other times has brought devastation to the land. The samurai relationship developed out of an economic dependency between lord and vassal. In modern times, it has returned to its economic origins as a bond between employees and employer. Articles of this ancient code can still be found applied to contemporary situations.

■ **The Samurai View of Death**

According to the samurai code, the life of a samurai is a mystical love affair with death. He is a *bushi* (warrior). The sole purpose of his existence is to serve and obey his master. His own life or death is of no consequence in comparison to his duty. He trains himself to think without reference to a future. Each breath he draws is his last. Thus he can kill or die without hesitation.

Today, Japanese corporations command this same sense of total commitment from their workers. The Japanese employee gets the job done for his employer as if it were a life-or-death matter. It is not written anywhere; it is just understood.

■ **The Loyalty of the Samurai**

A samurai in the service of the master will not only show his loyalty when the master is prosperous, but also in times of misfortune. A samurai will not leave his master's side, no matter that his thousand horsemen have been reduced to ten, or even to only one. A samurai will stand by and defend his master at the cost of his own life.

Perhaps this sense of loyalty contributed to the refusal of some Japanese to surrender at the end of World War II despite the fact that their master, Emperor Hirohito, had done so. Surrender is a strange concept to the Japanese. No master had ever surrendered before. Heretofore, death in battle had been not only the highest honor, but also the only alternative to victory.

The Japanese people think of their surrender in World War II as the tactical surrender of their armed forces, not the ultimate surrender of the people. In the emperor's surrender speech, he urged the Japanese to look to the future and unite their strength in the reconstruction of Japan, and especially to keep pace with the technology of the Western world. As loyal samurai, they followed the master's command and transformed defeat into a miraculous victory. I am sure Hirohito on his deathbed was proud of the nation's samurai.

■ The Samurai Judgment of Right and Wrong

Traditionally, a samurai is not simply a fighter. He must also be a learned individual of diverse intellectual accomplishments. He has read the Four Books of Confucius and mastered calligraphy as well. The modern samurai is, of course, well versed in mathematics, physics, engineering, economics, marketing, sales, and, above all, international trade.

A samurai is also one who can judge between right and wrong. But when a samurai's judgment conflicts with his lord's, he puts aside his own judgment and accepts that of his lord. Unquestioning obedience remains a strong—and dangerous—characteristic of the modern samurai.

■ Proper Etiquette and Grooming

The code required that a samurai cleanse his hands and feet each morning and night and bathe in a hot tub daily. He must be shaved and his hair properly combed each morning. He must dress in the proper ceremonial robes and wear his two swords as well as carry a hand fan. He must receive guests with the proper etiquette according to their rank.

When working with the Japanese, one must be aware that they expect to be treated with the kind of etiquette suited to their status. In return, they treat Westerners according to their rank and station. Improper attention to rank is a common mistake made by the less status-conscious Westerner in dealing with the Japanese, and is the cause of much difficulty.

I was present when a high-ranking Japanese diplomat presented the keynote speech at a trade convention in the United States. Afterward, he was approached by a young woman who had obviously liked his speech very much. The young woman complimented the diplomat profusely while reaching out to shake his hand. The diplomat was very familiar with American customs, but he was caught off guard and his Japanese heritage took momentary control of him. He jerked his hand away in anger and embarrassment that this woman of unknown rank should presume to approach him so informally. His aide stepped in quickly and smoothed over the moment while the diplomat composed himself.

■ | Silence Is Golden

The samurai must refrain from useless, idle talk. Avoidance of idle conversation is the norm among Japanese. The Japanese are not like the Chinese, who appreciate the Westerner's openness and talkative informality. In Japan, a wise man who speaks much is considered a fool. A silent fool passes as wise.

An eighteenth-century work, the *Hagakura* of the samurai Ya-mamoto Tsunetomo, puts it thus. "The essence of speaking is in not speaking at all if you can convey the idea without uttering a single word. If you can not, you should speak with a few wise and well-chosen words."

Through the centuries, the Japanese have honored the ability to communicate without words. A glimpse of the eyes, a facial expression, a slight movement of the body, all effectively communicate. The only time the modern samurai might grow voluble with a Westerner is at the dinner table after a few drinks.

■ | Never Let Down Your Guard

The code required that a samurai must be physically and mentally prepared for combat at any time, in any place, under any conditions. The Japanese have always been combative. For centuries it was common among all classes of Japanese men, not only samurai, but also farmers, artisans, and merchants, to carry a weapon at all times. It was a principle that even the lowliest servant should never, even for a moment, be without a short sword. Even during peacetime, a samurai took pride in participating in duels and competitions to the death. Yuzan, in *The Code of Samurai*, quotes an old saying, "When you leave your front gate, act as if an enemy is in sight. A samurai who does not maintain an offensive consciousness, despite displaying his swords, is nothing but a farmer or peasant in a warrior's skin." Yuzan's book was not written during wartime, but during the longest period of peace in Japanese history.

It is difficult for the Westerner to grasp such an unrelenting combative posture in an entire people. In the modern Western world, peace is seen as the normal and desirable order of things; war is viewed as a horrible aberration. Among the Japanese, the opposite has always been true.

Many Americans feel that the growing Japanese investment in the United States is not something with which we should be concerned. After all, as former Speaker of the House "Tip" O'Neill pointed out, the Dutch and English own more of America than do the Japanese. But it should be added that the Dutch and English are not the Japanese. They have not exhibited national characteristics of aggressive militarism and a sense of implacable determination to achieve revenge for past wrongs.

■ | **The Bravery of the Samurai**

During the protracted battles of the sixteenth century, seats were arranged each evening in camp in two sections—one for the brave warriors, the other for cowards. Each night, according to each individual warrior's performance during the day, he was shown to his proper seat. Daidoji Yuzan said, "A samurai lacking in bravery and courage, despite all good intentions, is not effective. As a matter of fact, he is not a samurai at all."

■ | **The Duties of the Samurai**

Samurai have traditional duties in two areas: military and civil. During wartime, a samurai functions as a warrior. In peacetime, samurai are assigned to construction or production projects. They bring into the civil arena the same sense of duty, loyalty, and courage that they bring to their military duties.

■ | **The New Samurai**

Although the old samurai are gone, there is a new samurai class in Japan. They are the Corporate Samurai, the workers, managers, and executives who bring to their work the same attitude that their ancestors took to the battlefield. A Japanese worker produces in one day what it takes an American worker two days to produce. To the Western world, the Japanese stress the importance of free trade because they know the Western worker is no match for the Japanese samurai worker.

■ THE WARRIOR'S ART

When I was a seven-year-old in Taiwan, I saw a Japanese movie called *Miyomoto Musashi*. It left an impression that has lasted all my life. It was the life story of Sword Saint Miyomoto Musashi, who became a childhood hero of mine and is, to a certain extent, still a hero to me.

Musashi was born in 1584, at the end of four centuries of internal warfare and the beginning of Tokugawa's 250 years of peace. A samurai descended from noble ancestors, he fought his first duel at the age of thirteen. By the time he was twenty-nine he had killed more than sixty skilled samurai. He never lost a duel. But he was not my hero simply because he was so adept at cutting people up.

When Musashi was sixty, he wrote a book called *Go Rin No Sho* (The Book of Five Rings), a treatise on dueling and swordsmanship. Because *The Book of Five Rings* is as much about the psychology of winning as about the techniques of wielding a sword, it is commonly studied by Japanese businessmen today. Any Westerners who must deal with the Japanese would be well advised to familiarize themselves with the principles Musashi elucidates, because they may rest assured that their Japanese associates know them well and use them habitually.

1. Musashi said: "The warrior is one who uses the pen and sword with equal skill. When victory is gained by clashing swords or engaging in battle, we can then attain power and fame for ourselves and our master. This is the virtue of warrior skill."

In other words, all knowledge is interrelated. To gain mastery of one discipline, it is necessary to study many. A samurai must be a scholar of diverse subjects. Accordingly, the modern samurai should have a breadth of knowledge beyond the narrow bounds of his field of specialization.

2. Musashi also said: "It is impossible to understand the Way through the study of swordsmanship alone. One must understand the mystery within the smallest as well as the largest, the shallowest as well as the deepest."

Swordsmanship is not simply proficiency in the mechanical movement of a blade. It involves the attunement of oneself to the Tao. In the exercise of swordsmanship, the student must seek to discover the unchanging principle. It is the same in the stroke of a sword as in the stroke of a calligraphy brush, or in the positioning of a bud in an arrangement of flowers.

This training to recognize the unchanging element in the ever-changing is fundamental to the uniquely Japanese ability to take new technology from the West and by extracting the central principle to find uses for it and create products from it that were never dreamed of by the actual developers of the technology.

3. Musashi said: "The void is that which has no beginning and no end. Attaining this means not attaining that. The Way of warrior skill is the Way of nature. When you are in line with the power of nature, knowing the rhythm of all situations, you will be able to cut and strike the enemy naturally. All this is the Way of the Void."

Musashi spent the latter part of his life in solitude, searching for the Void. The Void in Zen Buddhism is that which is beyond form and formlessness. It embraces and rejects everything and nothing. The Void is the beginning of the beginning, the end of the end, the mother of ten thousand things. It is the force from which the universe is made manifest. In such a state—the Way of the Void—Musashi would only see the oneness of the universe. There would be no differentiation between Self and Other, Enemy and Friend. The art that he studied on his path to the Void would then be of no utility because there would be no need to cut or strike any enemy.

As I gained maturity, I felt that Musashi had ultimately mistaken the means for the end. He sought in spiritual realms for the first principle by which he could perfect the mundane art of swordsmanship. I felt that the exercise of a mundane art is only a path by which one comes to the Void which is an end in itself.

Because of works such as Musashi's, in Japan proficiency in martial arts such as swordsmanship has always been equated with some degree of spiritual accomplishment. Too often, however, the outward expression is substituted for the inward grace, technique is emphasized while the spiritual component is unrealized.

To those who come out of a Judeo-Christian background, it is difficult to understand how the art of skillfully butchering your fellow man can be regarded as a path to spiritual fulfillment, but that is the way it is seen in Japan and throughout Asia. And because most practitioners do not grasp the subtleties of the spiritual component, they are left with good technique and a vague sense that the act of killing with the sword has a mystical significance beyond the value of the life that is taken. It is perhaps this attitude that can explain how thoughtful, scholarly men could participate in acts so seemingly barbarous as the systematic atrocities committed by the Japanese in Nanjing in 1937.

4. Musashi said: "You must contemplate on the Way of the warrior skill so you will be able to beat a man in combat by the use of your eye. With diligent training, you will be able to beat ten men in combat by using your spirit. The study of the Way of warrior skill is the path which will help one gain honor and respect, and prevent others from defeating your spirit."

Japan's military defeat in 1945 only kindled the fire of determination in the Japanese people to win the final battle. American experts and policymakers sometimes seem to understand only columns of figures: GNP, balance of payments, industrial output, and so on. But these are useless in understanding the Japanese postwar miracle. Witness four decades of erroneous prediction, underestimation, and complete misunderstanding by American observers of what was going on in front of their eyes. These experts have never understood the power of the human spirit. The people of Japan understand Musashi, even though they may never have read his words. His philosophies are buried deep in the soul of every Japanese—past, present, and future.

5. Musashi said: "Be calm in combat and daily living. Do not let emotion influence your body, or let your body influence your emotion. Be neither high nor low in emotional expression. These are signs of weakness. Do not reveal emotion to your enemy."

Unlike the Japanese, the Chinese and Koreans are much more expressive with their emotions, even though they may be expressing an emotion that they do not truly feel in order to gain some advantage. The Japanese businessman, on the other hand, diligently practices to control and conceal emotion.

6. Musashi said: "It is necessary to maintain a combat posture in your daily life, and make your everyday posture your combat posture. You must study this well."

In the samurai's mind, he is in combat every moment. In the mind of the modern Japanese executive, he too is in combat every minute. International trade as mortal combat is the theme of all Japanese executives' daily meditation.

7. Musashi said: "Do not be distracted by insignificant movements of the sword. You must study this well."

The corollary to this is: Distract your enemy by insignificant movements of your sword. For example, a small group of American businessmen arrived recently in Tokyo for an important contract negotiation. Their Japanese hosts greeted them at the airport and whisked them away to a lavish reception. In the course of the afternoon's small talk, one of the hosts politely offered to help them make arrangements for their return flight if they had not already done so. He was thanked and told that it was all taken care of, they were booked to leave on a certain day at a certain hour. During their stay they were entertained with a variety of dinners, lunches, parties, and sightseeing tours. In fact, their schedule was so full that they were not able to get down to negotiations until just before they were scheduled to leave. They were in a position of needing to come to quick agreement with their Japanese hosts or going home to tell their boss that they'd had a wonderful time but hadn't managed to achieve a deal. Can you guess who came out ahead in the deal they struck just before the Americans had to leave for the airport?

8. Musashi said: "In single combat, when the enemy loses his timing, you must not let this temporary advantage pass. The enemy may recover and not be so vulnerable thereafter. Concentrate on your enemy's disadvantages and pursue them relentlessly so he may never recover."

Japan's basic trade policy with the United States is relaxed from time to time when American feelings are running high about the tremendous American deficit. Japan will make some minor but well-publicized concessions in order to defuse the situation, but there will be no permanent change if it is left to the Japanese to decide. A sense of fair play has not been a part of Japanese culture and is not a part of the consciousness of the people. Their understanding of the game of competition is win or lose, kill or be killed.

■ | ## THE SAMURAI'S MASTER GAME

According to the ancient code, a samurai makes each move with calculated precision. Nothing happens by accident. Outwardly, he appears to present no threat to his enemies. While he is drinking with his enemy, apparently enjoying the geisha's dance of the spring cherry blossom, his concentration is really focused on his sword and the sword of his enemy. He acts with great respect toward his guest (enemy). He toasts to his guest's health and long life. If he is a true samurai, he will become his enemy and feel his enemy's emotions, needs, and desires.

In the fall of 1989, Fjisankei Communications Group, a media conglomerate, hosted former President Ronald Reagan and his wife, Nancy, in Japan for two twenty-minute speeches by the former President. The fee for the two speeches was $2 million and an additional $5 million for expenses. The event was discussed and debated in public and private all over the world. Ronald and Nancy Reagan might have had a private celebration of their personal good fortune, but the people who had real cause to celebrate the event were the Corporate Samurai, the Japanese political and business leaders who had orchestrated the Reagans' visit. Certainly, in an earlier age, the samurai would have gathered in the great hall in their ceremonial robes and fans to toast such a magnificent victory. Their accomplishments were manifold:

1. They demonstrated to the world that Japan has arrived. Only forty-five years after its defeat, Japan has been transformed from a poor, starving, war-torn country to a major world power able to put a price tag on the President of the United States.

2. They purchased Reagan's future influence: Ronald Reagan continues to be a popular figure with American voters. His endorsement and support were essential to President Bush's election and to the continuity of the Republican Administration. The Japanese believe that Mr. Reagan still wields a great deal of power in shaping the policies of the current administration and perhaps future administrations.

3. They gained Ronald Reagan's vocal support for Sony Corporation's recent $3.4-billion takeover of Hollywood's Columbia Pictures Entertainment Corporation. Mr. Reagan remarked, "Maybe Hollywood needs some outsiders to bring back decency and good taste."

4. They sent a message to the United States Congress: By paying Reagan a sum so disproportionately large for his services, they sent a clear message to American political leaders: If during a politician's career he cooperates with the Japanese, then the Japanese will take care of him after retirement. There is no law against paying a former member of government for a few speeches after he has retired from public service.

The Corporate Samurai not only bought the most popular American President of recent history, but they got him at a bargain price. During the eight Reagan years, America had slipped from its position as the world's wealthiest country to becoming the world's largest debtor nation, with Japan as its major creditor. Japan is now providing financing to keep the U.S. government running. Reagan made a great personal contribution to the achievement of Japanese economic goals, and made their realization possible much sooner than expected.

A Japanese business associate once exclaimed in my presence, "Thank God that Reagan is your leader, and thank God even more that he is not ours!"

9

Morita
and
Ishihara

Co-authored by Akio Morita, the CEO of Sony, and Shintaro Ishihara, the former Japanese minister of transportation, *The Japan That
Can Say No* was first published in Japan in 1989. What Morita and
Ishihara wrote must have struck a respondent chord in the Japanese,
because the book became an instant best-seller, going through
eleven printings in eleven months.

When I read the book, my reaction was one of shock. It was not
so much the outrageous things that were written that shocked me,
but why they had been written and to whom they were addressed.
If the book had been addressed to an American audience, it might
be possible to defend it as a frank statement of long-suppressed
dissatisfaction with the U.S. But the book was not published in the
U.S., nor has it been officially translated into English. The book was
intended for the Japanese people alone, and as such it can only be
seen as a piece of demagoguery by Ishihara and Morita.

A pocket-sized volume of only 160 pages, the book is a collection of eleven more or less independent essays, six by Morita, five
by Ishihara. The basic theme that runs through the essays is that
Japan has now arrived at a position of world leadership and that her
behavior, especially toward the United States, should change as a
result of her new economic and technological importance. There is

a strong sense of a Japan that, after having been victimized for decades, is suddenly waking to discover that she is now stronger than her oppressor. Even the titles of many of the essays are provocative:

1. *The Necessity of Revolutionizing the Japanese Consciousness*
   (Ishihara)
2. *America's Downfall—Looking Only Ten Minutes Ahead*
   (Morita)
3. *The Root of Japanese Bashing—Racial Prejudice*
   (Ishihara)
4. *Bashing Japan Gets Votes*
   (Morita)
5. *America Is the Unfair One*
   (Morita)
6. *The Criticism of Japan as an Imitator Is Unfounded*
   (Ishihara)
7. *America, the Protector of Human Rights?*
   (Morita)
8. *The Japan That Can Say No*
   (Morita)
9. *Don't Let Japan Give In to America's Bluster*
   (Ishihara)
10. *Japan and the U. S. Are "Inescapably Interdependent"*
    (Morita)
11. *Japan Should Live in Harmony with Asia*
    (Ishihara)

Of the two authors, Ishihara is by far the more vitriolic. His choice of words is incredible for a man of his position. In reference to the U.S.–Japan Security Treaty, he refers to the Americans as "mad dogs" rather than watchdogs. "Ugly" and "nasty" are other adjectives he uses to describe Americans. His arguments are blatantly racist. He ascribes America's evil intent toward Japan to the common interest of the white race against the yellow race. Clearly, he is verbalizing forty years of suppressed anger and hatred of the conquered toward the conqueror. And clearly, judging from the book's popularity, the Japanese people are sympathetic to his message.

The most disturbing element in Ishihara's arguments is that they are illustrated largely by military examples. His solution to Japan's problems with the United States seems to hinge on the superior military technology of Japan. He feels that Japan's technological lead over the United States is irreversible. He feels that Japan can and should stay ten years ahead of Western technological development. He makes the point that the military technology of both the West and the East is already dependent on parts available only from Japan and that this condition will become even more pronounced in the future. He advocates abrogation of the agreements between Japan and the U.S. concerning joint development of military projects. He would like to rescind the U.S.–Japan Security Treaty and have Japan maintain her own military capability.

Especially chilling is his description of the Mitsubishi FSX jet fighter in a dogfight with an American F-15. His reason for opposing the joint U.S.–Japanese development of the FSX is to keep it out of the American arsenal. He maintains that the U.S. could contribute only the engines to joint development, and for that contribution it would demand control of the project. He offers three alternatives if the Americans get "nasty":

- The Japanese could probably develop a better engine in a reasonable amount of time.
- They could go to the French and buy engines just as good as the American ones.
- They could even buy from the Soviets. He notes that the Soviet engines aren't as powerful as the others, but the FSX is so superior to other existing aircraft that a slight lack of power would not affect its dominance.

With obvious relish, Ishihara describes the American reaction to the Japanese FSX as surprise, shock, and fear.

The future as Ishihara sees it is divided along racial lines. The past has belonged to the white race; the future belongs to the yellow race. To support his accusations of racist motivation in U.S. dealings with Japan, Ishihara appears to champion the downtrodden Asian. But Ishihara has no feeling for the yellow race that transcends his virulent Japanese nationalism. Their Asian neighbors distrust the Japanese far more than do white Westerners.

American racism is an easy target to hit. The United States' internal racial problems have been reported openly and discussed for years, and that has created a climate in which charges of racism against the United States are accepted without a great deal of substantiation. Americans are so used to confronting their own racism that they will give a serious hearing to even the wildest accusations. That is not to say that racism does not exist in the United States, or even that it does not color our relations with nonwhite nations, but only that Ishihara is using accusations of racism simply to stir up racial feelings among the Japanese.

Ishihara is a true believer. He believes that Japan has a destiny to fulfill in the world. He credits the postwar economic success of Singapore, Taiwan, and Korea in part to the Japanese administration they enjoyed during World War II. In passing, he does mention that there might have been some negative aspects to the Japanese administration in various countries of Southeast Asia during that period, but they were offset by the benefits of exposure to Japanese culture.

He contrasts this to American actions in the Philippines. He quotes a Truk Islander who laments the departure of the Japanese and the work ethic that they brought with them. He charges that the Americans promoted laziness in the population by giving the people aid in the form of money and food instead of the means of producing the necessities for themselves.

This is typical of the book as a whole. There is a framework of very critical but defensible observations about the shortcomings and mistakes of the American people. But on this framework are hung the most outrageous accusations and conclusions. It is true that the United States has made some poor decisions in its relations with the Philippines, but for a Japanese politician to compare American conduct in the Philippines unfavorably to that of the Japanese occupation forces is beyond belief. It brings us back once more to the fundamental question: Why is Ishihara making these statements in this most inflammatory style, addressing them not to the Americans, not to the world at large, but to the Japanese people alone?

Ishihara is employing the thirtieth of the 36 Strategies that we have discussed—provoking strong emotion. He is provoking the emotions of the Japanese and fanning the flames of resentment toward the U.S. But to what purpose?

Morita's observations are more moderate, well-reasoned, and certainly less strident. His points about the shortsightedness of American businessmen and politicians are painful to acknowledge but undeniably true. As he sees it, the decline of American economic and industrial strength results in large part from our unwillingness to sacrifice short-term profits for much more important long-term benefits. He seems to view us as a nation of spoiled, selfish, and greedy children. He makes a good case for his view.

If Morita's essays had been presented in a different forum, they would fall under the heading of harsh but constructive criticism. But we must ask ourselves what purpose was served by his publishing them intertwined with Ishihara's nationalistic rantings, and in a book intended for circulation only in Japan.

When word of the book reached the United States and unauthorized translations started circulating among those who were not able to read the book in Japanese, a storm of American outrage broke out against Morita and Ishihara. Morita later expressed regret that his views had appeared in print beside the more radical views of Ishihara.

Morita is a brilliant and thoughtful man. He does nothing by accident. You can be sure that, prior to publication, he examined every ramification of associating himself in print with a man of Ishihara's views. His attempts to dissociate himself from Ishihara are less convincing than the association he demonstrates through the many references he makes to Ishihara's essays in his own writing.

The Japan That Can Say No reflects not only the opinion of its authors, but that of the Japanese government as well. Traditionally, there is little difference between the objectives of the private and public sectors in Japan. Morita is clearly as authoritative a spokesman for the Japanese political establishment as is anyone. He has the added advantage that nothing he says carries any "official" weight as it is understood in the West. He is simply a private citizen exercising his right to express his opinion.

Shocking as the expression of these attitudes might have been to most Americans, they come as no surprise to Japan's Asian neighbors. They are alarmingly similar to the ultranationalistic attitudes voiced by the Japanese in the years leading to World War II. Japanese leaders are now openly extolling a twenty-first century dominated by Japanese technological and military supremacy.

■ | **A MAN OF DESTINY**

Akio Morita, age seventy, is chairman of the Sony Corporation. He is a handsome man with a head full of silver hair, a gentle manner, and a pleasant smile. When he concentrates, however, the smile disappears; his facial muscles and lips pull downward, revealing Akio Morita, the man of destiny. Looking out through his striking brown eyes is a person possessing a strong sense of determination. He is disciplined, energetic, arrogant, and self-righteous; and, most of all, he is ruthless in pursuit of his goals.

In meetings, he prefers to lecture rather than listen. Since publication of his *Made in Japan* in 1986, he has acquired the habit of dismissing questions even from important American business and political figures with a terse, "Just read my book." Morita is possessed of an uncanny ability to read people and events quickly and accurately. He knows exactly how far he can push his opponents. He also has the rare ability to insult without angering.

Morita graduated from Osaka Imperial University during World War II with a degree in physics. At the time of the Japanese surrender, the young Morita was serving in the Imperial Navy. The overwhelming American industrial and technological superiority that led to the sudden end of the war left a deep impression on him.

His homecoming was bitter. In *Made in Japan* he describes the charred remains of Tokyo and of his hometown, Nagoya. He confronted the awesome power of Western technological superiority from the most personal perspective.

Akio Morita is the first-born son in the fifteenth generation of one of the Japan's most venerable sake-brewing families. It is a wealthy family, deeply rooted in traditional Japanese culture and values. His grandfather's grandfather was decorated by Emperor Meiji for his contributions to the community, and a statue was erected in his honor. His mother comes from a samurai family of great distinction. Morita takes understandable pride in his ancestry.

Like most wealthy Japanese of his day, young Akio slept in a Western-style bed rather than on a tatami mat. It was not out of a shallow sense of fashion that the Morita family adopted such Western customs. Modernization and Westernization were mandated by the emperor. As community leaders and patriotic Japanese, the Morita family naturally set an example.

Akio Morita was groomed as the heir apparent to the family business. But even as a child he felt called to a greater destiny than the brewing of sake. During World War II he enlisted in a special naval program that allowed him to continue his scientific studies rather than throw his life away in some futile sea battle a thousand miles from Japan. He felt strongly that he had a role to play in Japan's future, and that it was his duty to Japan to preserve himself for that future.

Morita has accumulated a great deal of wealth and power in his life, but he is neither a Donald Trump nor a T. Boone Pickens. It is essential to understand that everything he has accomplished he has undertaken out of a sense of his destiny to shape the future of Japan.

■ MORITA'S COURAGE

One must congratulate Mr. Morita on his courage. A substantial portion of Sony's assets as well as Morita's personal fortune have come out of the pockets of the American consumer. A liberal trade policy by the U.S. government has allowed him unrestricted access to those pockets. Yet Morita has demonstrated by the publication of

The Japan That Can Say No that he is not afraid to offend either the people or the government of the United States.

He is not overly concerned, however, that anything he says would result in an American boycott of Sony products or a sterner trade policy in regard to Japan. He has analyzed the situation and believes that the American consumer and the American government are motivated only by personal interest. As long as Sony continues to provide superior products, Morita is confident that Americans will buy them without a thought. With the strongest lobby in Washington, he is not overly concerned about the adoption of stricter trade policies.

Morita and the Japanese nation have been playing the strategy of "Pretend to Be the Pig in Order to Eat the Tiger." But now that he feels the tiger is caught, he can finally speak his mind. And speak his mind he has.

Morita believes that the time has come for Japan to speak frankly and forcefully to her trading partners in the West. A basic misunderstanding has resulted because, in the past, the Japanese have been reluctant to say to the Americans what should have been said. He attributes this reluctance to the traditional Japanese dislike of saying no directly. However, Mr. Morita knows that what the Japanese have long wanted to say could only be said from a position of strength. That position of strength has been attained only recently.

Morita is much more courageous than many of our state governors who travel throughout Japan bowing deeply to anyone who they think might influence Japanese investment in their respective states. They are far too timid to do anything that might provoke the anger of the Japanese. Japanese businessmen and politicians privately describe them with a Japanese word that means "beggars." Japanese investment is so very important to these American politicians because they have tacitly accepted Morita's assessment that the United States will never again regain its place of eminence in the world economy. Some of our governors seem to believe that courting the Japanese is a better bet than encouraging the development of their native industries.

I live in the beautiful state of Oregon, a state whose economy has become heavily dependent on Japanese investment. Recently I was invited to participate in a discussion entitled "Are the Japanese Buying Oregon?" televised by the local ABC affiliate in Portland. Also invited were representatives of a number of Japanese firms and high-level officials of the state government. The Japanese did not seem to be overly concerned about what I would have to say, but just before the show began, a director from the governor's office came over to ask, "You are going to be nice, aren't you?" I said, "Sure. I'm always nice."

I consider that telling the viewers that the Japanese did not have our best interests at heart is nice.

■ MORITA'S MOTIVATION

Even though Morita thoroughly calculated his risks in publishing *The Japan That Can Say No*, it is still a question as to why he would allow himself to be perceived as biting the hand that feeds him. What could be his reward for all this? He certainly didn't do it for the money. The answer is that his actions came out of his sense of destiny.

Since the mid-nineteenth century, Japan has had to submit humbly to the will of the Western colonial powers. Time and again, the great gunboats impressed on the Japanese their inability to oppose an industrialized and technologically advanced enemy. It was not until after her victories over the Chinese and the Russians in the early years of the twentieth century that Japan began to feel she had become a world power in her own right. A series of easy military victories led her seriously to overestimate her powers and plunged her into a war she had no chance to win. As mentioned earlier, since her humiliating defeat in World War II, Japan has been working single-mindedly to regain a position of dominance in the world community.

Emperor Hirohito's surrender was broadcast over Japanese radio. He spoke of "enduring the unendurable and suffering the insufferable." He was not speaking of the destruction of his cities or the physical suffering of his subjects. Since the beginning of history, wars have raged across the landscape of Japan, wars in which quarter has never been asked for or given. The Japanese are capable of enduring great physical suffering. They are less capable of enduring humiliation and defeat. At the moment of defeat, when the emperor urged his people to unite their strength in the reconstruction of the nation and especially to keep pace with the technological progress of the world, he was urging them to remedy the cause of their defeat. His few simple words became the unspoken will of the nation. The frenetic energy with which the Japanese attacked the problems of reconstruction came from their desire to wash away the shame and humiliation of defeat.

In *Made in Japan*, Morita tells a story about his father. Due to

some reverses in his business fortunes, the elder Morita was forced
to sell three very valuable artifacts from his private collection in
order to settle an obligation. He made a vow that he would mend
his fortunes and someday buy back the pieces. It especially impressed Morita that his father never forgot the vow he had made and
eventually redeemed the pieces.

Akio Morita himself made a vow nearly a half-century ago. He
vowed to help rebuild his burned and ruined land and restore it to
its place of greatness. He has never forgotten that vow.

■ MORITA'S STRATEGY

The publication of *The Japan That Can Say No* served Morita's
purposes in a number of ways.

■ Send a Clear but Indirect Message to Americans

In *Made in Japan*, his earlier book, Morita did not express his
discontent with the United States directly. Yet, if one reads between
the lines, that discontent is very apparent. However, the majority of
American readers are not sufficiently attuned to the subtleties of
the Asian mind to have understood much of what Morita left unsaid.
Most important, the majority of his American readers let his war,
battle, and combat metaphors pass without much serious thought.
Part of his message was that on the side of the Japanese, trade with
the United States is conducted as a war. The goal is the defeat and
domination of the enemy.

Morita felt a need to restate himself more directly in *The Japan
That Can Say No*. Because he speaks so bluntly, Morita needed to
address his remarks directly to a Japanese audience, but it was
important that his words get to American readers and more important that they arrive indirectly without "authorization." Shintaro
Ishihara is making a lot of unpleasant noises about the bootleg
translations in the United States, but there is a persistent rumor that
the unauthorized translations circulating through the State Department and the offices of the news media after the book's publication
in Japan can be traced back to a leak at Sony Corporation.

■ **A Declaration of Victory**

Why would Morita go to so much trouble to let America know that she has been engaged in a war with Japan without even knowing about it? Because he feels that the war is virtually won.

The Japan That Can Say No is a proclamation of victory. After forty years of submission to the U.S., used to thinking of themselves as a conquered people and third-rate world power, the Japanese people need such a statement to bring their image of themselves into alignment with their true status in the world today.

For such a statement to carry any satisfaction, it must be acknowledged by the enemy.

■ **Using Another's Hand to Kill**

Although Morita has made some attempts in speaking to the American media to distance himself from Ishihara and his views, his partnership with Ishihara was deliberate and well calculated. Their collaboration served three purposes:

- Morita did not personally have to make the most offensive statements but managed to get them said just the same. Morita did not want to dirty his hands, therefore he borrowed Ishihara's hand to do the dirty work.
- Ishihara, although a former cabinet minister, does not have the international stature to command the attention for his views that a collaboration with Morita would ensure. Morita's imprimatur lends credibility to Ishihara's rabid nationalism, but Morita retains deniability in quarters where that is to his advantage.
- Ishihara's hostile and aggressive style sets the tone for the book. It is a note that Morita could never strike himself, but one that he feels is necessary in a book primarily designed to stir up a nationalistic fervor in the Japanese people.

■ | MORITA'S CONCERN

The Japan That Can Say No is addressed especially to the younger generation of Japanese who, the older Japanese feel, do not properly understand Japan's Heaven-ordained destiny. They did not directly experience the humiliation of defeat and the hardships of the years after World War II. Reared in a more affluent and permissive era, they pay too little attention to traditional Japanese values and too much attention to decadent Western customs. Furthermore, Morita's generation views the younger Japanese as lacking the fiery commitment to the glory of imperial Japan that characterized their own generation. The new generation is very unlike the one that stumbled through the ruins of Tokyo after the incendiary bombings, or endured the horrible aftermath of Hiroshima and Nagasaki.

The Japan That Can Say No is an attempt to instill in the younger generation some of the sense of purpose that has driven their fathers and grandfathers. Since the Meiji Restoration, the Japanese have shared one mind and one purpose in regard to the barbarians from the West. For the first time there is a generation that is not fully involved in that purpose, and that is a cause for great concern on the part of Morita, Ishihara, and others like them.

■ | MORITA'S ETHICS

Traditional Japanese culture honors ethical conduct and prescribes a strict code of ethics derived from Buddhist and Confucian principles. The Japanese consider that their reverence for and practice of ethical conduct in all aspects of their lives is what distinguishes them from the barbarians of the West.

There is a principle of Confucian teaching that is known and practiced in all Asian cultures and for which the Japanese have a deep respect. It is most easily described by a Chinese phrase: *Yin shui si quan*. Literally translated, this means, "While one is drinking the water, one should thank the well."

Asian cultures stress the importance of never forgetting those to whom you owe your success and those who lent a helping hand when you were in need. If such a debt cannot be paid back in one's own lifetime, it becomes the obligation of one's children and grandchildren to repay the debt. If anyone receives a great favor but is unwilling to repay the obligation, he and his family are badly disgraced. If they go so far as to offer offense to those who have done them the favor, they would disgrace their ancestors and destroy whatever reputation the family had acquired through many generations.

In the 1930's, Japan embarked on a program of conquest in Southeast Asia. She launched a sneak attack on American forces at Pearl Harbor and as a consequence expanded World War II throughout the Pacific. After her defeat, Japan received billions of dollars in U.S. aid. From 1950 to 1980, the United States provided Japan with $810.3 million in military assistance and close to $4 billion in nonmilitary assistance. If this aid had not been provided, there would be no modern Japan or Sony Corporation. There would no arrogant billionaire writing *The Japan That Can Say No*.

The first major contract that Morita landed was funded by U.S. foreign-aid dollars. The predecessor of Sony, Tokyo Tsushin Kogko, was underfinanced and underequipped. It occupied a shabby building without the simplest of amenities. Nevertheless, the American brigadier charged with awarding the contract to build a large audio mixing unit for NHK, the Japanese broadcasting network, decided to take a chance on Morita. It was this contract that allowed the company to stay afloat. It was also an American officer at NHK who loaned Morita's partner Ibuka the tape recorder that he took apart and studied in order to develop Sony's first tape recorder.

It appears that Morita's interpretation of *Yin shui si quan* does not extend to Americans.

■ MORITA'S WISDOM

Although Morita's motives may be suspect, his observations cannot easily be dismissed. He has a keen eye for what is wrong with America today. Many of his comments seem to come under the heading of rubbing salt in the wounds rather than constructive criticism, however. Among other things, he charges that:

1. *The United States no longer makes things; it only takes pleasure in making profits from moving money around.*

It is difficult to argue with this statement. No one is seriously trying to retool the antiquated steel industry in the United States. Too many of the best financial minds in America are instead engaged in such nonproductive activities as engineering corporate takeovers.

Ultimately, the blame for this condition must rest with America, but the Japanese did play a role. In the 1960's and 70's, a healthy U.S. manufacturing industry was undermined by Japanese penetration of American markets through legal *and* illegal means. Both means were sanctioned and sponsored by the Japanese government.

Illegal methods included industrial espionage and the outright theft of proprietary technologies. For example, a few years ago a large American telecommunications company and a Japanese firm were negotiating the purchase of U.S. technology. The negotiations were extremely protracted. While the executives were negotiating, the Japanese technicians were observing the U.S. operation. Being entirely naive about Japanese methods, the American engineers freely shared their information with these people they considered fellow scientists. Suddenly the negotiations were broken off by the Japanese without resolution. Why should the Japanese company pay hundreds of millions of dollars for something they had already obtained through subterfuge?

It is also a common practice for Japanese companies to send employees to work in the U.S. so that they can then bring home valuable technology gleaned from their U.S. competitors.

Illegal dumping by the Japanese is a favorite and very effective method of squeezing American competitors out of the market. Japanese firms will sell items below cost in the United States and usually substantially below the selling price in Japan until its American competitors give up the struggle. Being guided by the ideology of the free-trade system, lacking experience with the Japanese, and lacking any practical method to detect and prevent such actions, the U.S. has allowed these unfair trading practices to go on until the present day.

The Japanese would never allow their industries to be attacked in such a way. While they decry any U.S. attempt at protection as unfair, they themselves have always practiced protectionism. Although it is true that America does not produce goods the way she used to, if the people who shaped our trade policies thirty years ago had realized that there was an undeclared war going on with the Japanese, perhaps American industry would be in substantially better shape.

Morita sees the shift from the production of wealth to the mere manipulation of paper as in corporate takeovers a symptom of American decadence. He does not note that the world's ten largest banks are all Japanese. Without the participation of these banks, a great many corporate takeovers would not be possible.

2. *The United States is shortsighted; it prefers the one-minute manager to the ten-year plan.*

Morita compares the shortsighted approach taken by American managers to the long-term planning done by Japanese corporate executives. He cites the example of an American currency trader who told him he could not plan further than ten minutes into the future.

From an Asian point of view, Americans are spontaneous and ingenuous. It is America's nature to be fond of simplicity. A situation is encountered, a decision is made, and action follows. Books such as *The One-Minute Manager* are so popular because they address that attitude.

Americans are fond of listening to their hearts. They are more straightforward than the Japanese and so tend not to see the duplicity in others. This naivete often places them in a vulnerable position in the U.S.–Japan trade battle.

The Japanese, like most other Asians, are trained from childhood in the art of strategy. While Asians are studying *The 36 Strategies*, Americans are studying *All I Need to Know I Learned in Kindergarten*. The American economic system is having a hard time accepting the reality that international competition with the Japanese cannot be accomplished with a handshake and a bow. The American ethic of fair play will neither be understood nor reciprocated by the Japanese.

Actually, Morita was making a considerable understatement in maintaining that Japanese companies commonly plan ten years ahead. The Japanese government as well as private corporations plan and execute strategies that often require far longer to bring to fruition. The Japanese are still adhering to a plan laid down by the Emperor Meiji upon his restoration over a century ago.

3. *Americans are angry that the Japanese will not buy American-made products, but in fact, Americans won't buy them either.*

Morita tells a story about an American businessman who is constantly chiding him about the Japanese refusing to buy American goods. During a round of golf, Morita pulled out an American-made driver; his critic pulled out a Japanese club. When asked why he used that particular make, the American replied that it gave him more distance. After the match, Morita accompanied the man home, where he found a Japanese boat in the driveway, a Japanese recreational vehicle in the garage, and Sony TV's, radios, and stereo equipment throughout the rest of the house. When he asked his critic if he proposed that the Japanese buy products that even Americans found inferior to their Japanese counterparts, the man had no answer.

It is hard to dispute Morita's point as far as it goes. But he attempts to draw from it the conclusion that there is no official policy of denying American firms access to Japanese markets. True, America is not going to sell many television sets in Japan, but agricultural products, if they could make their way through the deliberate complexities of Japanese trade regulations, would do very well with Japanese consumers. They are paying as much as ten times more for rice, beef, and fruit than American consumers.

■ | **MORITA'S PATRIOTISM**

Morita, like all patriotic Japanese, has a unique interpretation of the history of World War II.

In *Made in Japan*, Morita attempts to make the case that American sympathy for China's Chiang Kai-shek and his charming, American-educated, English-speaking wife turned into a national consensus that drove a wedge between the United States and Japan, and eventually led to war. He ignores the fact that Japan's conflict with China was an indefensible act of aggression on Japan's part. Even so, the American people were never seriously involved enough to go into a war with Japan, whether Madame Chiang was charming and articulate or not. The United States went to war with Japan in 1941 because three thousand Americans were killed and a substantial portion of its Pacific fleet was destroyed in a sneak attack by the Japanese at Pearl Harbor. Morita overlooks that entirely.

To former Secretary of State Henry Kissinger, Morita suggested that America bore some responsibility for World War II by enacting high tariffs on Japanese goods, by forbidding Japanese immigration to the United States, and by cutting off Japanese petroleum imports in order to force Japan out of China. Perhaps if the U.S. had not been so shortsighted about Japan's activities in China, Morita went on to suggest, the U.S. and Japan together might have kept communism from gaining a foothold in Asia.

Morita's position seems to be that it was America's humanitarian impulse to stop providing strategic supplies for Japan's genocidal attack on China that caused the war in the Pacific, and that it was America's interference with the Japanese attempt to destroy the anticommunist forces of Chiang Kai-shek that led to a communist takeover in China. It is difficult for an American to believe that a brilliant man like Morita not only said these things, but also, like most Japanese, that he usually believes them.

■ THE TWOFOLD PURPOSE OF THE JAPANESE CRITIQUE OF THE U.S.

In September 1989, in order to manifest its new "direct and forceful attitude" toward its trading partners, the Japanese government sent the Bush Administration a critique of U.S.–Japanese trade relations and a set of very specific suggestions for improving certain areas.

It is interesting to note that in 1894, Japan sent Korea a similar critique and demand for changes in the internal affairs of the nation. Then, as now, the Japanese had no real interest in the reforms themselves, but only used them to divert attention from their true agenda. In that case, it was to provoke an outbreak of hostilities and regain the Korean markets that they were steadily losing to the Chinese.

The recent action has the ostensible purpose of smoothing trade relations between our two countries, but, in fact, it is a gambit by the Japanese to preserve and increase the trade advantage they already enjoy.

■ The Best Defense Is a Good Offense

While South Korea and Taiwan were retreating and making extensive concessions in order to avoid being included in the proposed American reprisals against nations engaging in unfair trade practices, Japan launched a frontal attack with its 1989 critique. Rather than addressing the issues involved, Japan clouded them by introducing a host of other issues.

If the United States wants Japan to make changes, the authors of the critique said, the United States must be willing to make some changes too. The recommended changes included the reduction of the federal deficit, an increase in savings rates, upgrading of American schools, adding a gasoline tax, and removal of Alaskan oil export prohibitions. Except for the last, they are all excellent suggestions and would help put the American economy back on track, but that is not why the Japanese made them.

The Japanese know that the Americans will make a serious response to their critique and thus divert themselves from their first real attempt to do something about unfair trade practices and the huge trade deficit. When this diversion has run its course, the Japanese will come up with another.

The only item in their American critique that the Japanese seriously care about is access to Alaskan oil. Japanese investment in the United States is not about Paramount Studios or Rockefeller Center. It is about natural resources. And the Japanese are taking it one step at a time. First, they want to be allowed to buy Alaskan oil. From there it is another short step to buying the fields themselves.

■ Reinforce the Japanese National Victim Syndrome

The Japanese version of World War II contains very little of Pearl Harbor, Nanjing, or Bataan. It contains much about Hiroshima and Nagasaki and gives a detailed description of the suffering of the Japanese in the postwar years.

The Japanese version of its present differences with the U.S. contains very little about the trade imbalance. It contains a lot about the Western giant picking on the poor little Japanese again.

The critique served a domestic purpose for the Japanese government. It is being used as an illustration of how America is blaming all its problems on Japan and insisting that Japan change its time-honored way of life because Americans can't solve the problems they have brought on themselves. Like *The Japan That Can Say No*, it is being used to mobilize anti-American sentiment in the Japanese people. By the time it is forced to tear down the artificial barriers to trade, the Japanese government will effectively have created a mental barrier in the Japanese consumer against any American import.

Not too long ago, I was discussing *The Japan That Can Say No* over lunch with a Japanese businessman. He agreed with Morita on every point, as did every Japanese he had talked to about it. I asked him a simple question: "Please tell me, if Japan were in America's place right now, what do you think it would do?"

"We would invade."

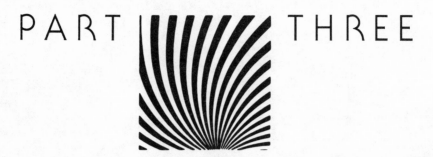

PART THREE

THE
MATRIARCH

■
———

To understand Asia, one must first understand China. Because of its much greater antiquity, Chinese culture is the root of other Asian cultures. Much of what I have to say about China and the Chinese applies to some extent to other Asian nations and Asian peoples.

Chinese feel themselves to be one people, bound by a common heritage, whether they live in Beijing, Hong Kong, Taipei, San Francisco, or London. Much of what I discuss about the Chinese in Asia can be applied to some extent to Chinese living anywhere in the world.

10

The Hurdles

■ THE FRENCHMAN'S STORY

On a spring morning in 1986, a Frenchman was arrested by the police in Tiananmen Square in central Beijing. He had been screaming wildly and making obscene gestures at passers-by. The Chinese authorities subdued him and immediately put him on a plane for France. Upon his arrival in Paris, he was diagnosed as the victim of a complete nervous breakdown. He was committed to a sanitarium for a lengthy period of rest and recovery.

The man was André Pierre. He had arrived in China some nine months earlier as the representative of the French firm Petrofuture International. He had come to negotiate a $500-million contract to build a petrochemical refinery in a Chinese province. Less than twenty-four hours before his abrupt departure, he had been congratulating himself on a job well done.

Certainly the time it had taken to set up this deal had been difficult, uncomfortable, and very confusing for this Westerner alone in Beijing who had had to deal with the strange tactics of his Chinese negotiating partners. But, as the contract was signed and

151

bore a comfortable profit margin for Petrofuture, he felt happy that he would no longer have to endure the strange Chinese ways and would soon be on his way home. There was only one small cloud on the horizon. A man named Li, a high-ranking official in the Ministry of Foreign Trade and Economic Relations, had requested to see him that afternoon in his hotel room.

As he waited for the meeting, Pierre's mind worked over the last nine months and the early mistakes he and his company had made in dealing with the Chinese.

In retrospect, the first mistake was Petrofuture's decision to send Pierre alone. He would be dealing with teams of Chinese bureaucrats and technical experts. He was also poorly trained for his mission. Although the firm had hired China specialists to brief Pierre, these "experts" had only scholarly knowledge of China, not personal experience. They warned him the Chinese would be tough negotiators but gave no clue as to how to deal with them.

Upon his arrival in Beijing, there was a round of welcoming banquets that left Pierre tired and confused over such an elaborate and large-scale welcome. Furthermore, after explaining his company's position to one set of negotiators, they would suddenly, inexplicably, disappear to be replaced by another team. More than once a team disappeared and, just as suddenly, reappeared. It seemed he would be explaining his company's position endlessly.

At each session he varied his words, his phrases, his arguments. He looked for the best way to make an impression on these unimpressionable people. Pierre's variations on the same theme and his minor self-contradictions were carefully noted by the Chinese. In subsequent negotiations, they were subtly thrown back at him in order to upset his mental balance.

The plans for the petrochemical plant, which had been carefully put together in Paris, were slowly picked apart. The Chinese, eager to conserve foreign currency and to make better use of their factories, insisted on providing some of the parts for the project. The quality of these parts was questionable. Pierre insisted, over the repeated objections of the Chinese, that Petrofuture could not take responsibility for the result if such parts were used. His stubborn refusal to budge on this point cast a cloud over the negotiations.

Pierre set the initial price too high. He had been told often about what pitiless negotiators the Chinese were so he thought it best to leave considerable room in which to maneuver. To his chagrin, he quickly learned that the Chinese were aware of the actual prices for such equipment and that they had been negotiating for the same plant with Japanese, Italian, and German companies over the past two years. Petrofuture was sought out not so much for its high-tech expertise but as a way to energize the fierce competition. In order to stay in the race, he had to lower his price; so he chose to make a dramatic impression by dropping his price 15 percent in one single move.

At the end of the third month, the talks were suddenly broken off with no explanation. Pierre assumed a decision was imminent so he waited by his telephone for weeks. Finally, the Chinese officials informed him that they were dropping their demand about Chinese-made parts. This meant that the negotiations had to start over from the beginning. He went back to the province and restarted the talks. Those he met seemed to have forgotten everything that had been discussed before.

Pierre began to develop a fierce hatred of China, the Chinese people, Chinese food, Chinese hotels, and the deadening life he was forced to live in Beijing. The position the Frenchman held was increasingly uncomfortable but, like a roulette player whose losses keep mounting, it seemed to make sense to keep going, even though a French banker had warned him, "In China you have to know when to stop or you'll lose everything, including your sanity."

Pierre was in his sixth month in China when he finally received some encouraging signals. Various intermediaries, all claiming connections with people in high office, began coming around. Petrofuture had done business with Eastern-bloc countries, and had learned it might need to grease some palms; it was prepared to go as high as $25 million. Pierre settled on an intermediary named Wang. Wang was supposed to expedite the contract once a down payment of $5 million had been deposited in the bank account of a middleman in Hong Kong. Pierre signed the transfer order and Wang disappeared, never to return. Meanwhile, the Chinese negotiators returned to one of their prolonged periods of silence.

Eventually a meeting was scheduled. Pierre was face to face with the head of the import agency charged with the development of this project. Pierre's exasperation at the progress of the negotiations caused him to give the Chinese official an ultimatum. To his surprise, rather than asking the usual questions, the official remained silent; they sat without a word for forty-five minutes. Finally, he signed the documents Pierre had prepared. It was finally over. Back in his room, Pierre broke down and cried with joy.

On his final afternoon in China, as Pierre sat recollecting the difficult nine months, Mr. Li arrived for their meeting. He came to notify Pierre that although the agreement had been signed by the import agency, since it included certain tax breaks for Petrofuture, it needed approval from the Finance Ministry and this approval had been denied. Therefore, the talks would have to start over once again.

That was it for Pierre. The next morning the police found him raving in Tiananmen Square, subdued him, and sent him home.

André Pierre is not this man's real name, nor is Petrofuture the name of the company, but the story is essentially true. It is a story that should strike a sympathetic chord in every person who has negotiated with the Chinese. Although an extreme example, this story demonstrates a pattern that can be recognized by any Westerner who has had to deal with the techniques used by Chinese negotiators. Strangely enough, it is an example of a successful negotiation. The Chinese were willing to overlook the unpleasant incident and eventually signed a contract with Petrofuture.

Western business analysts tend to call this an example of "tough adversary negotiation" and "shrewd bargaining." Actually, Pierre's story is not so much an example of the Chinese being overly shrewd or such tough adversarial negotiators, as it is a story that points to the foreigner's lack of understanding of Chinese negotiating style.

■ THE TWO-EDGED SWORD OF FRIENDSHIP

> Friendship among good men is as light as flowing water.
> Friendship among small men is as sticky as honey.
> —Chinese proverb

Among the Chinese, friendship is a two-edged sword. It is a fulfilling and rewarding relationship, but at the same time it can be terribly burdensome. In China, as in the West, a friend is someone who can be counted on to support you in good times and bad, someone with whom you share a sympathetic bond. In China, however, friendship carries with it an additional set of obligations that are not common in the West. For example:

- When you are ill, your doctor friend will treat you without charge.
- Your lawyer friend will always help you with your legal problems without charge.
- If you must go on an extended trip, a friend will care for your children at his own expense, even if you are gone for a year or more.

- Your merchant friend will sell his goods to you at a substantial discount. If he is a very good friend, he will sell at or below his cost.
- If a friend is traveling to an area where you have relatives or other friends, he will deliver anything from messages to furniture for you.

A few years ago, a famous Chinese movie star and her husband, a noted writer and director, purchased a hotel in Hollywood as an investment. So many of their friends and relatives from Taiwan, Hong Kong, and Singapore came to stay free at their hotel and eat free at their restaurant that the hotel started losing significant amounts of money. The couple chose to sell the hotel rather than deny their friends free room and board.

These expectations are not confined to China alone. Most Asian cultures share similar ideas about friendship. During one of my recent seminars, I was explaining the differences between Asian and Western conceptions of friendship to a group of American businessmen. At one point in my talk, one of the participants, whom we will call Mr. Jones, suddenly blurted out, "So that's what happened." I asked him to explain what he meant and he told this story:

For months Mr. Jones had been courting a Japanese businessman who was planning a multimillion-dollar purchase of the agricultural commodities that he dealt in. For a variety of reasons, Mr. Jones felt he had the inside track on his only major competitor, a midwestern broker. He and the Japanese buyer developed a strong rapport, and the deal was all sewn up when the buyer asked him for a favor. He wished to have his son study in the United States for a year and wondered if the boy could come live with Mr. Jones. Unfortunately, Mr. Jones said, his life was not arranged so that he could conveniently care for the boy and he was forced to decline. Soon thereafter, his Japanese client signed a contract with his midwestern competitor, who, not coincidentally, had some room in his house to put up the client's son. At last count, Mr. Jones's unwillingness to undertake the obligations of friendship as understood by his Asian friend had cost him $10 million worth of business and the total is still climbing.

A Westerner who goes to China or engages in business or political negotiations with Chinese immediately notices that the word *friendship* is used over and over again. In contrast, friendship is rarely mentioned between friends in China nor is it mentioned often at business or political functions. The word is used primarily in situations where a real feeling of friendship is not present. In order to fill a silence in a meeting among strangers, something may be said about friendship.

What does the word *friendship* mean to the Chinese business-man when he is dealing with an American, a person with a totally different conceptual frame of reference, a person with whom he often cannot even converse directly? There are two considerations in the Chinese businessman's mind. First, there is a personal consideration: It is currently considered fashionable in China to have a friend in the West. In this context, the word *friendship* is used to express the desire for personal aggrandizement. The second consideration is professional: When he has established a successful and profitable venture with a foreign company, a Chinese businessman is considered to have achieved something admirable.

Westerners are led to believe that the first step in doing business with Chinese is to make friends. The Chinese keep a mental ledger of the obligations owed to friends and the obligations owed them for past favors. They fully expect that their expostulations of friend-ship will be reciprocated by tangible concessions on the part of Western business associates.

As do all Asians, the Chinese view the marketplace as a battle-field. They are in it to win. The word *friendship* is often used to create trust where it is not always warranted.

On behalf of a large American corporation, I hosted a group of Chinese businessmen visiting the U.S. We traveled from city to city on a private jet and were lavishly entertained at each stop, all at the expense of my client. At every opportunity, the Chinese toasted their friendship to their generous hosts. Just prior to their return to China, however, they attempted to engage me to contact their host's closest competitor for them after their departure.

Friendship is a tool used by Asians with other Asians. Simi-larly, it is a very effective tool in dealing with Westerners. The Chinese are proud of their worldliness in dealings with Westerners. They use the word *tean-zan* (childlike) to describe the friendly, ingenuous Americans.

■ ARROGANCE AND TIMIDITY

Of Westerners who deal with them, the Chinese recognize two distinct types.

Lin Yu-tang, in his book *My Country and My People*, wrote the earliest, and perhaps best, description of the more offensive of the two, the China Expert. It is not a flattering portrait that Lin paints, but it must be said that he did not apply it broadly and indiscriminately. He had words of praise for many Westerners, and an especially deep and abiding friendship for the writer Pearl Buck, who he felt was a compassionate and understanding friend of the Chinese.

Details have changed a bit in the fifty years since Lin's book was published, but the China Expert is still around. The modern China Expert is someone who has been living perhaps in Hong Kong or Taiwan. He believes himself to understand Chinese culture and Chinese history far better than he actually does. He can use chopsticks and knows how to say "*Ni how?*" (How are you?). He reads the English-language dailies over his breakfast of ham and eggs and feels that, in doing so, he is staying close to the political situation in China.

He cannot pronounce words of three *pin-yen* (a group of sounds that make up a syllable), yet considers himself fluent in the Chinese language. To conduct his daily business, he depends on his English-speaking Chinese colleagues. He ordinarily surrounds himself with English-speaking people—Americans and Chinese—but when with visitors from the United States, he insists on giving incomprehensible instructions to the taxi driver and the hotel waitress in what he believes to be excellent Chinese. He takes his American friends bargain-hunting through little back alleys in Hong Kong away from the "tourist traps," unaware that they are cheated just as badly there.

He believes and revels in the flattery he receives from Chinese officials on formal occasions. Although he has no real knowledge or understanding of Chinese history or philosophy, he enjoys speaking of the Ming Dynasty, Lao Tzu, and Confucius. He is proud of being considered a friend of the Chinese, but thanks his lucky stars that he was not born one. When he returns to the United States, he gives speeches and writes articles for newspapers and magazines. But after all his years in China, he has no idea what it is like to be a Chinese or how the Chinese mind works. He spent most of his time in private clubs and on golf courses. The idea of eating hot soupy rice for breakfast still makes his stomach turn. The Chinese tolerate him and praise him to his face, but they far prefer the second style, the nonexpert, any time.

This second type, the timid American, does not offend the Chinese as does the expert, but he is generally so worried about not knowing the culture and customs of the Mysterious East that he is afraid to speak his mind or ask questions for fear he will offend the Chinese. He acts the way he thinks the Chinese want him to, and jeopardizes his bargaining position by appearing too eager to please.

There is a third type, a well-informed, better-balanced individual. He is neither intimidated by Chinese culture nor arrogant about his knowledge of it. He, instead, is guided by his genuine desire to understand China and the Chinese people as they are, the good, the bad, and the ugly.

■ THE UNINFORMED INFORMING THE UNINFORMED

In 206 B.C., China organized the world's first government bureaucracy. After two thousand years of existence, it has woven itself into a cocoon of red tape that is nearly impossible for anyone, even the Chinese themselves, to unravel. Often, dealing with China has been a game of the uninformed informing the uninformed. Some Western organizations, after years of exchanging friendship and technology and expending millions of dollars to gain favors, have found out they were dealing with the wrong ministries.

I was once invited to an informal gathering to mingle with some important Chinese officials who were, according to my American host, essential to the achievement of his organization's objectives. I listened as the American drew them out on their position in regard to his proposals. Afterward, one of the Chinese officials told me, "We really have nothing to do with this. The authority belongs to another ministry. We are so embarrassed. Over the past eight years, almost everyone in our ministry has visited the United States at this organization's expense, and they have presented us with state-of-the-art factory equipment as a gift."

A Chinese businessman once told me, "China is like a mystery palace and Americans don't know where the door is. The Japanese don't spend any money entertaining us, they just sit and watch until they find the door, then they go right in."

■ WHO'S THE BOSS?

Americans think in terms of "Who's the boss?" "Corner the boss and you will get your deal." In China, the highest-ranking person is not always the boss. Seniority and personal connections carry more weight than titles. The Chinese call this structure *Ho-Tai*. It means literally "backstage," and it plays an important role in decision-making.

If a person under the director is senior in age and has a greater involvement in the government and party, or if he has a strong Ho-Tai (perhaps his wife's uncle is a high-ranking official in Beijing), he is often the true leader. His nominal superior will look to him for decisions. The official government version of things is that this ambiguity between the nominal and the actual leadership does not exist, but the reality is quite different. It is of primary importance for a Western businessman to identify and cultivate the real boss.

■ | **LANGUAGE BARRIERS**

The barrier of language is, of course, the main source of communication problems between the East and West. In May 1986, during a business trip to Hong Kong, I chanced to read a newspaper article reporting an address by Burton Levin, the United States consul-general in Hong Kong, delivered at a luncheon given by the American Chamber of Commerce. He stated: "It's remarkable how simple truths sometimes seem to be overlooked, such as hiring bilingual agents who understand the difference of operating in a Chinese business environment, being patient, and the value of having a representative spend enough time in an area to develop a first-hand knowledge of the market and the personal ties so important to doing business in China."

Mr. Levin's words demonstrate a clear understanding of an essential problem facing American companies trying to do business in China. As Levin pointed out, language is the number one problem facing most foreign businessmen in China. He said, "I am sure most of you have sensed that the skills of the interpreters assigned to you in China are wanting. Heed my warning, your interpreter is more likely to confuse than clarify the issue." He advised people in business either to master Mandarin or to hire someone with unquestionable fluency in both Mandarin and English.

On many occasions, I have witnessed interpreters simply make something up rather than admit that they didn't understand what was said and ask for further explanation. In China, the position of interpreter is a full-time and glamorous profession. Many interpreters feel that it would compromise their professional image ever to admit that they do not understand something that has been said.

In the course of my consulting practice, I have spoken with a great many Americans doing business in Asia, as well as their Chinese, Japanese, and Korean counterparts. I have found that most Americans do not consider it necessary to learn the language of the country with which they are conducting business. Yet, when I ask the Asians, they tell me they consider it very important to learn at least a little English and to study American customs. It *is*, however, important for American businessmen to learn some of the native language as a token of their interest in the culture and the people with whom they do business. It will give them a tremendous edge over competitors who have not demonstrated this desire.

■ | ## Accurate Translation of Written Materials Is Vital

Accurate translation of company name, literature, and business cards is vital. An improper translation can lead to disastrous results.

Western businessmen and politicians dealing with the Chinese should be very careful to have their names translated, rather than transliterated. They should choose words that are pronounced similarly to their Western names or that have the same meaning. If the word is chosen because it is pronounced similarly, *careful attention should be paid to the meaning of the word in Chinese.* I know of one American diplomat whose name sounds like a word that means "stupid" in both Chinese and Japanese, and that is exactly how his engraved business card read to those who received it on his tour through Asia: "Mr. Stupid."

To the Chinese and other Asians, a name is very important. They do not simply pick a name for a company or product. They often consult scholars and may take months combining words to create the right image. Western companies must take the same care to ensure that the chosen translation of their name conveys the proper image and that their literature is translated correctly.

I have seen sales literature and business cards for a single company that were translated by several different translators. Each translator, left to himself, created a different name for the company. The result was that the Chinese formed the impression that the company's products were available from several entirely different companies.

In order to find a reliable translator, your company should follow a few basic guidelines:

- Because Asian languages are so different from Western languages, it is preferable that the translation be handled by someone who speaks the language as their native tongue rather than by a Westerner who has learned it as a second language.

- It is easiest for a Westerner to verify the translator's ability by having the translator read some of the company's material and then explain the contents.
- Once the translation is done, the company should obtain another native translator to check the quality and sophistication of the first translator's work.

You would not hire just anyone to write your promotional material simply because they could write English. You should not hire someone to translate it simply because they know both English and Chinese. Both the writer and the translator should be experienced in marketing, in understanding how to use words to create the proper image for your product. Do not be afraid to spend some money guaranteeing that your message is getting across the way it should.

■ THE CONCEPTUAL BARRIER BETWEEN EAST AND WEST

The barrier that is even more difficult to overcome than the language barrier is the barrier imposed by the differing conceptual frameworks of the Asian and the Westerner.

Even though the words may be understood and agreed on, the mental pictures associated with those words are quite different. Let's take as an example a relatively uncomplicated idea: an airplane trip to London. The phrase is easily translated without ambiguity, but the Westerner and the Chinese will have an entirely different set of ideas associated with it.

An American can decide over breakfast to fly to London and be on the plane before lunch. The procedure goes something like this: Call the travel agent. Make sure the passport is in order. Grab some traveler's checks at the bank, and make sure that the American Express card is in your wallet. Pack a couple of suitcases and take a cab to the airport. Wake up in London.

For the Chinese it is a procedure that can take months. It goes like this: Obtain a letter of invitation from a British business or government agency requesting you to come to England. Take the letter to the proper ministry and apply for a visa. Wait. Wait some more. Perhaps get a visa; perhaps not. Make application through official government channels to obtain the foreign currency needed. Wait for approval. Reserve airline tickets weeks in advance and hope that everything else falls into line before then. This illustrates how, even though the two parties may think they agree on the meaning of the words, they are really talking about two entirely different procedures.

Misunderstandings like this are common between Chinese businessmen and foreign suppliers. Chinese officials sometimes lack a knowledge of standard practices. When the Chinese purchase equipment, for example, they assume the purchase price covers all components necessary to run the equipment. Often it is the U.S. industry standard that each component must be purchased separately and the supplier erroneously assumes that the Chinese know this.

It is of the greatest importance that these elements be understood by all parties very early in the negotiations. The amount of paperwork necessary in China to acquire foreign currency to make purchases is staggering. Once an amount of foreign currency is requested and obtained, it is difficult to go back to the government and ask for more to buy components. Such misunderstandings are frequent.

I asked the general manager for Chinese operations of a major Japanese auto maker about certain allegations made by the Chinese. The Chinese complain that the Japanese sell their best cars in the United States, their second best in Europe, their next in line in the Middle East, and the bottom-of-the-line cars in China. The Chinese feel that the Japanese are taking advantage of them.

The general manager denied that the Japanese sold inferior cars in China and offered this explanation of the Chinese misunderstanding: The United States, Europe, and the Middle East have equipment requirements for air-pollution control. The equipment placed on automobiles to meet pollution standards is fairly recent technology. The Chinese have no special pollution-control requirements, therefore their cars are equipped with very straightforward engines. He said the Chinese have interpreted the lack of this more recent technology to mean that the cars they get are technologically outmoded, when, in fact, it means that they are more efficient, more economical, more reliable, and easier to repair.

■ | **THE ROLE OF SUPERSTITION IN ASIA**

Most Asians are extremely superstitious. When faced with an important decision, they seek auspicious signs. They consult oracular books to decide the best time to get married, bury the dead, break ground for a new house, or open a new business. The Chinese communist government has attempted to eradicate superstition but it still plays an important role in Chinese thought.

On a trip to the Oregon coast, a group of visiting Chinese saw a deer cross the road. Because the pronunciation of the Chinese word for "deer" is the same as the word for "prosperity," the leader of the group interpreted it as a very good omen that the proposed business venture with their American host would go well. Such an incident might seem trivial to the Westerner, but many Chinese truly believe that the future is foretold by such omens.

It is a belief among Buddhists that during the seventh lunar month that normally falls in August, all the ghosts in Heaven and Hell return to Earth. There are usually no weddings in this month and some people hesitate to make important decisions or to conclude negotiations until it is past.

The Chinese people also give special significance to color. In certain parts of China, a green hat is the traditional mark of a cuckold. While a delegation from Taiwan was touring a farm in the Midwest, the farmer, in a gesture of hospitality, placed a green hat on the delegation leader's head. The leader was so offended by the gift that he tore the hat off and threw it on the floor.

The colors of black and white, separately or in combination with one another, have a complex significance to the Chinese. A Westerner should avoid the use of these colors unless he has the expert advice of someone well-versed in their significance. White in conjunction with yellow or black is an especially inauspicious combination, being associated with funerals. In Japan, China, and Korea red is the color of happiness, joy, and all good things.

■ | USE CULTURE AS A WEAPON

Asians can hide behind cultural differences when it is to their advantage. They are well aware that Westerners are intimidated by the mystery of Asian culture, and they will use culture as a weapon to gain advantage over them.

The Japanese in particular are masters of this practice. In response to American charges of protectionism, the Japanese government ascribes the greater part of American difficulties to ignorance of Japanese customs rather than to protectionist policies on the part of the Japanese government. They emphasize that the Japanese are very different from Americans and that the real problem is the unwillingness of American companies to learn what they need to know in order to do business in Japan.

On the other hand, when it is to their advantage, they will minimize the differences between the Japanese and American cultures. They can take either side of the issue, depending on which one is more convenient, because they know that the Americans do not have the depth of understanding of Japanese culture to judge what is true and what is false.

Recently I listened to a Japanese businessman address a conference of American businessmen. He told them that the Japanese and Americans were really no different. We are all businessmen, he said, we are all interested in making money. In regard to the recent wave of books critical of the Japanese, he maintained that emphasizing the differences between the cultures is a good way to sell books, but that in reality there is very little difference between the peoples. As I sat and listened to this man, I couldn't help but wonder if he really believed what he was saying.

In his efforts at damage control, Shintaro Ishihara went to a great deal of effort to make exactly the opposite point, that the two cultures are so different that Americans are incapable of understanding the intent of his essays. My mind turned to the World War II kamikaze pilots. The greatest difficulty the Japanese military had with the kamikaze program was finding enough aircraft for the tremendous number of young men who were passionately willing to sacrifice their lives in one fiery, glorious moment. That image alone pointed to a profound cultural difference.

There are undeniable cultural differences between Asia and the West. Asians make a practice of emphasizing or deemphasizing these differences to make the foreigner believe that culture is to blame for negotiating problems. It is important for the American businessman to understand which situations are the result of true cultural differences and which are just manipulation strategies.

11

China Views the West

■ **FIRST EXPERIENCES WITH THE WEST**

In the eighteenth century, Voltaire wrote that the morality and organization of the Chinese empire was "the best the world has ever seen." Travelers' tales of China's fabulous wealth stimulated the imagination and greed of European empire builders. George III of England dispatched Lord Macartney as special envoy to the Chinese imperial court with the intent of opening up trade between the two countries. When Lord Macartney arrived in China, he was nonplussed to find that the Chinese were not overwhelmed with the honor done them by King George's notice. In fact, they treated his visit as that of a vassal paying tribute to a great lord. The emperor thanked Lord Macartney for coming so far to pay his respects but, in a polite but condescending manner, required him to tell his master that China did not have the slightest need for English goods.

That unquestioned sense of superiority applied not only to the fair-haired barbarians but to China's Asian neighbors and even to many of the ethnic groups that make up the Chinese people. For thousands of years, the only people considered to be truly civilized were the Han people who lived along the Yangtze River, the cradle of Chinese civilization.

Today, Chinese still feel an innate sense of cultural superiority to all other peoples. They call foreigners *lao wai*, a term of denigration that translates literally as "outsider." This xenophobic attitude has been shaped partially by the treatment the Chinese have received at the hands of the foreign barbarians during the last few centuries.

For much of its long history, China maintained a self-imposed isolation. This was not out of a fear of the outside world, but out of a sense that there couldn't be much of interest or value outside of China. Trade with other nations went on in a small way, but there wasn't a great deal of interest in the outside world. It wasn't until the middle of the nineteenth century that China was forced to deal with foreigners.

■ The Opium War and the Treaty of Nanjing

Through the early years of the nineteenth century, the British had been steadily increasing the flow of opium from India to China. At first, the Chinese chose to ignore it. By 1840, however, the deleterious effects of the opium trade on his subjects caused the emperor to order the seizure and destruction of all of the British opium. The British retaliation was swift and decisive. They demonstrated beyond argument that medieval Asian weaponry was no match for Western military technology.

The Nanjing Treaty of 1842 settled the Opium War. It was a treaty dictated by the conqueror to the conquered. Under the articles of the treaty, China was compelled to open five ports to British trading vessels and to concede a ninety-nine-year lease of Hong Kong to the British. Western nations were invested with legal jurisdiction over their nationals in China, and China was made to pay an indemnity of $21 million to Britain.

■ British and French Troops in China

In 1856, Britain and France requested permission to send ambassadors to Beijing. The young emperor, Hien-Feng, was outraged by the request. To even suggest that the Son of Heaven should have to behold these barbarians was an intolerable offense. "Since my ancestors established the Ching Empire," the emperor raged, "there has never been such a ridiculous proposal." Because of the vehemence of his denial, Britain and France decided the only way to achieve their ends was by force.

Later in that same year a pretext for hostilities presented itself. A British ship registered in Hong Kong and flying a British flag was boarded by Chinese authorities in Canton harbor. The Chinese were unfamiliar with the concept of a ship's registry and the sovereignty accorded it by Western maritime custom. Twelve Chinese seamen who served on the ship were arrested. The Chinese, unaware of the symbolism that his flag has for a Westerner, offended the British when they discarded the British flag by throwing it overboard. (Until the 1900's China had no flag of its own.)

Britain's Envoy Extraordinary, James Bruce, petitioned the Cantonese governor, Yei, to issue an official apology and release his twelve imprisoned seamen. Governor Yei released the prisoners but ignored the ambassador's request for an apology. Subsequently, a British battleship attacked Canton. In retaliation, the people of Canton burned the British commerce building, shouting, "Kill all the barbarians. Not one should be left alive."

In the following year, 1857, Britain and France combined their forces. They issued an ultimatum to Governor Yei, demanding that he appear for discussions at a specific time some ten days hence. Governor Yei chose to deal with this ultimatum in a fashion typical of the Chinese bureaucracy: He ignored it. When the day of the ultimatum passed without Yei responding to their demands, the combined forces of the English and French attacked Canton and arrested Governor Yei. The governor was imprisoned in India, where he died in the following year.

In 1858, British and French troops sailed north and conquered Tianjin. The twenty-year-old emperor was reluctant to sign the treaty that his conquerors were pressing on him. His advisors suggested to him that the treaty was merely a piece of paper and, being just a piece of paper, did not have to be complied with. Signing it, however, would rid them of the French and the British troops. "When the treaty is signed, the troops will leave Tianjin," they said. "Then, after they are gone, we will simply not fulfill our agreement. Later, we will tell the foreigners that those who are responsible for not fulfilling the treaty agreements will be severely punished." It was with these intentions that the emperor signed the Treaty of Tianjin.

In order to intimidate the Chinese into compliance with the terms of the treaty, in 1859, British and French warships appeared off of Taigu, the seaport serving Tianjin. The emperor's envoy warned the Western commander not to attempt to enter the heavily defended harbor, but instead to land ten miles to the north at Beitan. The Westerners thought little of Chinese defense systems and so ignored the warning. Although the United States was technically neutral in this conflict, in the ensuing attack on Taigu, the British and French were joined by American warships. Despite the American help, the Chinese sank four ships and heavily damaged six others in successfully repelling the attackers. The elated emperor celebrated this victory as a turning point in China's conflict with the West.

■ **The Burning of the Summer Palace**

But in 1860, Western warships returned to Taigu and captured both that port and the city of Tianjin. Despite the best efforts of his forces, the superior military technology of the West again placed the emperor in the position of having peace terms dictated to him. On this occasion, however, the British Envoy Extraordinary, James Bruce, insisted on presenting the treaty document to the emperor personally. In three thousand years, no one had ever been in the emperor's presence without kneeling and bowing. This arrogant barbarian now demanded to stand face to face with the emperor.

Peace negotiations began in September of 1860. In violation of one of their own most sacred laws of diplomacy, and even though the emperor's brother, Prince Tsai-Yuan, personally led the Chinese peace delegation, the Westerners attacked the Chinese negotiators. The justification they offered was that the Chinese themselves were planning treachery.

Prince Tsai-Yuan believed a Chinese-speaking foreigner, Harry Parkes, was at the root of these machinations and that, if Parkes were removed, the Western forces would be much less formidable. The Chinese arrested Parkes and thirty-eight others, twenty-five British and thirteen French. The emperor issued orders for their execution, but before the executions could be carried out, a Chinese official helped Parkes and the rest of the British prisoners to escape. The Frenchmen were executed.

Upon learning of the arrest of Parkes, the Western troops attacked Beijing, forcing the emperor to flee. The Chinese surrendered Beijing to the combined British and French forces. Beijing had been conquered before, but this was the first time the city had fallen into the hands of Europeans. Beijing's conquerors in the past had been the Mongols and Manchurians, barbarians also, but they were at least Chinese barbarians, not European "foreign devils."

The British and French took revenge for the men who had died in jail by looting and raping throughout Beijing. They culminated their revenge by looting and then burning Yuan Min Yuan, the emperor's summer palace.

It had taken over three centuries to construct Yuan Min Yuan. The Chinese watched mournfully for three days and nights as the beautiful summer palace burned. They recalled the Chinese people's great sacrifices during its construction. Prince Tsai-Yuan, in anger and bitterness, signed the Treaty of Beijing.

In the years following the Beijing Treaty, China was sliced into pieces by foreign powers. Major and minor powers of the world each claimed a piece for themselves. There were divisions of as many as eight to ten foreign territories in a single city.

■ The Russians in China

In these first encounters with the West, the Chinese had difficulty understanding their opponents. Governor Yei had misjudged the Western reaction to his decision to ignore the ultimatum they had sent him. The emperor and his advisors had misjudged the effect of signing and then ignoring the terms of the Treaty of Tianjin. The first hostilities had arisen from a simple misunderstanding of the symbolic significance of a flag. The Chinese had first thrown the British flag overboard and then refused to apologize.

Observing these difficulties, the Russians offered themselves to the Chinese court as intermediaries to help convince the British and French to remove their forces from Beijing. But the Chinese distrusted the Russians as much as they distrusted the British and French and therefore rebuffed their offer.

The French and British had never intended to occupy Beijing for any length of time and had been making preparations to depart even before the Russians had made their offer. By coincidence, shortly after the Chinese had spurned the Russian offer, the British and French ran into some logistical problems that forced them to delay their departure. Although the two events were unrelated, the Chinese felt that the Russians, in retaliation for the snub they had received, had somehow caused the British and French to change their minds about leaving. Sometimes the Chinese are so smart that they outsmart themselves.

Believing now that the Russians really did have the influence they claimed to have with the British and French, in exchange for Russian friendship, the Chinese ceded to Russia 270,000 square miles of territory in northeastern China that included the seaport of Vladivostok, still today Russia's only access to the Pacific.

In the latter part of the eighteenth century, both the Russians and the Chinese had difficulty controlling the Moslem minorities along their common border between Xinjiang Province and Siberia. The Russians used these periodic riots and rebellions as pretexts to encroach on Chinese territory by sending troops far into China to quell the disturbances. Because the Beijing government was so far removed from Xinjiang, it was the Russians' hope that the Chinese would tacitly accept Russian control of this area. Instead, the Chinese sent troops into Xinjiang to assert their rights to the territory. The Russians agreed to withdraw, but in compensation for their efforts in protecting Chinese interests, they demanded and received 240,000 square miles of territory in northwest China, including three huge lakes totaling 17,500 square miles.

In all, the Russians acquired 625,000 square miles of Chinese territory, an area three times the size of France and five times the size of Japan. These acquisitions were made without firing a shot.

The Russo-Japanese war of 1904 was fought neither in Russia nor in Japan but on Chinese soil. Chinese civilians were the victims of that war and only Chinese property was destroyed. In subsequent years, China lost Vietnam to France and Korea to Japan. In the first century after opening itself up to the outside world, China suffered a territorial loss of 3 million square miles.

■ | ## THE CHINESE PEOPLE RISE UP

From the beginning of the Opium War until the end of World War II, China was a subject of foreign powers rather than a sovereign nation. At various times during that period the Chinese people attempted to rid themselves of this domination.

The Boxer Rebellion in 1900 occurred in response to these depredations by foreign nations. In Western popular literature and movies it has been portrayed as a treacherous and bloodthirsty rampage by the heathen Chinese. In China it was regarded as a patriotic attempt to throw off the yoke of foreign domination.

On May 30, 1925, the killing of a Chinese worker in Shanghai by a Japanese merchant once again ignited the smoldering resentment of the Chinese people. Three thousand students and workers demonstrated in the streets. An English patrol opened fire on the demonstrators, killing or injuring more than thirty people. Fifty others were arrested. The English later fired upon a second group of demonstrators, killing four people and injuring ten. On June 3, thirty thousand students struck in Beijing to protest the killings of Shanghai. A general strike followed in Shanghai on June 10. Demonstrations spread to Canton where, on June 23, the Anglo-French forces shot and killed sixty more people. On June 25, the Chinese expressed their outrage at the foreigners' indifference to the taking of Chinese lives. They staged a nationwide general strike that shut down Chinese businesses, factories, and schools.

■ THE CHINESE DISTRUST OF FOREIGNERS

China has been victimized repeatedly by outsiders throughout modern history. Perhaps that explains in part the attitudes that the Chinese bring to present-day business and political negotiations with the West. Today a residue of bitterness still remains from China's encounters with foreigners. The Chinese people have a strong sense of history. Even as late as the outbreak of World War II, there were signs on buildings in Shanghai's British quarter that read, "Chinamen and Dogs Not Permitted to Enter." Decades later, these humiliations are still fresh in the Chinese mind.

Since long before Marco Polo visited China during the Ming Dynasty, China has received foreign guests with courtesy. But the events of this last century have created an understandable distrust of foreigners.

■ THE CHINESE VIEW OF AMERICANS

In interviews I have conducted with nearly two hundred immigrants from Japan, Korea, China, Hong Kong, and Taiwan in the United States, most expressed a preference for doing business with Americans to doing business with each other. They feel that dealing with American businessmen is much less complicated. Asian business negotiations can be extremely exhausting and tiresome even to Asians.

Asians believe that Americans are open, big-hearted, friendly, and trusting. Americans are known to give generously to the needy and to support projects to lessen human suffering. They usually conduct business dealings at a relatively high level of integrity, and Americans remain, despite certain disillusionments of recent years, an idealistic people. Asians admire these qualities. However, those qualities that the Chinese find endearing are also the qualities of which they may take advantage in business and political negotiations. Openness and trust can cause Americans to be vulnerable when negotiating with Chinese. It is relatively easy for Asians to take advantage of American weaknesses.

Asians also find Americans to be sometimes too superficial. They allege that Americans often look only at the surface of problems while Asians search out the underlying causes. This superficiality, they claim, makes dealing with Americans both easy and difficult.

Americans' trusting nature can sometimes work against them. But the naivete of the American results, at times, from arrogance. The American may simply lack the interest or commitment necessary to learn enough about his Asian counterpart to understand his counterpart's actions and attitudes. Americans are often more interested in studying trade statistics than in studying culture or history.

Americans can be short-sighted. Many American companies are notoriously impatient. They put a great deal of pressure on their representatives to achieve results that will show up on the next quarterly report.

Asians feel that these negative qualities impair the Americans' understanding of Asia and impede progress toward better trade and political relationships.

The Chinese people describe the Americans with the term *teanzen*, which means "childlike." They feel that American history is simple, uncomplicated, short, and rather pleasant. It is a history of growth and relative peace. Americans have not endured hardships like those of the Chinese. The Chinese carry the burden of five thousand years of war, suffering, and the endless struggle for survival. Human life has been cheap throughout China's history, with the resulting loss of innocence. It is little wonder that the Chinese may feel they have the right to take advantage when the opportunity is presented.

The Western business person would be wise to recognize the shadow cast by the past 150 years of mistreatment the Chinese have suffered.

12

Historical and Cultural Connections Among the Asian Peoples

■ | **THE CHILDREN OF YAN DI AND HUANG DI**

Before there were Japanese, before there were Koreans, there were the Chinese. Chinese written history begins in 2697 B.C. It is written that the Chinese people are the children of Yan Di and Huang Di. Chinese mythology describes Huang Di as the god of gods who gave up his divinity to abide on Earth and help mankind. Huang Di taught men to write and gave them the compass. His wife, Leizhu, taught them sericulture (the raising of silkworms for the production of raw silk) and silk weaving. Yan Di was the Sun God. He was the god of growing and healing, the patron of agriculture and medicine. The intermarriage of the people of Huang Di and Yan Di created the Han people who lived along the Yangze River. The Han people were regarded as the progenitors of the Chinese race and the creators of Chinese civilization.

In 219 B.C., Chin Shi Huang, the first emperor of the Ch'in Dynasty, sent Shufu, one of the learned men of his court, on a quest to find the fabled island of Peng Lai where the gods dwelt. He wished Shufu to bring him some of the herbs that grew there and were believed to confer immortality. Because he was going to the home of the gods, Shufu was attended by thousands of pure maidens and youths. At sea, the expedition encountered a typhoon which drove them off course and landed them in what is present-day Japan. The young people married among themselves and with the native islanders and thus begat the Japanese race.

Although the story of Shufu is wrapped in myth, there is a kernel of historical truth to it. The traditional belief is that the Japanese imperial line is descended directly from the Sun Goddess; many Japanese scholars make a case that the emperor is descended directly from Shufu. A great many Japanese believe this; however, the imperial house much prefers to think of itself as descended from the gods rather than the Chinese.

In 1121 B.C., during the Chou Dynasty, the Chinese emperor claimed Korea as a Chinese territory and appointed a Chinese governor. Subsequently, Chinese people began to settle there and intermarry with the original inhabitants. Throughout most of its history, Korea has been, to a greater or lesser degree, under Chinese influence. In 1895, it was lost to the Japanese, who wrested it from the Chinese under the pretext of declaring it an independent country. Soon after its separation from China, the Japanese occupied Korea as their colony.

The people of China, Japan, and Korea are very closely related. They share similar values through the agency of a similar culture and philosophy. Nevertheless, though the national characters of the Chinese, Japanese, and Korean peoples are similar in many ways, there are important differences.

Geography had a great deal to do with shaping some of the differences between the Chinese and Japanese. Japan is a tiny country, surrounded by the sea. China is a vast landmass. China has simply absorbed the many external perils that have threatened it over the millennia. Wave after wave of invaders have marched into China and disappeared into the fabric of Chinese culture.

The Japanese have always seen their survival as more precarious than China's, and, consequently, they have developed a uniquely insular character. They refer to it as *shi ma gu ni kon jo*, which, translated literally, means "island country root nature." Like the crew of a storm-tossed ship, the Japanese are bound by a deeply felt sense of common destiny. They place enormous importance on the concepts of duty, loyalty, and cooperation, and very little importance on individualism.

Japan does not enjoy the abundance of natural resources that China does. Economic survival has always required an intense and aggressive effort on the part of the Japanese. Consequently, they have acquired an intense, aggressive nature. In comparison, the Chinese are much more easygoing.

The Chinese and Japanese have differing interpretations of bravery. There is a Chinese maxim that says, "A good man does not fight a losing battle." In a country as large as China, there is always somewhere to run. The Chinese see the attainment of their long-range goals as more important than displays of personal bravery. They have no compunction about retreating from a superior force in order to regroup and attack at a more favorable time. In Japan, however, an army most often has the sea at its back. It must conquer or perish. The Japanese have evolved a sense of martial honor that makes it difficult for them to retreat or surrender in order to fight another day. They are eager to die in battle and extremely brave on the battlefield.

Korea, although not an island, is a peninsula on the fringe of the vastness of China. The land was and is inhabited by a stubborn, resourceful people who have managed, against great odds and many invaders, to maintain a surprising degree of racial homogeneity. Korea developed along its own path and falls somewhere between China and Japan culturally.

■ THE MAIN CURRENTS OF ASIAN PHILOSOPHY AND RELIGION

To gain a deeper understanding of Asians with whom you must deal in the world of business, you should, as I have indicated earlier, make some effort to understand the principles by which they live. Asian culture has no clearly defined division between religion and philosophy. Faith and philosophy are lived each day as a way of life. In Asia, the teachings of sages are not generally regarded as the revealed word of God, but as guides to living in harmony with Heaven.

Chinese religion has no direct equivalent to Western scriptures, but there are mythologies as well as moral and ethical philosophical writings. The oldest and most complete book of Chinese mythology is the *Mountain Sea Scripture*. It is a combination of works from the Hsia Dynasty (2205–1766 B.C.) and Chou Dynasty (1122 to 770 B.C.), the Autumn-Spring Period (770–476 B.C.), the Warring States (476–221 B.C.), and the early Han Period (206 B.C.). The *Mountain Sea Scripture* contains several versions of creation. Another version of creation is found in a collection of books called *Huai-Nan-Zi*.

Both the *Mountain Sea Scripture* and the *Huai-Nan-Zi* relate the creation process as a combining of Yin and Yang forces; the female and male aspects of energy. The concept of Yin and Yang dominates every aspect of Asian life and thought. The Koreans chose the symbol of Yin and Yang as the main device depicted on their flag, a circle evenly divided into areas of light and dark. In Asian philosophy everything has a positive and negative side: a black and a white, a good and an evil, a dark and a light, a female and a male aspect. Yin and Yang are considered to balance the universe.

■ TAOISM

The Tao that can be voiced is not the everlasting Tao.
The name that can be expressed is not the everlasting name.
The nameless is the beginning of Heaven and Earth.
The named one is the mother of ten thousand things.
Contemplate the "nothingness" to see its mystery.
Contemplate the "existence" to see its manifestations.
These two came from the same source but differ in name.
Of all things profound, these are the deepest;
The gate to the mystery of all.

The highest virtue is like water,
It benefits ten thousand things and does not strive.
It flows in lowly places that men reject.
So its nature is just like Tao.
It dwells everywhere.
In meditation, it is calm as water.
In dealings, benevolent.
In speech, truth.
In ruling, justice.
In business, proficient.
In action, rhythm.
Such a man acts without struggle,
in harmony with peace.

Honor and disgrace bring distress.
Misfortune is the human condition.
Why do honor and disgrace bring distress?
When honored, one is up,
When disgraced, one is down.

When one gains, distress,
When one loses, distress.
Why is misfortune the human condition?
The source of my misfortune comes
from having a body.
If I have no body,
How can I have misfortune?
When one surrenders oneself humbly to the world,
Then, to such a being can be entrusted the care of the world.
When one loves the world as one's own self,
Then, such a being can be entrusted with the sovereignty of the world.
—Lao Tzu, *Tao Te Ching*

The philosophy of the Tao preceded the Taoist religion. Lao Tzu and Zhung Tzu (circa 300 B.C.) did not proclaim a religion. They merely taught the Higher Truth existing in the universe as they experienced it. It was later disciples who established Taoism as a religious doctrine and proclaimed Lao Tzu as their spiritual avatar. Lao Tzu's teachings became intertwined with superstition and magic.

■ The Wu Wei Principle

Lao Tzu saw the whole universe as the perfect manifestation of Tao (or God, or Creator, or whatever you like). The essence of his teaching is summarized in two Chinese characters, *wu wei*, which together mean nonaction.

The principle of nonaction does not mean sitting and doing nothing. Rather, it evidences an understanding that all actions are gifts from Tao. The heart beats, the lungs breathe by the grace of Tao. Human beings perform their daily actions by the grace and harmony of Tao. *Wu wei* directs them to act to the best of their abilities and leave the outcome, the fruit of their action, to Tao. By giving up the attachment to the fruit of their actions, they acknowledge that all things are accomplished by the grace of Tao.

The fruit of an action is the reward we all look for in our daily lives. It comes in different forms for different people. A cinema star is looking for the reward for her efforts in a successful film. A writer is seeking the fruits of his writing in a best-seller. Politicians measure the fruits of their actions in election results. It is not a principle of Taoism that we should not look for or expect our actions to bear fruit; rather, it is that we should first act in harmony with nature, give our best effort, and then leave the outcome to Tao. *Wu wei* is the principle of detachment from the fruits of action.

Unfortunately, men not spiritually equipped to comprehend the truths hidden in Lao Tzu's writings have misinterpreted them for popular consumption. The harmony of action proposed by the concept of "nonaction" was literally construed to be a call to not act.

Many Chinese believe that the way to get by is to do nothing. The Chinese have practiced nonaction for over two thousand years and truly believe that the more you do, the more trouble you bring down upon yourself. This corruption of the concept of "nonaction" has contributed to the decline of Chinese society and technological stagnation.

■ ZEN BUDDHISM

In A.D. 645, a Chinese monk returned to China from a long pilgrimage to India. He brought with him the seeds of Chinese Buddhism. Because Taoism and Buddhism are two ways to acknowledge a single Truth, Buddhism easily wove itself into the Taoism of China with few modifications. The Chinese never embraced the Buddhist discipline of homeless wandering as a proof of nonattachment, because Chinese values are rooted in the family and the land, but the essential elements of Buddhist philosophy, mingled with the philosophy of the Tao, flourished in China. The Chinese called this form of Buddhism *Zhan*. During this era, which was China's Golden Age, it was common for Japanese scholars and monks to come to China to study culture, art, history, and philosophy. They were exposed to China's new-found religion and carried it back to Japan, where it evolved into Zen Buddhism.

The essence of Zen is that each individual contains the seeds of divinity and has the potential to realize his divine nature. The object of the practice of Zen is not to reach enlightenment, but rather to realize one's own divine nature. Zen teaches that an individual may wander from lifetime to lifetime without awareness of his true nature, subject to the ephemeral pains and pleasures of life. Life is like a dream when a person is ignorant of his divine nature, and the dreamer often suffers from his delusions. Through meditation, devotion, disciplined living, grace, and selfless service to his fellow man, the disciple can dispel the illusion that he is a mere mortal and can come to the realization that "God dwells within you as you."

But rather than elevating the mundane to divine, the practice of Zen has often been reduced to the mundane. Zen became the art of doing things: the Zen of flower arrangement, the Zen of swordsmanship, the Zen of gardening. Of course, when one is in harmony with the divine, one will naturally be master of any discipline, but too often the effect is mistaken for the cause.

■ THE TEACHINGS OF CONFUCIUS

The man who is full of wisdom and sees the Tao clearly has no doubts in his heart. The man who is full of virtue and benevolence has no selfish thoughts; therefore, he examines himself with no guilt. The brave man is in harmony with the truth and virtue; therefore, there is no fear within.

The virtuous man is full of Tao, such that within every word he speaks there is the essence of the Truth (Tao). The one who can speak skillfully, with seemingly sweet words, is not necessarily a virtuous man. The benevolent one, his whole heart full of eternal Truth with no self-interest, when his duty of life is called upon, will fulfill it at all costs. The courage is naturally within him. But a brave man will fight because of his temper or anger or to serve his pride, not necessarily to be benevolent.

When you are poor, having great difficulty clothing and feeding yourself and yet have no resentment or hatred in your heart, it is most difficult. When you are rich and full of wealth yet you can be contented and have no pride, this is easier to do.

When you are examining yourself in every movement, every word, and every action, you will make very few mistakes.

A learned man is very careful and timid in every word he says; but in action, he works very swiftly and is not lazy.

The virtuous man is not alone; his virtues will ever be his companions.
—From *The Teachings of Confucius*

Confucius was born in 551 B.C., during the Spring-Autumn Period, when China was divided into warring feudal states. In this chaotic period, Confucius laid down principles that came to be the foundation of social order. He taught that it was the duty of the rulers to govern with benevolence and justice and that it was the duty of the people to obey and respect their leaders. At the time, no one listened to him. It was not for many generations that the rulers discovered the advantage of popularizing Confucius's teachings to promote obedience and respect for their authority.

The intention of Confucius was to reestablish law and order in a chaotic and divided country by codifying the proper relationship of the governors to the governed and delineating their respective duties in that relationship. But it was usual for the rulers to pay little attention to the part of Confucius's teaching that enjoined them to govern with benevolence and justice. This perversion of Confucius's teachings resulted in two thousand years of political and social repression, the effects of which are still being felt throughout Asia.

The subject of Confucius's teaching is the proper conduct of the individual, or *Dharma*. His teachings concern service to society as well as the performance of the domestic and daily duties required by one's station in life. He placed the ideas of service and duty in the context of understanding and becoming in tune with the Tao and Heaven. He taught that only when a man learns to cultivate his own virtue can he expand his concern to the family, the country, and the world. He taught that what you do not wish done unto you, do not do unto others—a statement later echoed in Christianity's Golden Rule.

■ **Zung Yung**

The essence of Confucian teaching is preserved in a book called Zung Yung, which means Eternal Center.

> Split many times from the middle, it becomes ten thousand things. In the end it will be united again into one Truth. If this Truth is let loose, it will fill the whole universe, but when you fold this Truth, it will hide in the smallest and most secret place. The essence of this Truth is endless. This is the True knowledge. The learned individual should contemplate and meditate upon this. The knowledge will reveal itself. When you take this true knowledge to all the aspects of your daily life, there is an endless supply.
>
> —Zung Yung

All ten thousand things under the sky are nothing but consciousness. If you do not contemplate on this consciousness, what you have is only the limited knowledge. If you understand this principle of consciousness within all things, then all knowledge can be interchanged. This is the essence of knowledge.

—Chu Tzu, Neo-Confucian Scholar of the South Sung Dynasty

The teachings of Confucius deal largely with mundane examples. His disciples feared that the higher truth of the master's words would be lost to future generations. The Zung Yung was written so that people might understand the eternal principles that underlie Confucius's practical examples.

Zung Yung, called the middle path, has been popularly misinterpreted as an indecisive, noncommittal way. As a result, it has often been used to justify vacillation and hesitation and to buttress the common Chinese opinion that it is safest not to rock the boat. The Chinese have often used the words of Confucius to justify their mistakes and shortcomings.

In doing business with the Chinese, do not be surprised to encounter noncommittal, indecisive people. Just understand that they are the product of two thousand years of Confucianism.

■ | TOLERANCE

Throughout Western history, wars have been fought over religious differences, from the Crusades to the Catholic-Protestant struggle in present-day Ireland. The American continent was first settled by people seeking a place to practice their religious beliefs in peace.

There have been no religious wars in Chinese, Japanese, or Korean history. Asians believe all creatures of the universe are created by the One, call it what you may. Whether one is a follower of Buddhism, Zen, or Taoism, they believe salvation is achieved through self-discipline and meditation leading to self-purification.

■ | THE INFLUENCE OF CHINA'S PHILOSOPHY ON JAPANESE AND KOREAN SOCIETY

Both Japan and Korea have been deeply influenced by the Chinese way of thinking. Both societies respect Confucianism. The Japanese learned it well and established an orderly society based on obedience, discipline, and strong family commitment. One consequence of this was social repression at all levels of Japanese society. The Koreans have also created a society based on order and obedience and, along with these, on social and political repression. The Chinese people have endured repression for thousands of years.

China, Japan, and Korea have each adapted and interpreted the wisdom of Chinese philosophers. The following two stories, the first Chinese, the second Japanese, demonstrate the strong similarity in the two countries' values.

The Chinese story concerns misfortune:

A man named Sei Weng owned a beautiful mare which was praised far and wide. One day this beautiful horse disappeared. The people of his village offered sympathy to Sei Weng for his great misfortune. Sei Weng said simply, "That's the way it is." A few days later the lost mare returned, followed by a beautiful wild stallion. The village congratulated Sei Weng for his good fortune. He said, "That's the way it is."

Some time later, Sei Weng's only son, while riding the stallion, fell off and broke his leg. The village people once again expressed their sympathy at Sei Weng's misfortune. Sei Weng again said, "That's the way it is." Soon thereafter, war broke out and all the young men of the village except Sei Weng's lame son were drafted and were killed in battle. The village people were amazed at Sei Weng's good luck. His son was the only young man left alive in the village. But Sei Weng kept his same attitude; despite all the turmoil, gains and losses, he gave the same reply, "That's the way it is."

This Japanese story concerns a young monk named Hakuin:

Hakuin lived all alone in a little farming village where he meditated and followed a rigorous and austere spiritual discipline. He was not involved with a worldly life and was praised by his neighbors for his virtue. A beautiful young girl who also lived in the farm village was discovered to be pregnant. The girl's family asked her who the father of her child was. The girl cried and said, "Hakuin, the monk." The family went to Hakuin and condemned him for the dishonorable thing he had done. The young monk said, "Is that so?" When the baby was born, the girl's family gave the newborn son to Hakuin to raise. The monk took the boy and raised him as his own, while still maintaining his austere, spiritual existence. Hakuin never proffered an explanation for what had happened. Years passed during which the village people despised the monk for his hypocrisy. At last, the girl's conscience could stand it no more. She told her family that the father of her child was not the monk, but rather it was another young man of the village. Her family and the people of the village went to the monk and apologized to him for abusing and dishonoring him for so many years. Hakuin said, "Is that so?" And uttered no other words.

The Chinese have always been flexible in the interpretation and reinterpretation of their fundamental philosophies under the changed conditions wrought by the passing of centuries. The Japanese and Koreans who adopted their beliefs from these Chinese sources tend to be more dogmatic and inflexible in the application of these ancient principles. A case in point is the Confucian idea of a woman's place in society and how differently it is understood today in China, Korea, and Japan.

Confucius taught that women were lesser beings than men. But he taught more than two thousand years ago during one of the darkest periods in Chinese history. Society was chaotic and violent. Much of what Confucius taught is timeless, but much is specifically addressed to the social conditions of those times. If Confucius were teaching today, his view of a woman's role in society would be very different. In China today, the attitude toward women has changed dramatically compared to Korean and Japanese attitudes. I recently tried to discuss women's rights with an educated and articulate Korean man. He took a great deal of national pride in the fact that Korean women are in their "proper" place. He attributed this to the Koreans' stricter adherence to the teachings of Confucius on the subject.

■ | ANCIENT AND MODERN ANIMOSITIES

Recently, at a meeting I was attending, an American lady came to me and asked if it were true that the Koreans do not like the Japanese. She said she had been told this by a Korean businessman at a party she had attended the previous night. I told her that relationships among Korean and Japanese individuals may transcend national feelings, but that Koreans as a general rule do not like the Japanese. Within living memory of many Koreans, Japanese troops occupied Korea and treated the Korean people with systematic brutality. This experience has left the Korean people with bitter feelings toward the Japanese. To this day, the fear of economic or military domination by Japan still lingers among the Korean people.

Even though throughout history China has been in and out of Korea, the relationship between these two countries has been much more genial. Although China sometimes acted as the protector of Korea, she has more often taken on the role of conqueror. But whether the battles were won or lost, the Chinese have had a tendency to return home. They are not driven by the desperate need for human and natural resources that fires the Japanese, nor do they impose themselves so forcefully on the culture of their subject peoples. Hence, they have not incurred the same resentment.

From the late 1800's to the end of War War II and the unconditional surrender by Japan, the imperial Japanese government had essentially the same plan for China as it had for Korea. The Chinese people too have difficulty forgetting the actions of the Japanese.

As I have said, my family is from Manchuria and my parents grew up during the Japanese occupation. My mother told me that in her hometown, the path to the Japanese police station was clearly identified by a trail of blood on the ground. As a young child, she had to step over it each day on her way to school. She told me that traveling from one place to another was often very dangerous. The Japanese would interrogate and often torture travelers right on the railway platform if their identification papers had the slightest hint of irregularity.

Although both my parents can speak Japanese fluently, having received their formal education in Manchuria and Japan, now that they are not compelled as they were under the Japanese occupation, they will not speak Japanese for any reason whatsoever. Even though it is sometimes advantageous in business to speak Japanese with Japanese people, they will not. Like all of the older generation, my parents vividly remember the occupation of China by the Japanese. My generation learned of Japanese brutality from our parents' stories and from written histories.

The Chinese people still bitterly resent the brutal actions of the Japanese in China. A Westerner will seldom hear this resentment spoken, however. It is seen as a matter between old acquaintances that an outsider would not understand. The Asian peoples share many similarities, yet the attitudes developed through centuries of interaction, and inflamed by the occurrences of recent history, have woven among them complicated and intricate relationships that are not easy for a Westerner to grasp.

13

The Inner Chinese

■ | THE CHINESE CLASS SYSTEM

Up to the current century, Chinese society had been organized into a class system that had not changed for thousands of years. There were four classes in traditional Chinese society: The scholar class occupied the highest position, followed, in order of decreasing rank, by the farmer, laborer, and merchant classes. Class membership was largely hereditary, but there was one important avenue of social mobility, the examination system for entry into many jobs. Scholarly achievement could quickly elevate the humblest peasant to a position of wealth and rank within the scholar class.

The Chinese have always attached an inordinate amount of importance to intellectual accomplishment. The scholar was the ideal toward which the best of men were supposed to strive. Only scholars could hold government positions. Other occupations, though productive and equally important to society, were held in lower esteem. Over the course of centuries, this attitude contributed to China's economic stagnation by creating a society top-heavy with a great many thinkers and few doers.

The Chinese communist government has tried to glorify the laborer at the expense of the scholar class, but class prejudices ingrained over the course of twenty centuries cannot be changed by decree. I remember touring a prosperous agricultural collective in Fujian Province in 1985. The business of the collective was raising hogs, and it was done very successfully. What was remarkable was that the collective was worked only by the women. The men held positions in the government bureaucracy. Even though hog farming was the source of their prosperity, the men held desk jobs because they could not bear to be thought of as pig farmers rather than scholars.

The merchant has always occupied the lowest position in the social hierarchy. As far back as the Ch'in Dynasty (221–206 B.C.) there was an attempt to wipe out this "lowly class of peddlers." The first emperor of the Han Dynasty, who ruled from 206 to 195 B.C., forbade merchants to wear silk or ride in a vehicle. He also levied an extremely heavy burden of taxation on them.

Today in China and Taiwan, these class distinctions are becoming somewhat blurred. The knowledge explosion has created a fifth class, the technocracy. A successful merchant today is very different from the old-time haggler in the marketplace. He must understand finance, accounting, marketing, management, and a hundred other subjects. He is a scholar. A successful farmer must study horticulture, soil science, and many other disciplines. He, too, is a scholar. Consequently, today's scholar-merchant and scholar-farmer have brought the prestige of the scholarly class to occupations that previously were considered menial.

■ THE NORTHERN CHINESE VS. THE SOUTHERN CHINESE

The Chinese themselves feel that there are notable differences between the people of northern and southern China, and every Chinese person identifies himself with one group or the other. The identification with one group or another is not always decided by geography. For example, I was raised in the South, but my family for countless generations lived in the North. I am, beyond question, a Northern Chinese in spite of the southern influence in my upbringing.

Physically, the Northern Chinese tend to be large, strong, and stocky. The Southern Chinese tend to have a relatively smaller frame and less strength. Southern women are generally more delicate and are often famous for their beauty.

The Northern Chinese are commonly characterized as candid, sincere, and hardworking. They tend to dress simply. They have a keen sense of humor, but are often seen as hot-tempered because they are not accustomed to disguising their true feelings and do not suppress anger when they feel it.

The Southern Chinese tend to be more subtle, often devious thinkers. They excel in trade and commerce and are proud of their cunning in business negotiations. The Northern Chinese say of them that "they have longer intestines than other people," meaning that they think about things longer. They digest events thoroughly and mull over various strategies at great length.

The Southern Chinese are more given to elegance in their dress and in their pastimes. The temperamental difference between the Northern and Southern Chinese can be recognized clearly in their poetry. Northern poetry is straightforward and powerful. What it lacks in grace, it makes up in candor. The poetry of the Southern Chinese is more lyrical and descriptive, filled with tender emotions.

For Westerners, it is easier to do business with the Northern than with the Southern Chinese. The straightforward Northern manner is more understandable to the Western business man. The Southern Chinese more often have hidden agendas and engage in subtle and complex strategies to implement them.

■ WHAT THE CHINESE THINK OF THEMSELVES

One should not display the family shame to an outsider.
—Chinese proverb

Everyone in China is at least half philosopher. The Chinese spend a great deal of time examining their faults as individuals and as a nation. Among themselves, the Chinese are surprisingly frank in acknowledging faults that in Western culture might seem to be serious weaknesses of character. But what may seem bad in Western culture is not necessarily so in Chinese culture. At any rate, these shortcomings are not meant to apply to individuals. It is only as national characteristics that, among the Chinese themselves, they are commonly held to be true.

■ | **Creative Interpretation of the Law**

Over thousands of years, the Chinese have developed their own ways of taking care of business. Unlike Westerners, the Chinese do not like to fight the system. When it becomes a problem for them, they would rather work around it than confront it.

In the 1920's, the central government in Nanjing ordered all Chinese government offices within the Shanghai foreign territory to relocate outside of it. This order created a great deal of consternation among local officials in Shanghai, most of whom had homes and families established there. Compliance would also have thrown a great many people in Shanghai out of work.

The officials did not attempt to confront the central authorities and have the order rescinded. Their solution to the problem was simply to change the names of the various offices from those that identified them as official government offices to nebulous names such as the "Trading Management Company." The total cost was twenty yen for each new sign on an office's front door. No one had to move. No one lost his job. No one lost face.

This story is a classic example of how the Chinese circumvent authority without defying it. Foreigners often find out the hard way that the Chinese take the same attitude toward contracts and agreements.

■ | **The Chinese Love of Peace**

Though they have experienced countless wars, both external and internal, the Chinese people have never been warlike. China has always been an agricultural society and its people have always had more of the farmer in them than the warrior. That is not to say that they are not quarrelsome among themselves. Bickering, shouting, and yelling, as well as an occasional fistfight over something as trivial as a seat on the bus, are common occurrences on the streets of any Chinese city.

■ | **Accepting One's Fate**

> Don't concern yourself with the harvest,
> Concern yourself only with the proper cultivation of your fields.
> —Chinese proverb

The Chinese believe that things happen as a result of fate. They believe that man has limited ability to shape or alter his destiny, and that the more he fusses with it, the worse it will get. They believe that they should accept things as they are. One consequence of this attitude is a lack of initiative.

■ | **The Endurance of Hardship**

Throughout history, the Chinese people have endured hardships beyond the Westerner's experience. This has instilled a strength of character in the Chinese people, but it has also created too great a tolerance for the injustices thrust upon the individual by government and society. The Chinese have learned to accept repression at the hands of authority.

■ | **The Devious and Elusive Nature of the Chinese**

> Of the thirty-six strategies, escape comes first.
>
> A good man never fights a losing battle.
> —Chinese maxims

These are perhaps the characteristics that most often frustrate Westerners trying to deal with the Chinese. Because survival has not always been easy in China, the Chinese have developed a great respect for the ability to survive. There are many heroes in Chinese history who retreated, escaped, or, in defeat, abjectly begged for their lives, but who survived ultimately to win the war. There are also heroes in Chinese history whose valor compelled them to fight against overwhelming odds and who died in a losing cause. These latter are still admired for their courage and steadfastness, but as models for their daily lives, most Chinese much prefer the survivors to the valiant losers.

■ ## The Lack of Innovation

The Chinese once led the world in technological innovation, but the conditions of Chinese society have, over the centuries, discouraged experimentation with new methods. Traditional Chinese education has always emphasized the humanistic disciplines at the expense of science and mathematics. Chinese culture tends to suppress individual initiative and often tames the spirit of the most resourceful and superior individuals, rather than encouraging the sometimes erratic fire of creativity.

■ ## Mooching

Mooching among the Chinese is a popular and accepted form of behavior. If a Chinese person purchases a few eggs and some greens at the market, it is expected that the vegetable seller will throw in some green onions or a few carrots. A peddler who does not do so will not remain in business for very long.

This expectation of a little something extra extends to international trade. The Chinese often expect something to be tossed in for free when they buy goods. When dealing with the Chinese, it is important to build a small contingency into your price to cover the costs of mooching.

The Chinese also like to discount a seller's price. The Westerner may think a professional should set a fair price and stick with it. In China, however, everyone, from early childhood on, is trained to bargain. The Chinese sometimes bargain simply for the sake of bargaining. A British plastics dealer told me that he always adds 2 to 3 percent to the price of his goods. That way, when the bargaining begins, he can give this margin to the Chinese, allowing them to save face.

Although the root of this behavior may seem simply pecuniary to the Westerner, it is not so. The Chinese truly believe that all people are connected by some bond and that the bond confers obligations. Brothers will transact business with one another on the best of terms. When a peddler finds out that he and his customer both come from the same remote province, he is obligated to give him a better deal than he otherwise would. If they share the same surname, the terms must be better still. The conditions of each party to a transaction also determine the terms that must be offered. A poor man must be given a better price than a rich man.

Suffering acute jet lag after a flight from Los Angeles to Beijing, I was pacing my hotel room restlessly at three o'clock one morning. It was a few weeks after the Tiananmen Square massacre and there was a curfew in the city. Although my hotel was very close to the square, I decided to go walking anyway. I thought it might be a good time and place to get some information about events in the city since the incident. I didn't feel that I was placing myself in much danger; born and raised in China and traveling on a U.S. passport, I could be either Chinese or American, as the situation called for.

Wandering through the streets, I ran across an old peddler who was still awake beside his cart. I struck up a conversation and we talked for a long time. We discovered we were both from Manchuria. Then he found out I was American. His immediate response was, "Then why don't you give me some money?" There was no doubt in his mind that he had a clear right to some reasonable amount. Our families came from the same region. He had befriended me, alone in a big city. He was poor and I, being an American, was unquestionably rich. With all those bonds between us and the inequity in our wealth, most Chinese would have felt the same.

The Chinese carry that same attitude into international trade: China is poor; the West is rich. Therefore, it is right and proper that China get a little better deal than wealthier nations.

■ | **Avoiding Involvement**

One less responsibility is better than one more.

Unnecessary efforts bring unnecessary problems.
—Chinese maxims

The Chinese avoid involvement because it tends to bring responsibility along with it—and responsibility means accountability. In a communist-socialist society, there is no incentive to be burdened with unnecessary accountability. The Chinese are more interested in their individual welfare than in the collective good.

In 1989, I went to Chinese National Radio about purchasing time for a one-hour weekly radio show to be produced in the United States and underwritten by American advertisers for broadcast in China. Not only was the American currency of interest to station officials, but they also recognized that programming on state-run radio was not as imaginative or interesting as it might be, and were interested in a show produced in America. We reached an initial agreement about the format of the show. It was to feature Western music and interviews with Western celebrities and business leaders whose ideas might be of interest to the Chinese people. The only issue left to talk about was the money. The financial negotiations took several months, but we finally came to an agreement. Just when I thought it was all wrapped up, I got a letter informing me that the format had been revised. They were not going to permit interviews. In fact, there was to be no speaking at all; just music.

Without being told, I immediately knew what had happened. They badly needed the American currency, they had complete editorial and censorship control of what was broadcast, and everyone had originally thought that it was a wonderful format. But when it came right down to an official at Chinese National Radio accepting responsibility for what went out over the airwaves, there was no one who would take it on himself to approve the idea of foreigners expressing their views over Chinese radio, especially with events in Eastern Europe to underline the danger of exposing the Chinese people to Western ideas.

■ | **Selfishness**

Food is God.

—Chinese saying

China has always been a place of too many people and too little of the basic necessities of life. Some of the Chinese tendency toward selfishness is the result of the realities of survival. Unselfishness is a virtue most often practiced where there is enough for everyone.

Another factor that contributes to this selfishness is a misinterpretation of the ancient Chinese philosophy that teaches the cultivation of the Self in order to function in harmony with the Tao. The Self in this context refers to the Higher Self. Over time, however, this has been misinterpreted to mean the individual self. The result, rather than a striving to cultivate the spiritual Self, is simple selfishness.

■ **A Lack of Regard for Public Property**

The selfish attitude of the Chinese has led to a total disregard for public property. The extent of damage inflicted upon public buildings in China by abuse and neglect is extreme. Even relatively new buildings are in such a state as to cause disbelief among Westerners.

Littering and spitting in public places are examples of the Chinese disregard for public property. Even a Chinese official will tidy up the interior of his car by throwing trash into the street. Although it is not done in hotels and restaurants that Westerners frequent, in Chinese restaurants patrons think nothing of spitting and throwing trash on the floors.

■ **Lack of Unity**

The Heaven is high; the Emperor is far away.

—Chinese maxim

By this saying, the Chinese mean that, despite rules or policies to the contrary, they are free to do as they please within their own sphere.

Sun Yat-sen, the founding father of modern China, was deeply concerned about the lack of unity among the Chinese people. He likened them to a plate of sand, a billion individual grains without coherence or strength. Every Chinese school child is taught the example by which Sun Yat-sen illustrated the importance of unity. He took a pair of chopsticks in his hands and broke them easily. Then he took a dozen pair and struggled to break them, but was unable.

Chinese leaders repeatedly call for unity. But neither in business nor in government is there unity. Each Chinese has an individual agenda that is far more important to him than the common goals of the Chinese people.

■ Lack of Communication

Trouble is born out of the words you speak.

—Chinese maxim

The Chinese feel that unnecessary communication can only lead to unnecessary trouble. This is a common attitude in government bureaucracies in both China and Taiwan. A profit-oriented enterprise must be result-oriented, so this behavior is not as prevalent in that sector. But bureaucracies are not oriented toward producing results as much as toward not getting into trouble.

Consider the case of two Chinese bureaucracies, a commodity-production division and an import division that shared a building. Though separated by only a few feet, neither division communicated with the other. The production division often produced the same commodity that the importer sought abroad. Often, however, communication would have made little difference because the production unit was much more interested in generating hard currency from export sales than in producing for domestic consumption. It did not matter to them that hard currency reserves next door were being depleted to acquire the same commodity. That was someone else's problem.

■ Disagreement Between Heart and Mouth

What the Chinese say is often not what they mean. The Chinese speak in euphemisms and often by circumlocution. This is especially true when they speak humbly. If a Chinese person says he doesn't feel qualified for a particular responsibility, he does not mean it. What he means is that he is qualified but humble. It is for the listener to perceive the virtue in his humility and then to convince him of his worthiness. To accept his protestations at face value might be to make an enemy for life.

■ Impatience and Patience

Westerners think of the Chinese as long on patience. Time appears to move slowly in mainland China, although Taiwan and Hong Kong move at a more Western pace. Time has never been equal to money, as it tends to be in the West. In China, time is time and money is money. The Chinese take everything slowly, perhaps because the faster you go, the more you have to do. When a scholar comes to work, he takes his time. He may smoke a pipe while enjoying a cup of tea and engaging in a little discussion of past history and present gossip. Then he opens the day's paper and reads it thoroughly as he slowly sips another cup of tea. When he has finished, he calls a meeting to discuss pressing business. After a reasonable amount of discussion, he displays a scholarly prudence by adjourning the meeting with the words, "We will consider this further at a future date." He has put in a good day's work and it is time to go home.

But these same men often lack patience in their daily lives. There are no lines, for instance, at the bus stop; the Chinese wait for the bus to arrive and then muscle their way in. They may even fight with the bus driver, then with each other for a seat on the bus. They display the same aggressive impatience when boarding pre-assigned seating on an airplane where such behavior makes no sense whatsoever.

Often, because of this impatience, the Chinese choose not to follow the rules. The best example of this is their behavior in traffic. Automobiles are the leading cause of accidental death in China. That is an incredible statistic if you consider how few Chinese own cars, but those who have driven in China will not be surprised by this statement.

This is one of the contradictions in Chinese culture. On one hand, the Chinese function as if time were eternal. On the other hand, individuals often act aggressively, selfishly, and panicky in the events of their everyday lives. A client of mine who had been traveling with me in China for over a month characterized China as a society in panic.

■ | **Jealousy**

The Chinese believe that they have a greater capacity for jealousy than Westerners. Many are jealous of the success of others, especially their friends and competitors, and even people they don't know. But strangely, there is an unspoken rule that their jealously be directed toward each other and not toward foreigners.

■ **The Fondness for Strategic Thinking**

As I have mentioned, the Chinese are a strategy-oriented people. Situations that, in Western minds, are handled by intuition or common sense are the subject of formalized strategies in Chinese thought. Even young children learn strategies for dealing with a wide variety of everyday problems.

■ **Worry Now**

The Chinese feel that if you don't worry about the future, trouble will quickly descend upon you. Most Chinese would rather worry about the possibility of trouble in their future than enjoy the present and deal with trouble if and when the time comes. They "worry now" in hopes that they will have no worries in the future. This contrasts sharply with their acceptance of fate once it arrives.

■ **Shortcomings in the Chinese Work Ethic**

> Horse, horse. Tiger, tiger.
>
> —Chinese saying

The meaning of this saying is "I am not sure if it is a horse or a tiger, but it has four legs and a tail." In other words, it will get by.

Lack of quality control is often a problem in the Chinese workplace. It is an especially great obstacle to international trade with China. Chinese workers and managers often do not have the slightest idea of the standards of quality required in the international market and often feel that the foreigners fuss about nothing.

■ **The Chinese Tendency Toward Indecision**

> The sky has unexpected thunderstorms, and humans have unexpected misfortune.
>
> —Chinese proverb

The Chinese believe that the state of all things is unpredictable and temporary. Therefore, they are hesitant to make final decisions. Decisions are often made with the word "temporary" attached to them.

A classic example of Chinese indecision is the choosing of the Chinese national anthem. On September 27, 1949, the Preparatory Committee, after fourteen years of soliciting for a suitable anthem, declared "The March of the Volunteers" a temporary anthem. During the Cultural Revolution, there was a period when "The East Is Red" was substituted as the national anthem. In 1979, long after it had been restored as the temporary anthem, the lyrics to "The March of the Volunteers" were changed by order of the People's Congress. In 1982, the People's Congress restored the original lyrics and finally adopted "The March of the Volunteers" as the official anthem.

The Chinese feel that any decision, agreement, or contract can be modified to respond to changed circumstances. Those engaging in business with the Chinese should not be surprised to have the Chinese request changes at any phase of a project, even long after the contract is signed and work has begun.

■ | **Having or Losing Face**

The fear of losing face is nothing more than the fear of having one's ego deflated. It can be caused by a broad range of things: having an expected promotion fall through, one's child failing an examination, one's daughter marrying a poor man, one's brother working in a lowly position, all the way down to receiving a gift that is inexpensive. The list goes on and on. The logical counterpart to this is that anything that enhances the ego and provides glory is considered "granting face."

There are two reasons that the Chinese prefer doing business with very large companies with worldwide reputations. One has to do with stability: The Chinese feel that large companies are more stable and that the business relationship is more secure. The second and more important reason is face. The Chinese do not want to be seen by their colleagues as ones who do business with second-rate companies. When they do business with the largest and best-known international companies, it causes them to gain face.

■ The Tendency to Be Judgmental

Slap your face until it is swollen.

—Chinese saying

The meaning behind this admonition is that to keep your neighbors from laughing because you are poor and emaciated, you must make yourself look fat and prosperous by slapping your face until it is swollen.

Many Overseas Chinese don't like to mingle with Chinese social groups. They feel that by exposing themselves unnecessarily to other Chinese, they risk exposing themselves to vicious criticism. This may be difficult for Westerners to understand because of their notions about the humble and self-effacing Chinese. In reality, Chinese often are vicious with each other. Envy of those favored by good fortune and contempt for the less fortunate are very powerful forces in the Chinese community.

I have lived in the United States for nearly twenty years. I have never joined or associated myself with any Chinese organization or group. I only associate with other Chinese on an individual basis. I am by no means peculiar in this regard. When in China, I often find that my fellow Chinese try to measure me against their understanding of American wealth. They try to determine how rich or how successful I am by American standards so that they can judge me accordingly.

■ A Fondness for Gossip

The Chang family long, and the Li family short.

—Chinese saying

This saying refers to the fact that the Chinese always have some gossip about every family. Without gossip, the act of social judgment alone would not provide much entertainment. The Chinese are always interested in what their neighbor is doing. Consequently, China is a society almost totally lacking in privacy.

■ Patriotism

The Chinese are extremely patriotic. Through a multitude of rulers and ruling parties, partriotism has been a popular force. No matter where in the world a Chinese may find himself, he holds the motherland dear. When a beloved ruler dies, the Chinese react with the same emotion as if they had lost one of their own family.

■ Kuan-Xie and Ho-Tai

Kuan-Xie and Ho-Tai are important concepts to understand if one is to function effectively in Chinese society. Kuan-Xie literally means "relationships"; Ho-Tai means "backstage." Together they refer to an individual's personal influence and powerful connections. In China, simple merit has never been enough to advance one's cause. A highly placed Chinese official once lamented to me, "In China, it does not matter how many laws and how much righteousness are on your side, without Kuan-Xie, you have nothing. Even if you are outside the law and there is no righteousness to your position, if you have the right Kuan-Xie and Ho-Tai, you can do no wrong."

Anywhere in the world, influential contacts can be a great asset. But one needs to magnify their importance many times to understand the significance of Kuan-Xie in China. For five thousand years, guilty individuals have been pardoned because of Kuan-Xie and the innocent have lost their lives because of lack of it. The ignorant have been promoted and the able have been discharged. It is rare for one to be judged solely by his abilities in China. All Chinese people are affected by Kuan-Xie and Ho-Tai or their lack of these assets.

Without Kuan-Xie, traveling in China is nearly impossible. In China you cannot make reservations for trains or airplanes as you can in the West. Tickets may only be purchased at the point of departure. To make a business trip from Beijing to Hong Kong by way of Nanjing, Xi'an, and Xiamen, the traveler must make private arrangements to have tickets purchased in each of those cities for the next leg of his journey. To travel any distance, a traveler needs to know people throughout the country who can buy tickets for him. If he does not, he will have to buy the tickets on his arrival in each of the cities. It is likely by the time he arrives that he will have to wait several days for an available seat on the train he needs. That is why one always sees peasants at the Beijing train station. Many destinations have no direct route, and Beijing is a common place to change trains. Getting on the proper train can often take several days. The peasants, most of whom don't have *Kuan-Xie*, sleep in front of the station because they are trapped waiting for their train. The system is so bad that even the simplest trip, not to mention important business travel, requires *Kuan-Xie*.

The importance of influential contacts is characteristic of all Asian societies. If you have an introduction or reference from the right person, you will receive a warm welcome. If you knock on the door cold, there is a distance created that is difficult to overcome. Western companies could save immeasurable work by arranging to have their representatives introduced by the right people. This is true elsewhere in the world, but it is not as necessary a prerequisite to doing business as it is in Asia. Use *Kuan-Xie* there and your way will be made smooth.

■ | **Regional Identity**

The Chinese recognize a strong bond to village and province. There is an instant rapport when you discover someone is from the same province or village, and this relationship plays an important role in the game of *Kuan-Xie* and *Ho-Tai*.

In large cities like Los Angeles and New York, Chinese from the same province or city will settle close together. Although some Chinese, as I mentioned, stay apart in order to avoid being the target of gossip, others enjoy the game. They socialize together and support each other, and have fun fighting within their own local association and with other associations and groups.

■ | **Family Ties Are All-Important**

Strong family ties are the pillars of Chinese civilization. It is these ties that have allowed the people to survive China's seemingly unceasing internal wars, and it is these ties that make the Chinese civilization indestructible.

Often among Overseas Chinese, those who share the same surname form associations. The Chinese believe that those who share the same surname are from the same ancient family.

■ | **Hao-she**

Hao-she means "love-sex." Extramarital sex is common among Chinese men, especially among those who are wealthy or in high positions. In Taiwan and Hong Kong, mixing sex with business is often considered good practice. A businessman often entertains clients in a uniquely Chinese institution, the Wine House. A wine house serves food and liquor and provides female companionship during the meal for parties of men. The wine house is not actually a brothel, but arrangements can be made there for the bar girls to visit the men in their hotel rooms later.

While these practices are common, not all Chinese men participate in them. In general, the Chinese man's attitude is that what his wife doesn't know won't hurt her. A Taiwanese business associate of mine told me that these infidelities are good for his marriage. He said that when he is feeling guilty about his infidelities, he treats his wife better. Many wives of Chinese businessmen accept the mix of sex and business as usual procedure. They ignore it as best they can.

Mixing sex with business is practiced only in all-male business circles. If there is a female executive in the group, this form of entertainment is deemed out of the question.

American businessmen should keep in mind that Asian businessmen often will have expectations concerning how they will be entertained when they come to the United States on business. Night clubs featuring semiclad or unclad women will be high on their list of expectations. Most Asian men will be too embarrassed to bring it up if you leave fleshpots out of their itinerary, but they will be very disappointed. One American executive I know keeps a number of expensive and attractive call girls on retainer to entertain his company's Asian clients.

Keep in mind that I am not condoning or recommending these entertainments. I am simply describing common practice.

■ | **Child Abuse**

Beating is tenderness; scorn is love.

—Chinese axiom concerning parental discipline

In early 1988, an article in the *People's Daily* examined the case of a nine-year-old child who had been beaten to death by his mother because his grades in two of his school subjects had fallen below 90 percent. For five thousand years, what we in the West would now consider child abuse has been common practice in China. This newspaper's social commentary was literally the first to suggest that child abuse should not be accepted. The article went on to report that the newspaper accounts at the time of the incident did not spur Chinese parents to examine their own behavior, but were rather used as warnings to their own children. "See what happened to this boy? If your grades are not good, I'll beat you to death, too."

A radio station in China did a survey which found that 90 percent of the children in China are discontented with their parents and 80 percent are beaten regularly. One child cried out, "When they beat me, I feel like I should die so I can hurt them back. I will never forget all the people who have beaten me. I hated them in the past, I hate them now, I will hate them in the future."

Recently, while in Taiwan, I saw a group of children's crayon drawings displayed in celebration of Chinese Father's Day. Most of the drawings depicted scenes of paternal discipline and children in pain. One of the drawings depicted a boy lying on his father's lap. While the father spanked the child, huge tears rained from the boy's eyes and formed a large puddle on the floor.

■ | **Wife-Fearing**

Japanese and Korean men insist on and are very proud of their wives' subservience. Chinese men, on the other hand, adopt the posture that real men are wife-fearing. By humorous self-deprecation concerning their own meekness in the face of their wives, they manage to convey a subtle tenderness as well as the implication that a real man does not feel threatened by a spouse who speaks her mind.

The first emperor of the Sui Dynasty (A.D. 581), Wen Di, united China after nearly two hundred years of civil war and division. Despite this accomplishment, it is popularly told that he was so afraid of his wife when she was angry that he would run to hide in the mountains and not return until someone rode out to assure him that her anger had abated.

Emperor Tai Zong (A.D. 626–649) of the T'ang Dynasty initiated China's Second Golden Era by helping his father overthrow the Sui Dynasty and establish the T'ang Dynasty. History tells us that Fong, prime minister and advisor to Emperor Tai Zong, was terribly afraid of his wife. Finally, when he could stand her tirades no longer, he went to the emperor for help. The emperor told Fong to send his wife to him and he would put her in her place. Fong's wife appeared before the emperor and they exchanged a few words, whereupon the emperor called Fong into his presence and told him that he too was afraid of Fong's wife and in the future Fong should just obey her.

In Chinese history, there have been women who ruled the empire and female warriors who defeated men in combat. Women fought and died beside men in the revolutions of the twentieth century. In the Chinese family the highest position is often held by the women of the house. The common Western notion that Chinese women are subservient and powerless is erroneous. That condition existed only during the Ming Dynasty (A.D. 1368–1644). The classic nineteenth-century Chinese novel, *Dream of the Red Chamber*, vividly describes the inner workings of the Chinese family and the woman's place in it.

■ **Chinese Humor**

Humor has always offered the Chinese people relief from the suffering that has often been their lot throughout China's long history. The ability to find humor in adversity has allowed the Chinese to survive in the face of famine, plague, domestic turmoil, and foreign invasion. The Chinese sense of humor is unique to their culture. What seems funny to the Chinese often does not seem to translate well enough to share with foreigners.

I was once chatting with some Chinese visitors to the United States during a long automobile trip. We laughed about the funny phrases that the Chinese use to describe the people from different parts of China. They refer to those from the city of Tianjin as having "a mouth that can talk a dead man to life." Citizens of Beijing are "as slippery as oil." Beijing is the traditional seat of political power, and that type of personality thrives in such an environment. Baoding is the home of one of the nation's most famous military schools. The natives are "leg-huggers" because they have mastered the art of being promoted by their classmate friends in their advancement through the military ranks.

We then moved the subject to China's foreign invaders, Japan and Russia. One Chinese said, "Japan has a very small house so they like to visit someone else's house, and Russia has a large house but Russians don't like their house so they like to stay at their neighbor's house." We laughed about these descriptions of our neighbors.

When I was last in Beijing, a story was circulating underground that when Brent Scowcroft, President Bush's assistant for National Security Affairs, came to China in the much-criticized rapprochement with the Chinese government after the massacre in Tiananmen Square, Scowcroft brought a gift to Deng Xiaoping, a very special telephone upon which you could talk to anyone living or dead, from any time: past, present, or future. Deng quickly made three calls: The first was to President Bush in Washington to thank him for such a wonderful gift. The second was to his deceased comrade Zhou Enlai in Heaven. The third was to Mao Zedong in Hell. The next month, when Deng received his phone bill, he could find only two toll calls listed, the one to Washington and the one to Heaven. He called the phone company to find out why his call to Mao had not been charged. The voice at the other end of the line replied, "Hell is a local call."

The Chinese have the ability to laugh at themselves. They laugh about their hardship and, through laughter, transcend it.

■ | **THE UGLY CHINESE**

The Ugly Chinese by Bo Yong was published in Taiwan in 1985. It became an instant best-seller there and was surprisingly well received in mainland China as well, although after the student riots of 1987 and the subsequent suppression of liberal thought, it was banned from further publication or distribution. Bo Yong was already familiar with government repression. He had earlier been arrested because of his outspoken criticism of the Taiwanese government. He has said that Chinese like him will experience the same fate at the hands of either the Taiwanese and the mainland Chinese government, depending upon who has dominion over them.

The book is an in-depth analysis of the Chinese through Chinese eyes. As the title indicates, it does not present a very flattering image, but it is honest.

Bo Yong sees the Chinese people as a culture rather than a nationality. They are a group of people who share a common heritage. No matter what country a Chinese may be living in, he will always remain Chinese first and other Chinese will continue to see him as Chinese.

Bo Yong described the Chinese as dirty, messy, and especially noisy. He said that no other people can compete with the loud voices of the Chinese. But Bo Yong believes the Chinese use a loud voice because they are basically insecure. The louder they speak, the more righteous they seem.

Bo Yong believes that the defining characteristic of the Chinese people is that they love to fight among themselves. They do not often agree with one another and they have no concept of cooperation, harmony, or unity. He wrote that one Japanese looks like a pig, while three Japanese look like a dragon; and that one Chinese looks like a dragon, but when three Chinese get together, each one looks like a pig. In other words, one Japanese may not be very formidable by himself, but when three Japanese get together, they create a very impressive force. In contrast, one Chinese might appear formidable, but when three of them get together they squander all their force in squabbling among themselves.

The Chinese have a parable about monks: One monk scoops the water and drinks it; two monks carry the water back to the temple and divide it between them; but when three monks go for water, nobody has water to drink.

Another special characteristic of the Chinese, according to Bo Yong, is never admitting that they are wrong. Never. And because the Chinese will never admit they are at fault, they will do anything to cover up a mistake. The Chinese have a saying, "Close the door and concentrate on faults." While this saying was intended to apply to personal introspection, Bo Yong believes that, in reality, the Chinese concentrate on others' faults, certainly not on their own. Indeed, the Chinese will create more mistakes to prove that an initial mistake was not a mistake. They may create ten mistakes to cover one, and one hundred mistakes to cover the ten.

Bo Yong also talked about how foreigners do not understand that what the Chinese say and what they really think are not the same.

According to Bo Yong, if a Chinese owns a business in a foreign country he will promote his non-Chinese employees before the Chinese. Further, when he needs to cut back, he will lay off the Chinese first to demonstrate that he is a truly fair person. If one of his Chinese workers does something wrong and gets turned in secretly, it will most likely be one of the other Chinese workers who has betrayed him.

Bo Yong speaks of the Chinese people's sensitivity to imagined affronts. If you look at a stranger too long or one time too many, you may "get a knife," as the Chinese call it. I was on a train with a Chinese official. As we passed a cabin, a Chinese man inside looked out at my host as we passed. My host turned in anger and snapped, "What are you looking at?" This is a typical reaction.

In Western society, you often shake hands after an altercation and are friends. In China, it takes three generations to mend relations.

The Chinese will never have equality among themselves, Bo Yong wrote, because in Chinese thinking, if you are not my master, then I am yours. There is always an inferior-superior, master-slave relationship. Bo Yong believes the Chinese have this same struggle within themselves. He observed that, while a Chinese is behaving with absolute arrogance, he is feeling inferior at the same time.

Bo Yong observed that when the Chinese copy anything new from a foreign culture, they imbue it with uniquely Chinese characteristics. For example, the Chinese translate the Western concept of democracy into a philosophy that says, "You do what you wish, I do what I wish."

Despite its brutal frankness, *The Ugly Chinese* is not ultimately a negative or cynical book. Bo Yong's observations could not be so acute if he did not have great feeling for the Chinese people.

■ │ **ZHENG REN**

Zheng means to turn something upside down, to reorder it into something other than what it was; it also means to cause hardship. *Ren* means human being. *Zheng ren* means to cause someone a hardship by creating difficulties where there were none before. It is a concept unique to the Chinese culture. Anywhere there are Chinese, you will find Zheng Ren, especially in government and politics.

There are bureaucrats in China who do nothing on the job but read the newspaper, drink tea, and receive their salaries. They are not bad people; they mind their own business. They might not be productive, but they are not destructive. There is also another kind of bureaucrat who does no useful work either, but who is ceaselessly active and dedicated to Zheng Ren. In accordance with the old Chinese adage that if you chop someone's head off, you will appear a head taller by comparison, he hatches plots to discredit his colleagues in order to be promoted past them.

These people are self-appointed watchdogs for the government. They interfere with others who are engaged in productive enterprises. Without their watching and creating trouble, China would be a much more productive place.

When these self-appointed watchdogs are encouraged and rewarded by a strong leader, it can result in phenomena like the Cultural Revolution. I once asked a Chinese friend, "What was the Cultural Revolution?" He answered simply, yet with the most descriptive and powerful truth: "The Cultural Revolution was when the whole country, everyone, became politicians."

During the Cultural Revolution, the practitioners of Zheng Ren reduced the country to chaos. Everyone became desperate to prove that they were the true daughters and sons of Mao's revolution by being more vicious than anyone else. Chinese politicians displayed their mastery of Zheng Ren by finding ways to bring down whoever was in power. Those who were the most vicious were promoted.

These are the same games the Chinese have been playing on a small scale since the beginning of history, limited in ancient times to the players in the imperial court. Mao found a way to expand the game to the whole of China, to include one billion players.

■ | **Mao Zedong—A Master of Zheng Ren**

Mao spent enormous amounts of time studying the power struggles in China's history. He studied instances of Zheng Ren in the old histories of the imperial court. He mastered each of the written and unwritten rules of Zheng Ren, and by his mastery, he consolidated his political power.

He knew how to use others to eliminate his enemies. People like the Gang of Four acted as his mad dogs, doing the barking and biting. Mao surrounded himself with people who were also masters of Zheng Ren. Through the machinations of Mao's inner circle, brilliant people like Zhou Enlai and Liu Shaoqi, the best China had to offer, were unable to contribute to the reconstruction of China.

An old party member who knew Mao Zedong well described him to me by saying that Mao was good at two things: guerrilla warfare, which got him into power, and Zheng Ren, which kept him in power. As far as knowing how to reconstruct China, however, Mao was inept.

▪ MUO DUN

Muo Dun is an ancient concept that Mao wrote about in 1939 in an essay titled *Muo Dun Lun*. The essay was studied universally and memorized along with other examples of the wisdom of Mao. Any Chinese who was old enough to read during the Cultural Revolution is familiar with Muo Dun. *Muo* means spear. *Dun* means shield. The spear and the shield, *muo dun*, are forces that oppose each other. The spear is for attack, the shield is for defense.

Natural phenomena are composed of opposing forces: action and reaction, positive and negative. In the dynamics of human relations there are also fundamental opposing forces. Mao believed you can control any situation by identifying the opposing forces and applying your effort where it has the greatest leverage to tip the course of events in your direction. Mao later created the Cultural Revolution by magnifying the principle of Muo Dun to apply to the whole country.

When it comes to business negotiations with the Chinese, you will have a greater advantage if you understand that some of your adversaries participated in the Cultural Revolution, an elaborate and prolonged negotiation for power and often survival. This experience has educated them in methods of deception beyond most Westerners' capacity to understand.

14

Taiwan's Prosperity Explosion

Twenty years ago, a young Taiwanese man walked into the office of the purchasing agent for a large chain of American department stores. Never having been in America before, he was nervous and awed by the plush, modern office. At the front desk, he opened the case he carried and carefully arrayed the toys inside on the desktop. Then he spoke the only two words of English he knew. He had learned them especially for that moment.

"Good," he said, smiling. "Cheap."

When the young entrepreneur returned to Taiwan, he carried with him enough purchase orders to launch a business that is now a large and successful manufacturing concern. In that same period, thousands of other Taiwanese were launching their own enterprises, mostly focused on Taiwan's supply of cheap labor and the availability of capital for small, entrepreneurial start-ups.

Alongside the economic miracle of Japan's postwar reconstruction, the sudden flourishing of the Taiwanese economy has gone almost unnoticed. But in some ways, the story of Taiwan's success is as dramatic as that of Japan. In the forty years since Chiang Kai-shek retreated with his army and his followers to this island province, the per capita annual income in Taiwan has increased almost a hundredfold.

■ A BRIEF HISTORY OF TAIWAN AND THE REPUBLIC OF CHINA

Taiwan has figured in Chinese myth for thousands of years, but the first important settlement there by the Chinese did not occur until the seventeenth century, until after the Dutch had occupied it for some years. After an unsuccessful attempt to overthrow the Ch'ing Dynasty, Zheng Cheng Gong retreated with his army and his people from their home in Fujian Province to the island of Taiwan. He drove the Dutch off the island. Zheng had intended to stay in Taiwan only long enough to regroup and then launch another assault on the Ch'ing emperor, but he died suddenly, leaving the leadership of his people to a son who did not have his father's ability. The forces of the Ch'ing emperor pursued the rebels to Taiwan and defeated them. The remnants of Zheng's followers remained on Taiwan and peopled the island.

In the last years of the nineteenth century and the early years of the twentieth, Dr. Sun Yat-sen led a revolution in China that eventually overthrew the corrupt and ineffectual Ch'ing Dynasty and established the Republic of China in 1911. But the establishment of the Republic did not establish peace. Essentially, China has been in a state of civil war for the entire twentieth century. First, the most ambitious and powerful of the warlords had to be subdued. After their suppression, there remained two major forces in China in opposition to one another: the government of the Republic of China, led by Sun Yat-sen's successor, Chiang Kai-shek, and the Communists, led by Mao Zedong. A bloody struggle between the two forces was interrupted by the Japanese invasion during World War II. At the close of the war, the Communists were armed by the Russians with weapons and munitions captured from the Japanese. Chiang's forces were defeated on all fronts and he was forced to retreat with 2 million of his followers to Taiwan to regroup.

The retreat to Taiwan was, and still is, seen by the leaders of the Republic of China (ROC) as a temporary expedient. Like Zheng Cheng Gong, they intended to regroup, return to the mainland, and establish themselves as the legitimate government of China. Since 1949, the Chinese mainland has been controlled by the Chinese Communist Party under the name of the People's Republic of China (PRC).

The ROC and PRC agree on several fundamental points. They agree that there is only one China. They agree that the island of Taiwan is a province of China, not a nation unto itself. They agree that there is only one legitimate government of the Chinese people. They disagree only on the question of who represents the legitimate government.

In the years after 1949, the Taiwanese lived under constant threat of invasion from the mainland. I can remember, as a young child, hearing the soldiers marching by in the streets singing.

> Protect our great Taiwan.
> Protect our great Taiwan,
> This, the garden of our race . . .

As the years passed and the invasion did not come, there was a sense of growing strength in Taiwan. By the time of my adolescence, the lyrics of the song that the soldiers sang had changed to:

> Attack! Attack!
> Back to the Mainland.
> The Mainland is our home . . .

■ Diplomatic Isolation and New Political Strategies

But in 1979, the ROC, a charter member of the United Nations, was expelled from that body and the PRC took its seat as the legitimate representative of the Chinese people. In the West and in the third world, the political power of the ROC began to wane as nations acknowledged the reality of Communist control of the vast majority of the land and the people of China.

At this point, the leaders of the ROC altered their strategy in regard to the PRC. As we have seen, it is a Chinese axiom that a good man does not fight a losing battle; he does not attack his enemy's strength. The ROC leadership, understanding that they could not compete with the PRC for influence with the nations of the world on political grounds, abandoned their policy of refusing to carry on diplomatic relations with any nation that recognized the PRC. They chose to redefine the struggle in economic terms. The People's Republic may be huge and powerful, but it is poor. And burdened with a population of over a billion people and a do-nothing socialist economy, it will continue to be poor.

The government of Taiwan adopted a policy that encouraged economic growth in every way possible. Effort was focused on developing a strong economy, expanding foreign trade, and accumulating foreign exchange reserves. Today Taiwan's total trade volume is $120 billion worth of goods annually and the country has accumulated over $80 billion in foreign currency reserves. The new economic strength is intended to make Taiwan a more attractive ally to the nations of the world. The cash reserves might be intended for the reconstruction of China after the leaders of the ROC again assume power on the mainland. At any rate, they have been reluctant to divert very much of their cash reserves for desperately needed development or maintenance of the Taiwanese infrastructure, undoubtedly because they have always regarded Taiwan as a temporary base.

The fruits of this new policy are beginning to ripen. In the recent past, the nations of Belize and Liberia have withdrawn their recognition of the PRC in favor of the ROC. Guinea-Bissau has recognized the ROC, although it is still trying to maintain relations with the PRC as well. These are poor, third-world nations that need friends who can help their fragile economies survive. More and more of them are seeing the ROC as a better choice than the PRC. Currently, the ROC is finding friends where one might least expect to find them, among the Communist-bloc nations of Eastern Europe. Since 1988 trade with Eastern Europe has tripled.

Quite recently, the Bank of Tokyo announced that it was planning to open an office in Taipei. The Bank of China, the official bank of the PRC, threatened to discontinue its relationship with the Japanese bank if it followed through with its plan. At this writing, the Bank of Tokyo has reaffirmed that it will open the Taipei office. This points to a significant change of attitude on the part of the Japanese government. Although, on the face of it, this is an affair within the private sector, there is really no purely private sector in the economy of Japan. This move by the Bank of Tokyo was carefully calculated, tacitly approved, and privately encouraged by the Japanese government.

■ A GOOD TRADING PARTNER

American firms doing business in Asia have discovered that the Taiwanese like American products. The Taiwanese government has made a good-faith effort to open domestic markets to foreign goods. Between 1985 and 1989, U.S. exports to Taiwan increased from $4.7 billion to $12 billion. Even more dramatic increases could be achieved if American businesses would be more aggressive in their approach to these markets. Even though the Taiwanese opened their markets in response to American threats of retaliation, it is the Japanese who have achieved the greater benefit from the new policies, simply because they went after Taiwanese markets much harder than their American competitors.

■ **THE JAPANESE LEGACY**

Taiwanese readily acknowledge the debt Taiwan owes to the United States for its postwar economic aid. But Taiwan also owes a debt to the Japanese for the benefits they conferred on Taiwan unintentionally during their period of control over the island.

Japan acquired control of Taiwan from the Ch'ing emperor in 1895 by the Treaty of Shimonoseki. The Japanese first intended to establish it as primarily an agricultural colony, but later they began to establish diversified manufacturing enterprises there. Not thinking that Taiwan would ever again be anything but a Japanese colony, the Japanese invested heavily in developing the island's infrastructure. They built roads, railroads, bridges, harbors, schools, and hospitals. They developed the telephone and telegraph systems. To a greater degree than elsewhere in Southeast Asia, these improvements escaped destruction in World War II.

But more than these physical improvements, the Japanese left behind a population profoundly influenced by Japanese attitudes toward discipline, hard work, and cooperation. The Taiwanese seem more Japanese than Chinese in their appetite for progress and their receptivity to technological change. Taiwanese agriculture is much more productive than the agriculture of mainland China; one reason for this is the technique of scientific and intensive farming learned from the Japanese.

■ **THE ENTREPRENEURIAL ECONOMY**

The economy of modern Japan is predicated on a few huge, diversified industrial conglomerates operating in close cooperation with the government. The economy of Taiwan is predicated on tens of thousands of entrepreneurs like the toymaker who came to America armed with two words of English and a sample case full of good, cheap products.

The Taiwanese are among the world's most enthusiastic capitalists. In Taiwan it is still believed that an individual with only a dream and a capacity for hard work can build an empire. Such an individual can easily find financial as well as moral support in Taiwan because the entrepreneurs are not the only ones who believe in the dream; everyone does.

■ Hu Hua

Hu hua means mutual benefit. As an institution, Hu Hua can be likened roughly to a credit union. It is found wherever there are Chinese. It has also been adopted by the Japanese and Koreans, but it is nowhere practiced more intensely than it is in Taiwan. Eight out of ten Taiwanese participate in Hu Hua. It is a way to generate many small pools of capital by gathering groups of people together to contribute stipulated monthly amounts to an informal organization that has as its purpose the funding of worthy projects by its members. Hu Hua might finance the start-up or expansion of a business, the purchase of a home, or an American education for one of its members' children.

The important thing about Hu Hua is that it is not regulated by the government. It is governed by traditional rules and is based on trust between people. In Hu Hua, the human element has not been removed from financial decision-making.

Imagine a conventional banker confronted by our friend the toymaker. The man has a plastic molding machine and an assembly line that consists of people of his village who put the toys together on a piecework basis in their odd hours. He needs enough money to buy a better machine and to finance a trip to the United States, where he believes he can sell a lot of these toys. He knows only two words of English. What do you think will be the conventional banker's decision?

But within his Hu Hua, the toymaker is known to be an honest, intelligent, and energetic person. Besides, some of the membership might actually be assembling these toys in their spare time; they will be much more likely to send him to America, where dreams are known to come true. It is this kind of imaginative, risk-taking capitalism at the grass-roots level that is the secret of Taiwan's miraculous economic growth.

■ **The Individual as Assembly Line**

On a recent visit to Taipei, I decided to tour a national historic landmark. As I was paying for my ticket, I noticed that the girl in the booth had a pile of tiny plastic parts that she was assembling when she was not busy with customers. Later, in the vegetable market, I noticed the same thing among the peddlers. Each one had some kind of piecework to occupy him between customers. In mainland China, these people would have been sipping tea, gossiping, or reading the papers. China has no small, private companies to employ them in this way and offer them the opportunity of extra income. There is certainly no incentive to stay busy at their work.

■ **THE COST OF TAIWAN'S ECONOMIC MIRACLE**

■ **Pollution**

Economic growth has not come to Taiwan without cost. The environment has been ravaged and there is, as yet, no real concern for the environment. Recently, a wealthy Taiwanese industrialist addressed the student body of a Taiwanese university. At the conclusion of his remarks, he responded to students' questions. In keeping with the man's age and position, the students were polite and deferential, but one young man asked if something might be done about the fumes from the man's factory that lay just upwind of the campus. The fumes came from the processing of PVC plastics; they not only had an intolerable odor, but were perhaps toxic to some degree. The industrialist replied that every age had difficulties to which it must adjust. In his youth, he said, it had been mosquitoes. People were forced to create smoke by lighting fires of dried grass at dusk to drive off the mosquitoes. He advised the student to accept the difficulties of his age; the young man's body would adapt to the PVC fumes just as his had to the grass smoke.

The air, the rivers and lakes, and the sea around Taiwan have all suffered serious pollution. In some parts of Taiwan, the earth has sunk because so much groundwater has been pumped out. Fish can be no longer be found in many of the rivers.

■ | **Crime**

Twenty years ago, crime was virtually unknown in Taiwan. Now there is a thriving underground of violent criminals. In Taiwan's sudden growth in prosperity, it was inevitable that some people should be left behind. With the fruits of affluence displayed everywhere around them, some of these have turned to crime to acquire wealth.

When I was young, military service was accepted as the most hazardous career. Soldiers expected at any moment to be thrown into battle with the Communist invaders. The policemen had little to do and less to worry about. Today in Taipei, however, criminals carry automatic weapons and the policeman's life is busy and perilous. The soldiers have little to do or fear.

■ | **Is Everybody Happy?**

Ta Gia Luo, which translates literally as "Everybody Happy," is the name of an illegal lottery that is a national passion in Taiwan. It has obsessed the Taiwanese people with a vision of instant riches. Taiwanese cemeteries are no longer deserted at night. They are full of people praying to the ghosts of their ancestors to give them winning numbers. Often a lottery winner will host a banquet to celebrate his good fortune, but the banquet hall will be deserted except for himself, the waiters, who are serving course after course of expensive delicacies, and the silent, invisible ghosts who are the winner's only guests.

The degree to which the Taiwanese are obsessed with Ta Gia Luo is symptomatic of something that is not quite right in Taiwanese life. Many people neglect the duties of their everyday working life, staking their future on the unlikely prospect of a winning number. I read a newspaper article about a family man who had staked the last of his money on the lottery. He planned to commit suicide if he did not win. He could not bear to go down into the street to see the winning number posted, so he told his wife, "Take your parasol down with you to see the number. If our number has won, leave it open. If we have lost, close the parasol." His wife discovered to her great joy that their number had won. In her excitement, she dropped the parasol. Misinterpreting her action, her husband leaped from the window of their apartment to his death.

Stories about desperate losers who have killed not only themselves but also their families are relatively common. The government has recognized Ta Gia Luo as such a serious problem that it stopped issuing bonds because the winning lottery numbers originally were derived from the bonds' serial numbers and issue dates. But this action has done nothing to discourage participation in the lottery. The numbers are now derived from similar bonds issued by the government of Hong Kong.

■ | **Tax Evasion**

Tax evasion is another game played almost as widely and enthusiastically as Ta Gia Luo. Keeping two sets of books is a very common practice among Taiwanese businesses, as is the giving of cash gifts to the tax collector on holidays or any time the excuse presents itself. I know one Taiwanese doctor with a very lucrative practice. His wife's primary function in the management of their business affairs is to see personally to the distribution of gifts at appropriate times to the various tax collectors who have jurisdiction over their account. She travels frequently throughout the world, but on the occasion of the Chinese New Year, she drops whatever she is doing and returns to Taiwan for the year's most important gift-giving occasion.

This doctor told me that he reported only about 10 percent of his true income. If he had to report his true income, his tax bill would be ten times higher.

Of course, not all tax collectors accept such gifts. Many are diligent in their efforts to collect the taxes owed, and a cat-and-mouse game ensues between the taxpayer and the tax collector. Often a tax collector will sit in a business or professional office for days counting the people who come and go and noting the transactions. He calculates from his survey what the true cash income ought to be, in order to determine the extent to which the business is cheating.

■ THE GARDEN OF EARTHLY DELIGHTS

Despite the many problems besetting Taiwan, there are certain areas in which the quality of life could not be better.

Taiwan's semitropical climate and scientific agricultural methods have produced a supply of food that is superior in every way to that found on the mainland. It is not as subject to seasonal availability as the food produced farther north. On a typical day, there are several dozen varieties of melons available in the markets. Improved cultivation and hybridization techniques have produced fruits and vegetables that are juicier, tastier, and larger than they were a few years ago.

The best Chinese cooking is not in China; it is in Taiwan. For the gourmet, Taiwan is heaven. The people who followed Chiang to Taiwan came from all over China. In Taipei, the epicure can find every style of Chinese cooking within an area of a few square blocks. This is true only in Taiwan; restaurants in the various regions of the Chinese mainland serve only the traditional dishes of that region. On the mainland, if one fancies Sichuan cooking, one must travel to Sichuan Province for it.

■ LEVELS OF GOVERNMENT

To understand the Taiwanese government and the governmental bureaucracy, it is important to understand that the ROC is seen as the national government of all of China, temporarily removed from the seat of government on the mainland by circumstances beyond its control. The government of Taiwan is the regional government of the Province of Taiwan. The cities of Taipei and Kaohsiung also have regional governments that are directly responsible to the national government and are not under the authority of the provincial government. The mayors of these cities have the same authority within them that the governor of Taiwan has elsewhere in the province.

■ THE POLITICS OF REUNIFICATION

Until 1986, the ROC was a one-party state. The KMT party held all power. Even today, although legal, other parties offer only nominal, if somewhat vociferous and colorful, resistance to KMT policies. Loud arguments and fistfights are common between members of the opposing parties on the floor of the Congressional Hall.

The most volatile political issue is the question of Taiwan's future status. Is it to remain in the political limbo of a government in exile? There is a minority that favors accepting the reality of two Chinas and establishing Taiwan as an independent nation, separate from mainland China. Both the KMT and the Communists violently oppose this idea. The PRC has openly threatened military intervention if such a move were attempted. The vast majority of Chinese also oppose Taiwanese independence. If there is one matter on which almost everyone agrees, it is that there is only one China.

The leaders of the ROC have never forgotten their original purpose, which was to return to the mainland and establish the legitimate government of China. Currently, the government of the ROC is still strongly influenced by the generation of men who actually fought the Communists. On the mainland, the policymakers are still the old soldiers of the Long March. Personal animosities stand in the way of reasoned diplomacy in the efforts to reunite China. But within the next decade or two, this generation will be gone. Then, perhaps, a meaningful dialogue on the reunification of China can take place.

When the day of dialogue comes, there are only two real issues that need to be resolved: What form will the government take and who will lead it? The purpose for which the leaders of the ROC are accumulating capital is to bolster their bargaining position. With billions of dollars in cash reserves banked around the world, the leaders of the ROC will be able to argue that they have the only thing that China lacks to become a first-rank world power, the capital to develop her abundant resources and to tap her huge labor pool.

The reunification of China is a problem that does not seem to have any clear solution at present. But China is five thousand years old. Dynasties have risen, flourished, and crumbled to dust many times. Forty years is but the flicker of an eyelash in the span of Chinese history. This problem, too, will resolve itself.

PART  FOUR

THE
SURVIVORS

■

Korean culture is a mix of ancient Chinese influences, Japanese energy, and nationalistic yearning for identity. Squeezed between two powerful nations, Korea has survived out of sheer will and determination. Now Korea is coming into her own as a major player in the global arena.

15

Great Expectations

On September 17, 1988, the Olympic Games opened in Seoul, South Korea. It was a proud moment for the city and the nation. The International Olympic Committee had selected Seoul by a wide margin over its only serious competitor, Nagoya, Japan. The selection was another indicator that the world was beginning to take notice of South Korea as an important world power. South Koreans are hoping that this recognition will have an effect on their national fortunes similar to the effect of the Tokyo Olympics of 1964 on the fortunes of Japan.

■ POSTWAR KOREA

Freed finally from forty years of brutal occupation by the Japanese, at the close of World War II the Koreans had expected to be able to get down to the business of rebuilding their ravaged land. They discovered, however, that by a secret decision among the Western powers at Yalta, Korea had been divided into zones of influence in much the same way that Germany and, indeed, all of Europe had been divided. At the suggestion of the United States, the 38th parallel became the line of demarcation between the Soviet-dominated North and the South, which was to be aligned politically with the Western democratic nations. As in Europe, an iron curtain was drawn across the Korean peninsula.

In 1947, the United Nations mandated general elections in Korea to begin the process of independence and unification. UN officials were not permitted entry into the North, however, and the elections that created the Republic of Korea in 1948 were held only in the South. A Communist regime under the leadership of Kim Il-sung came to power in the North.

In 1950, armed and encouraged by the Soviets, the North Koreans launched an invasion of the South. Within a month, virtually all of Korea was under their control. The United Nations sent a force under the command of General Douglas MacArthur to drive out the invaders. The UN forces were successful until the Chinese Communist forces entered the war and created a stalemate. After three years of bitter fighting, a cease-fire agreement again set the Line of Military Demarcation at the 38th parallel, where it still remains.

For the decade following the Korean War, the Republic of Korea remained in a state of instability and turmoil, under constant threat of invasion from the North. In May 1961, General Chung-hee Park took control of the government in a bloodless military coup. Park's regime stabilized the nation to the degree that Korea could finally begin her economic reconstruction.

■ | **THE FOUR DRAGONS**

Korea, Taiwan, Hong Kong, and Singapore are called "the four dragons." They are the newly awakening economic powers in Asia. Today, Korea is the foremost among them and second only to Japan as an economic power in Asia. Although Korea's ambition is to overtake Japan eventually as the leading industrial power in Asia, the immediate goal is to secure a position among the world's ten most technologically advanced nations before the end of this century.

In the race to industrialize and capture a share of the international market, Korea began ten years after Taiwan and fifteen years after her old enemy, Japan. But in the succeeding three decades, Korea's per capita GNP has soared from $75 to $3,800. Several factors have contributed to this miraculous growth. The first was the government's conscious decision to eliminate poverty without delay. Prosperity was considered the most effective weapon against the spread of communism.

■ | **KOREA, INC.**

Whatever else it might have been, the government of Chung-hee Park was a military dictatorship. It had a greater ability to intervene in the affairs of Korean business and industry than a purely democratic government might have. Because of those beginnings, a close interrelationship between the public and private sectors has evolved in South Korea. Asian business persons often see the whole of Korean industry as a single monolithic entity. They humorously refer to it as Korea, Inc.

Korea, Inc., sets national economic goals and smooths the path for the implementation of those goals. It weds the advantages of a centrally planned economy to the efficiency of profit-motivated free trade. The Japanese have achieved a similar bond between government and industry, but it has been forged from within, from the unique capability of the Japanese people to subordinate the interests of the individual or the individual business to the needs of the nation as a whole. In Korea, the connection has been imposed by the government.

Because of this close relationship between the government and industry it has been relatively easy for Korea to alter economic priorities in response to changing conditions in the world market and within Korea itself.

The original plan for the industrialization of Korea was built around labor-intensive light industries such as textiles. When it became apparent in the early 1970's that Korea was losing its competitive edge in labor-intensive industries, the emphasis turned to heavy and high-tech industries: steel, heavy machinery, shipbuilding, electronics, and petrochemical refining.

Because the Korean economy has developed along the same lines as the Japanese economy, being dominated by a few huge conglomerates, it has not achieved the more even distribution of wealth that has occurred in Taiwan and Hong Kong, whose economies are largely entrepreneurial. There is not a large middle class in Korea. Most Koreans are too poor to buy in sufficient quantities the goods that Korea produces.

Because of the lack of a domestic consumer base and an inadequate supply of domestic capital, the plan for the industrialization of Korea has, from its inception, been export-oriented. It was through trade with the West that Korea sought to accumulate the capital to further her industrialization. For this reason, the Korean economy was profoundly affected by U.S. demands to voluntarily rectify the trade imbalance or face economic sanctions. In 1989, economic growth in Korea slowed from double digits to 6 percent.

■ BUREAUCRATIC CORRUPTION

The Korean economy faces other difficulties as well. Corruption is rampant within the government bureaucracy. To do business in Korea, it is necessary to bribe the right people. That is a simple fact. The red tape involved in doing business can either be simple or absolutely overwhelming. If a Western businessman finds that his operations are bogged down in red tape, it might well be because he is not paying off the right people, or that he is not paying them enough.

An executive for a multinational high-tech company told me, "In other countries, whenever we replace the local distributors with our own people, business immediately soars. But so far, I am hesitant to do that in Korea. Our Korean distributors know whom to pay off and we don't, so we've got to keep them."

■ SOCIAL AND POLITICAL INSTABILITY

In May 1989 a firebomb exploded in the office of the United States Agricultural Trade Commission in Seoul. It was the latest in a long series of terrorist acts and violent demonstrations against the government of the Republic of Korea and against Americans, who are seen by Korean nationalists and leftists as allies of the government in maintaining a divided Korea.

Many Western firms have been reluctant to make sizable, long-term investments in Korea because of its uncertain political future. In the case of Taiwan and mainland China, the division at least came as the result of internal strife among Chinese. The Koreans essentially woke up one morning to discover that the Americans and Russians had decided that there were going to be two Koreas; one for each of them. Koreans bitterly resent the partition of Korea, and the political uncertainty will remain until the Korean people are reunited as one nation. If reunion cannot be managed peacefully, it will certainly come about through force of arms.

The two superpowers have caught themselves in a trap, and caught Korea between them. The Soviets provide military support to the North Koreans and the United States maintains a huge military presence in South Korea. Although recent indications are that both sides are willing to disengage, neither wishes to take the first step for fear that the other will step into the power vacuum created by its withdrawal. But perhaps the impasse is breaking down. On June 4, 1990, South Korean President Roh Tae Woo made a sudden and unannounced flight to San Francisco to meet with Soviet President Mikhail Gorbachev at the end of Gorbachev's visit to the United States. Their discussions were tentative, but the door has been opened for further negotiation.

■ URBANIZATION

To an uncomfortable degree, the population of South Korea has become urbanized. Six out of ten South Koreans live in a city. One out of four of them lives in Seoul. The government is attempting to reverse the migration from the countryside to the cities by relocating centers of economic activity throughout the country, but so far the effects of their plan have not been seen. It is expected that by the end of the century eight out of ten South Koreans will live in a major city.

■ THE KOREAN PEOPLE

The Korean Peninsula was peopled by successive migrations of Siberian, Mongolian, and Manchurian peoples who interbred with the aboriginal inhabitants. During the eleventh century B.C., Chinese Han people began to migrate into the peninsula as well. The Korean people coalesced out of this diverse mixture of cultures.

At the time of the first Han migrations, the inhabitants of the Korean peninsula practiced shamanism, a belief that not only people, but animals, trees, inanimate objects, and natural forces such as wind and rain possess spirits. A form of this shamanism still exists in Korea today. Shamanism was not derived from Chinese influences, but many other Korean cultural institutions developed from Chinese antecedents. As well as absorbing Chinese cultural influences, Korea also served to transmit these influences to Japan. Ancient migrations from Korea helped to people the Japanese islands. Later, trade routes from the Middle Kingdom to Japan through Korea developed quite naturally in order to shorten the dangerous ocean journey.

■ | ## THE INFLUENCE OF CHINA

Culturally as well as geographically, Korea is located between China and Japan. Because of her proximity to Korea, her size, and the antiquity of her civilization, China has been the primary influence in the development of Korean culture. The Japanese influence was superimposed on Korean culture at a relatively late date. While Japanese influence is readily apparent and even striking in some aspects of Korean culture, it is not as deeply imbedded as the Chinese. In many ways the Koreans are more Chinese than the Chinese. They have preserved traditional Chinese customs and habits of thought that have been abandoned by the Chinese themselves.

Recently, while watching a Korean film, I was especially struck by the breadth and depth of the cultural similarities between Korea and China. The story was set in Korea in a prior century. The architecture, clothing, calligraphy, art, all were indistinguishable from those of China in the same period. I might have been watching a Chinese film but for the difference in language and the uniquely Korean clothing and hairstyles of the women.

Koreans have adapted every aspect of Chinese culture, including the adoption of Chinese-like names. Chinese was the official written language in Korea until a century ago. As in Japan, in Korea even today one cannot be considered an accomplished or cultivated person without having mastered Chinese calligraphy.

The traditional Korean class system was very similar to China's. It was comprised of four classes. The top-level scholar class included all government officials, bureaucrats, and those holding military rank. The professional class was next in importance. The farmers and artisans were members of the third class. The lowest class was composed of those who worked at menial or unclean occupations: servants, butchers, carnival entertainers, for example. The single avenue for social mobility that existed in the Chinese class system did not exist in the Korean system. The examination for entry into important jobs was open only to those born into the scholar class. A lower-class Korean could not elevate himself by scholarly achievement.

The Korean class system virtually disappeared under the Japanese occupation in the early 1990's. The Japanese treated all Koreans brutally, without regard to social position. An anachronism in the latter half of the twentieth century, the class system did not reestablish itself after the liberation at the end of World War II.

■ | ## THE INFLUENCE OF CONFUCIANISM

Although Buddhism was the official religion for centuries in many of the states of ancient Korea and is still widely practiced there, Confucianism, both as a religion and a philosophy of social order, played a more fundamental role in the development of Korean values. The family is the fundamental unit of Korean society, and, more so even than in China, family relationships are defined in terms of Confucian principles.

Korean children are raised according to a severe code. Obedience must be complete and unquestioning. Severe and frequent beatings are the norm. Children are the absolute property of the parents and have no intrinsic rights. It is from this seed of acquiescence and obedience that the other Confucian principles are born. Children who are severely disciplined by their parents grow up to see their parents everywhere. They are submissive to their leaders, their husbands, and their fate. There is nothing intrinsically Korean or even Asian about humility, respect for authority, filial duty, or fatalism. Westerners raised according to the same principles would exhibit these same qualities.

In keeping with Confucian values, learned individuals are highly regarded in Korean society. The quality of the educational system is a high priority among Koreans. The family constantly impresses upon the children the importance of education.

■ | **THE INFLUENCE OF JAPAN IN KOREA**

Since the sixteenth century, the Japanese have viewed Korea as a stepping-stone to the invasion and conquest of China. After Toyotomi Hideyoshi unified Japan under his rule, he immediately directed his energy toward the conquest of the Ming empire. In the spring of 1592, Hideyoshi invaded Korea as the first phase of his plan. The Japanese decimated Korea. War brought famine; famine brought disease. The Ming emperor responded to the entreaties of the Koreans, who were tributary to him and entitled to his protection. He poured relief troops into battle alongside the Koreans. The conflict dragged on until the death of Hideyoshi in 1598.

At the beginning of the present century, Japan annexed Korea and ruled the country ruthlessly for nearly half a century. Japan's domination ended with her defeat in World War II. As a consequence of their past victimization, most Koreans even today consider the Japanese their mortal enemies.

I was present at a business meeting between an American businessman and a Korean delegation. The American had done business in Asia before, but only with the Japanese. Anxious to demonstrate that he was a fair-minded man and an admirer of Asian culture, the American took every opportunity to bring in anecdotes about his experiences in Japan and to praise the Japanese. Finally, the leader of the Korean delegation could stand it no longer. He exploded, "We despise the Japanese! Don't mention them again!"

Unlike the Taiwanese, who were not so brutally treated under their Japanese occupation, most Koreans refuse to acknowledge any benefits derived from their experience with the Japanese. Rather, they tend to dwell on Japan's vicious exploitation of Korea. More than 5 million Korean men were conscripted into forced labor camps. An untold number of Korean young women, wives and mothers, were taken by the Japanese army against their will to official military brothels and were forced to satisfy the sexual desires of endless lines of Japanese soldiers day in and day out. A witness to these events once described to me how, during periods of bad weather, the Japanese soldiers would write their names on a rock and use it to mark their place in line so that they could seek shelter during the long wait.

Nevertheless, Japanese influences during the occupation did contribute to the later industrialization of Korea. Like the Taiwanese, the Korean people benefited from exposure to the powerful

Japanese work ethic, even though it was brutally forced upon them. Pride in workmanship also was learned from the Japanese. Although the quality of Korean manufactured goods falls short of Japanese standards, it far surpasses the slipshod work of the mainland Chinese. After living under the rule of the perfectionist Japanese, the Koreans, like the Taiwanese, developed similar standards of product acceptability.

On a national scale, Korea has fostered the development of large, strong conglomerates by following Japanese models. The economic policies of the Korean government, like those of the Japanese, have been designed for the benefit of large, powerful companies.

Some Western scholars even argue that Korea's educational and legal system are products of Japanese influence. However, Korea's arduous educational examination system and the institutionalized indifference to human rights in the legal system are certainly derived from ancient Chinese models.

Although few of the older generation of Koreans would admit to the Japanese influence that shaped them as individuals, the influence is quite evident. It would be remarkable if it were not. The formal education of that generation was conducted entirely in Japanese. The history and literature taught were not Korean; they were Japanese. After graduation from high school, Korean students were encouraged to visit Japan. In this way, the Japanese conqueror hoped to forge a bond between the subject people and the motherland.

The area in which the Koreans most resemble the Japanese is in the conduct of modern business and trade. Business in Korea, especially as it regards dealing with the international community, is a phenomenon entirely of the twentieth century. Coincidentally, that is the period in which Korea was under Japanese domination. The Koreans and the Japanese learned Western business methods at the same time and made similar adaptations.

Members of the last generation raised under Japanese rule, many of whom hold important positions in business and politics today, tend to behave like Japanese in many situations. This is especially notable in their taciturn negotiating style, which contrasts sharply with the more open, voluble style of the younger generation of Koreans. Unconsciously, older Koreans observe the etiquette and values of Japanese society, the standards to which they were educated.

Another more startling manifestation of Japanese influence is the tendency of this older generation to start singing Japanese military songs after the liquor has been flowing and spirits are beginning to soar. Whatever conscious feelings they may have about the Japanese today, these were the songs of their youth.

It is probably due to the Japanese influence that the role of women in the family and in society has not changed in Korea in the last decades as it has elsewhere in Asia. Korea and Japan remain male-dominated societies. Left to its own devices, Korea might have developed differently. As late as 1895, Korea was ruled by a woman, the Empress Min. She was a strong leader who firmly resisted Japanese imperial ambitions in the peninsula. Eventually she was assassinated by the Japanese to clear the way for Japan's colonization of Korea.

■ COMMON CHARACTERISTICS OF KOREANS

The Korean character has much in common with the Chinese. Koreans are much more like the open and expressive Northern Chinese than the reserved and taciturn Japanese. Like Chinese people, they take delight in the openness of Americans. When a Korean likes another person, he rarely holds back the enthusiastic expression of his feelings. Conversely, when a Korean feels animosity toward another, it is much easier to detect such feelings than among Japanese people.

When confronted with a choice between the interest of the group or their own interest, most Koreans, like most Chinese, will decide in their own favor. Japanese people, on the other hand, will commonly sacrifice themselves for the good of the group. And like the Chinese, Koreans are less scrupulous than the Japanese in honoring their word. They feel that changed conditions can alter their obligation to fulfill commitments they have made. In the West, these qualities are intertwined with ethical considerations. It is important to keep in mind that for Koreans these are simply cultural differences; ethics play no part in them.

It takes only a short drive through rush-hour traffic in Seoul to realize that Korean and Chinese drivers learned in the same school. They create their own traffic laws on the fly. At first, the squealing of brakes and blaring of horns seem totally chaotic, but traffic actually flows pretty well. How else could six lanes of traffic negotiate a four-lane street except through the creative and impassioned interaction of all the participants? In Korea, as in China and Taiwan, traffic laws are learned only for the driving test. Immediately upon obtaining a license, they must be unlearned if one is to get anywhere.

Koreans are very much like both the Japanese and Chinese in looking for a little something extra in every purchase they make. But they realize that mooching is not a standard practice among Westerners, so they generally practice it only among Asians. Not long ago, I was shopping in a Korean-owned clothing store in Los Angeles. After the owner rang up my purchases, something over two hundred dollars, he carefully pointed out that he had not charged me for the twelve-dollar hairpin. As a Korean, he thought all Asian people expected him to throw in something free. I am so used to shopping in Western stores by now that this gesture had not even crossed my mind.

Koreans are extremely competitive, especially with other Asians, but such competition is not commonly exposed to Western eyes. Jealousy, gossip, and criticism are used to undermine the efforts of others, sometimes even among close friends. Like the Japanese and Chinese, Koreans also think in terms of who is superior and who is inferior to whom. The forms of social interaction between two people are defined by their relative status. Like all Asians, Koreans are also very concerned with saving and losing face.

Koreans worry. It is a way of life with them. Koreans do not believe that matters will work out all right on their own; they must be worried over. This attitude is fundamental to their need to strategize and calculate in all life situations rather than take them as they come.

A Korean proverb says, "If you wish to know a man's true nature, watch him play Go, gamble, or drink." Koreans, like all Asians, are students of human nature. In their observation of the most mundane details of daily life, they draw inferences about the nature of the people they observe. They believe that when a man plays Go, a traditional Japanese game of battle strategy, he reveals the capacity and depth of his mind. A drunken man reveals his true nature. The way a man gambles also reveals much about his character.

■ | **THE IRISHMEN OF ASIA**

Without question, the trait that sets Koreans apart from the Chinese, Japanese, and other Asians is their emotionalism. They are sometimes called the Irishmen of Asia. They are quick to anger and just as quick to reconciliation. They are the only Asians among whom you will commonly see public tears or public displays of affection.

They are hot-blooded, jealous, stubborn, and prone to laughter, sometimes displaying all of these traits within the span of a few minutes.

Koreans are fun-loving. They enjoy a physical kind of humor. Korean comedy has much in common with a Marx Brothers movie. They are also sociable. Koreans are famous for their drinking and their ability to hold their liquor. A Korean businessman described to me how he and his associates spend their evenings. "After dinner we will go from one bar to another. We don't stop. But we don't have any problem with alcoholism like they have in the United States." I asked him, "Do they do this occasionally or every day?" He answered, "We do this every day . . . but, we have no alcoholism."

Korean men are very emotional even when making business decisions. If you strike the right emotional chord, the Korean decision-maker will often respond favorably simply on impulse. On the other hand, a Korean, unlike a Japanese, will not be polite when you get on his wrong side. Korean tempers can get awfully hot. An exasperated Italian leather wholesaler told me once, "I don't know what to do with my Korean distributor. I don't know if I should kill him or kill myself."

Historically, Korea has always been threatened on one hand by absorption into the massive Middle Kingdom and on the other by Japanese militarism. Consequently, Koreans fiercely maintain a sense of national identity. Korea has been almost constantly at war defending itself against the depredations of its neighbors. In spite of this—or perhaps because of this—the Koreans are, by nature, peace-loving. When forced to fight, Koreans are brave and formidable warriors. Korean soldiers fighting in Vietnam as American allies earned a reputation as fierce fighters.

Korean stubbornness has been the cause of much consternation on the part of those who must do business with them, but it has proven to be a valuable trait. Even after nearly fifty years of Japanese rule, the Japanese were never able to snuff out the smoldering, stubborn resentment of the Koreans. Yet, after the same period of domination in Taiwan, the Japanese had made significant progress in altering the attitudes of the Taiwanese. When I was young in Taiwan, I often heard native Taiwanese remark how much better life was under the Japanese than under the Nationalist Chinese government. A Korean who publicly ventured such a sentiment even today would probably require immediate medical attention.

PART  FIVE

ENDGAME

16

Winning
Moves

■ | **REN QING**

The values of Japanese, Korean, and Chinese culture were profoundly influenced by the Confucian concept of Ren Qing. This concept is represented by the same Chinese characters in the languages of all three nations and translates literally as "human feelings." It dictates that the human element should never be removed from human affairs, that understanding and a sympathetic give-and-take should govern the relationships of men.

Although the ideal of Ren Qing is an informal and unselfish give-and-take among people, in reality, accounts are kept very strictly. Favors and obligations are weighed carefully and the balances owed between people are known as well as if they were put down in a ledger. As a matter of fact, a couple of years ago I came across a case in which they actually had been put down in a ledger. In a small Japanese village, the villagers were gathering together as they had from time immemorial in a communal effort to replace the thatch roof of one family's dwelling. Before the work began, one young man produced a book that had been kept by his family for generations. It was called *The Debts of Ren Qing*. In the late nineteenth century, his great-grandfather had recorded a debt owed to the family whose roof was now being replaced. That family had provided two days labor and a pot of sake to his family. The young man announced that he would provide two days of labor in the replacement of the roof, but would leave the pot of sake still owing.

The debts of Ren Qing are not often written down, or discharged so rigidly and exactly as in that case, but they are remembered in minute detail and enforced by deeply rooted feelings of guilt and shame in those who fail in the fulfillment of the obligations of Ren Qing. The Westerner should understand that he is surrendering very little to chance by making agreements according to the Asian custom of leaving many of the details open to interpretation. In fact, if he is skillful, he can incur obligations in his Asian counterparts that will lead them to grant informally more generous terms than they would be willing to grant in a detailed and inflexible Western-style contract.

Ren Qing often is used as the opportunity for the subtle manipulation of an adversary in a business negotiation. The art is to create an obligation through a gesture that costs you little and then to subtly call the debt due at a time when your adversary can only repay it with a more valuable concession. This procedure requires a delicate touch but it can be accomplished by a perceptive Westerner.

■ | **SPECIFIC MOVES**

We have discussed the similarities and differences between Asians and Westerners in fairly broad terms. The question remains, however, of what this all means for an individual who needs to apply this knowledge to his business, political, or personal interactions with Asians, either in Asia or the West. There are some specific things a Westerner needs to know in order to make his or her affairs in Asia go more smoothly. They cannot be deduced from principles. They are facts that must be learned, either by making a blunder and being corrected after the damage is done, or by being forewarned. These facts range from simple items of table etiquette to the subtle art of giving gifts graciously and effectively. There is no logical order in which to discuss them. What follows comes out of my experience in facilitating communication between Western and Asian businesspeople and politicians, and the areas of misunderstanding or difficulty that I have frequently observed.

■ | HUMANIZING BUSINESS

Because he more readily accepts emotion as a part of business, the Asian businessman is often easier to manipulate than the Westerner. If you come to an Asian businessman with a story of some personal problem that will affect your ability to fulfill your obligations under your contract, he is far more likely to give it a sympathetic hearing than his Western counterpart.

Among Asians, a written contract does not have the sanctity that it has in Western business, especially between parties who profess the bond of Ren Qing. Often it is no more than a memorandum concerning the duties and responsibilities of each party. If a problem arises, the parties generally sit down and hash it out face-to-face rather than pore over the contract text for a solution. Among themselves, Asians prefer a vague agreement because it leaves plenty of room for later adjustment if things aren't working out right. Asians understand that this deliberate vagueness is something that is neither understood nor accepted in Western business and in doing business with the West they have adapted to the need for specific and detailed agreements. Still, they see the Western compulsion to dot all the i's and cross all the t's as a cold, heartless, and ultimately futile attempt to eliminate the human element from business transactions. A wise Westerner will do all he can to dispel the perception that his head is entirely divorced from his heart when it comes to business matters.

Because the business of lawyers is to write ironclad contracts and to fret about details, many Asians feel that they cause more problems than they solve. Dealing with lawyers is looked on as an unavoidable evil in doing business with Westerners. If your business is so complex that you feel you need an attorney present during negotiations, you must make it clear to your Asian colleagues that you are in charge, not your attorney, that they are dealing with you as one human being to another. Your attorney must be presented as someone whose purpose is only to make sure that the spirit of the agreement you forge is properly translated into legalese. They must be made to feel that if problems arise about your agreement, you will work them out as one human being to another rather than delegate their resolution to an attorney.

Affairs that in the West would require the services of an attorney are handled routinely by Asians through human interaction. Malpractice and wrongful death suits are a serious problem for the medical profession in the West. In Taiwan, however, with all its modernity, these things are handled in the age-old manner. The family of the deceased carries the body into the doctor's waiting room and begins to mourn loudly. This, of course, is bad for business, and the doctor must do something quickly. The family can only carry the body in so many times, so they also are motivated to settle the affair. The litigation is limited to a few days. If the doctor feels that he was at fault to any degree, he will make a generous settlement. If he feels no liability, he will probably settle by paying the funeral expenses for the family just to get the affair behind him.

■ | **BECOME YOUR OPPONENT**

The idea of becoming your opponent is very familiar to the Asian mind but almost unknown in the West. There is a story about a Zen master who, to teach his pupil the discipline of meditation, set him to meditate on the form of a bull. The pupil tried to make his mind the mind of a bull, but was disappointed with his lack of success. A week after setting him to the task, the master returned. He approached the pupil's house and shouted for him to come out and greet his master. The pupil replied from inside the house, "I can't come out. My horns are too wide for the door."

The samurai warrior practiced entering the mind of his opponent in order to anticipate the other's movements. When doing business with Asians, you too should practice this transference or you will be at a distinct disadvantage to your Asian business associate. Before going into any important negotiation, consider carefully what your objectives are. Delineate them for yourself clearly and specifically. Then visualize all the people who will take part in the meeting. Put yourself in each one's place and consider what his goals would be, what objections he might raise to your agenda. Prepare yourself to disarm his opposition. Do not enter into the negotiation until you are absolutely sure of the direction you want the meeting to take. Thus prepared, the meeting will flow effortlessly in the way you want without any conscious direction from you.

You will also find that this method breeds a sympathetic understanding of your opponents and their objectives. Often you will be able to discover solutions that give everybody what they want, solutions that were invisible to you while you were focused narrowly on yourself and your own agenda.

The usefulness of becoming your opponent extends far beyond the world of commerce. It is an incredibly powerful force that can be applied to every aspect of your life.

■ UNSPOKEN MESSAGES

Western languages are linear and explicit. They leave very little to contextual interpretation. Asian languages depend much more on context. To understand his Asian associates properly, a Westerner must be very sensitive to the context in which their words or actions are framed. Even in translation, a great many important things are never stated explicitly; they are assumed to be understood from the context.

As well as the difference in language and the patterns of thought that language promotes, one must take into account the Asian custom of indirect speech. Asians avoid saying unpleasant or negative things directly. They seldom say no. You will instead hear phrases like these: *I'll see what I can do . . . I'll do my best . . . I'll think about it . . . It may be difficult . . . I'll try . . .*

While you should understand that these phrases probably mean no, their indirect nature leaves the door open for you to follow up later. This is a situation where your image as a naive Westerner can be used to your advantage. Since you are not expected always to understand Asian circumlocution, it is perfectly all right for you to call Mr. Chin the following week about that matter he promised to look into.

For the same reasons that Asians do not tell you no directly, you should not tell them no either. Even coming from someone who is not expected to know better, the word sounds abrupt and offensive to Asian ears.

Asians do not directly ask for things when they feel their correspondent should anticipate their needs or should understand the subtlest of hints. The fact that Westerners are not trained to listen for these subtle hints is often the occasion for misunderstanding and hard feelings.

■ HUMBLE MANNERS, SMILING FACES

Don't be disarmed by a warm smile and a friendly gesture. Reciprocate with your own warm smile and friendly gesture, but do not read into the situation more goodwill than is actually there. Asian people are generally polite, especially in business relationships. Some of your Asian business associates will have genuine warm feelings for you, others will be waiting for an unguarded moment to snatch the gold fillings out of your teeth. All of them will smile warmly at you. Nor should you accept an Asian's humility at face value. Remember that in Asia, humility is a weapon as well as a virtue.

■ KNOW YOUR COMPANY AND YOUR PRODUCT

This is a basic requirement for any business representative anywhere, but you must be able to apply the knowledge you already have to Asia. The people you will deal with simply don't care about the same things that a client in Los Angeles cares about. They want to know how your company and product fit the unique needs of their nation.

You must also be creative and flexible in adapting your terms and methods to the unique situations you will find in Asia. For example, the Chinese are poor in capital. Decisions are made by bureaucrats who are more concerned about the short-term cash cost of an item than the long-term cost. If you cannot sell an item to them for $100,000 cash, you might be able to sell it for $150,000 if you can finance it with little or nothing down at no interest on a long-term loan.

■ PLANNING, PLANNING, PLANNING

Again, this is basic knowledge that must be adjusted for the unique conditions you will encounter in Asia. Before you leave the home office you should know whom you are going to meet, when and where you will meet them, and what your objectives will be in those meetings. Work out the logistics of transportation and accommodation in great detail and then incorporate a healthy contingency factor. Travel in some parts of Asia is uncertain. Simply because the schedule says a train leaves Beijing at 3:30 P.M. for Nanjing, don't assume that it will.

If you are planning a business trip to China or Korea, keep in mind that these nations celebrate the Lunar New Year, which falls in late January or February. Almost no business takes place for a period of about two weeks. If you plan your trip for this time, you will spend several days alone in your hotel.

■ WOMEN IN BUSINESS AND THE PROFESSIONS

Japanese and Korean businessmen do not respond well to Japanese or Korean women in the world of business, but they have little difficulty accepting and working with Western women. Perhaps they do not view it as so direct a threat to their male-dominated societies. But in the professional world things are changing rapidly for Asian women. Ability alone can carry a woman to the top of her profession. Female politicians are beginning to be elected in Japan.

■ DEVELOP LONG-TERM OBJECTIVES

Go into an Asian market with long-term objectives. Do not count on quick profits. It can take a considerable amount of time to develop the necessary relationships. Many persons and organizations will not take you seriously until you have demonstrated your intention to stick around. The image you must project is one of reliability and continuity of purpose.

By the same token, you should avoid unnecessary rotation of your staff. It is very unsettling for Asian businessmen to have to deal with a new representative every few months. Business in Asia is built to a large degree on personal relationships. Once these relationships have been cultivated, they are far too valuable to throw away.

Establish yourself in the market at a competitive price. If your product or service is worth more, you must give your customers a chance to discover that for themselves. After you are firmly established you can slowly adjust the profit margin to the proper level. But if that is your plan, your Asian distributors and associates should be aware of it very early on so that they will not feel deceived. Also, if you employ distributors or middlemen, make sure that they are not taking advantage of your initial low profit margin to increase their own markup.

Once established, be careful not to jeopardize your position by sloppy business practices. Don't ship defective products. One unit that malfunctions attracts more attention than a thousand that work perfectly. Don't ship late. Be aware of all the import and export regulations and have them all covered. Be careful not to cause your Asian distributors and customers unnecessary expense through blunders on your part. If they have to warehouse a shipment for a week while the paperwork is put in order, the expense may not be great but the erosion of their confidence in your organization will be enormous.

■ KEEP YOUR WORD, KEEP YOUR SILENCE

Make only realistic commitments and be scrupulous in honoring them. Your spoken word must be as reliable as a written contract. Honor any confidences that are given to you. Especially, do not discuss the business relationship between you and any of your Asian associates. As an outsider to the culture, you may not always be aware of what might be sensitive information. It is always best to say nothing at all.

Everything that you say should be truthful, but it is not necessary to tell everything you know, either about your plans or the plans of others. Your adversaries at the negotiating table will be playing one card at a time. You should do the same. As well as it being imprudent to lay all your cards on the table, it will cause discomfort to your Asian associates, who may feel that you are attempting to obligate them to do the same.

■ THE ISSUE OF LOYALTY

In dealing with the Japanese especially, the issue of loyalty is very important. Once a business relationship is established, unless an associate does something extremely unethical, the Japanese will stand by it. They are not always shopping for a better price once they have found the firm with which they want to do business. The

Japanese often take a long time to establish such relationships. When dealing with other Asians, they place a great deal of importance on the family background and social status of prospective associates. A Taiwanese businessman told me that a Japanese firm went so far as to investigate his father and brothers. The Japanese understand that Americans come from a classless society and, when dealing with them, do not place the same kind of emphasis on social background.

In Taiwan and Korea, you will find traces of this concept of loyalty in business relationships remaining from the period of Japanese influence. In China, loyalty in business is regarded as laudable, but there is no tradition that it should come ahead of profit. The Chinese constantly shop for the best price. If you have an established relationship with them, they may come to you with the best price they have found and give you an opportunity to match it, but it is rare that they would stay with you if you could not.

■ RESPECT THE LOCAL CULTURE

The day of the Ugly American is long past, but his arrogance still lingers in Asian memories. Don't stir it up. Make an effort to understand the local culture. Accept the local methods of doing business. Don't make unfavorable comparisons of local customs to American customs. It doesn't matter how it is done in America, because you are not in America.

Learn a few words of the native language. You don't need to master the language. As a matter of fact, many Asians feel uncomfortable speaking their native tongue with a Westerner. Many simply don't trust a Westerner who is fluent. However, it is essential to learn a few simple words of greeting. It demonstrates that you respect the country and the culture enough to make an effort.

Don't attempt to demonstrate your knowledge of Asia by discussing other Asian cultures in relation to the local culture. Historical and anthropological truths are one thing; local perceptions are quite another. The Japanese don't want to hear about the Chinese roots of their cultural institutions; the Koreans don't want to hear about Japanese virtue.

Don't try to be Asian. You would do well to study and adopt to some extent the Asian habit of strategic thinking, but do not attempt to be too Asian in your behavior. Be a good Western businessperson rather than a bad imitation of an Asian businessperson. A well-mannered individual who manifests a respect for the culture, even though he may make occasional blunders, is better received than the Asia "expert" whose self-assurance borders on arrogance.

■ DON'T FORCE THE ISSUE

Be enthusiastic in your dealings in Asia, but avoid appearing aggressive. Don't attempt to close a sale by forcing a decision, and never ask your prospective client if you have a sale. In general, avoid all showdowns or ultimatums. It is difficult for an Asian businessman to respond favorably to your proposition if it is presented as an ultimatum. To acquiesce to your demands would cause him to lose face. Move things along as well as you can by polite inquiries as to whether your prospective client needs any additional information in order to make his final decision. If you are the seller, you are expected to be deferential to the buyer. To act any other way is considered rude.

■ THE HOME-COURT ADVANTAGE

Do not always concede the home-court advantage to your Asian associates. Whenever possible, have them come to you for negotiations. Although for business purposes your Asian associate knows he would be in a stronger position in his own country, many Asians love to travel in the West. Propose your offices as the site of the negotiations. If that is not acceptable, propose a neutral site, a resort perhaps, or a place of great scenic beauty.

■ SEIZE EVERY LITTLE ADVANTAGE

The Westerner who is proficient with chopsticks has the advantage over one who must find a fork and spoon for every meal. The one who can greet his Asian associates with a few words in their native tongue is better regarded than the man who can only say hello. The man with the expensive suit and the Rolex watch will create a better impression than the man who wears an off-the-rack suit and a Timex. Asians are judgmental. They will score you on every aspect of your personal and professional demeanor. You must grab points whenever and wherever you can.

■ SPEAKING AND BEING SILENT

Unless you have been paid to speak at a banquet or gathering, it is always better to say little and observe a lot. The idea that a wise man speaks little has been ingrained in the Asian consciousness. This is especially true in Japan. The Chinese and Koreans, however, like to be open and talkative in many social and business situations. In such situations, a silent person may seem aloof and can make them feel uneasy and sometimes unfriendly.

When you speak, paint simple, understandable mental pictures with simple words. Don't attempt to show off your erudition. Remember that your listeners may be fluent in everyday conversational English, but if you use uncommon expressions or obscure words, you may lose them. An Asian who takes pride in his command of English is not going to stop you to ask the meaning of a word, especially in front of his colleagues.

Be good-humored but stay away from humor as a conversational gambit. A story that seems funny to a Westerner often seems pointless to an Asian. Sometimes it turns out to be offensive. Especially do not joke with or tease any of your Asian associates. Good-humored ribbing is not a part of Asian culture. It is seen as an affront to one's dignity. Asians do enjoy their own humor, but they do not understand Western humor any better than Westerners understand theirs.

Sincere expressions of praise or admiration are always welcome, but avoid flattery. Throughout Asia, in the feudal relationships of prior centuries and the machinations of the ancient imperial courts, a man advanced himself by currying personal favor. Consequently, Asians came to understand flattery very well. Even today they are not easily taken in by insincere or overdone praise.

Don't be afraid to apologize, even if you have done nothing wrong. Asians apologize because an unfortunate incident has occurred, not necessarily because they feel that they are to blame for it. It is considered very virtuous to be the first to apologize in order to smooth over some unpleasantness. Do not be afraid that some unwarranted blame may fall on you. An apology is not an admission of guilt.

■ USE LOCAL INTERMEDIARIES

In any locality, there are many important items of information that only a local insider could be expected to know. In any culture, there are customs of which a foreigner could have no knowledge. You should seek a local advisor and intermediary to keep you from making inadvertent blunders. A local intermediary also functions well as a medium of unofficial communication between the parties to a negotiation. Often when things are put on the negotiating table, there are public positions that must be maintained. Retreating publicly from a previously stated position can involve loss of face. Lines of unofficial communication can help resolve difficulties without loss of face to either party.

■ THE IMPORTANCE OF STATUS

Asians are obsessed with status symbols: designer clothes, German luxury cars, membership in exclusive clubs, visibly expensive jewelry. An Asian's business card often carries numerous titles and prestigious associations in addition to his name, company, and his position there. I have the card of the president of a large Asian food-processing firm. He has five titles listed on the front of his card and thirty-two more on the back. These are not the tasteless extravagances of a nouveau riche. It is customary and accepted in Asia to display and even exaggerate your wealth and importance.

Similar displays are common among Westerners, but they are often considered in questionable taste, at least when it is someone else attempting to display his affluence or importance. If it is not your style to brag, by all means don't. On the other hand, don't minimize the status you have. If your uncle is a senator, you should find some way to bring that into the conversation. If you happen to have a picture of you and your attractive spouse leaning against the Bentley in the courtyard of your summer estate in Maine, you ought to find some way to get it out of your wallet. It will really help.

Most Asians are clothes-conscious. Although many wear company uniforms during working hours, they will accessorize them with Gucci belts and Vuitton wallets. On their days off, they will dress up to a degree that is surprising to many Americans. The clothes you wear will be scrutinized carefully. They need not be on the cutting edge of fashion, but both your business attire and casual wear must be of excellent quality. Following the American propensity to slip into a sweatshirt and a pair of faded jeans on your day off will get you nowhere with the typical Asian businessperson.

THE SPOUSE

In Japan, China, and Korea, you will seldom have the opportunity to meet your associate's wife. In general, wives in those countries do not participate in the social activities that accompany business. In Taiwan, Singapore, and Hong Kong you will have more occasion to meet your associate's wife socially. It is important to make a good impression. It has been my experience that an Asian wife may not make an effort to help your prospects with her husband even if you make an excellent impression, but she certainly will ruin your chances if she takes a dislike to you. Address her with courtesy and dignity, even if her husband does not. Never, never compliment her on her beauty or her femininity. A Westerner simply will not understand the subtleties involved in doing this without risking grave offense. Flirting is deeply offensive to an Asian woman. She considers that it makes her an object of amusement and entertainment among men and often considers it tantamount to rape.

THE PROTOCOL OF INTRODUCTIONS

Making introductions has never been taken lightly in Asia. In feudal Japan, a man who performed an introduction was thereafter responsible for the actions of the man he introduced. It was common that a man would pay with his life and the lives of his family for the misconduct of someone he had introduced.

You will forever be marked by the man who performs your introductions in Asia. If he is known and respected by those you meet, you will share in his good reputation. If he is poorly regarded, so will you be. Spend all the time you need and all the money it takes to ensure that your business introductions are handled by the best person. Make sure that he not only knows well the people he is going to introduce you to, but that they also know and respect him.

The Chinese and Koreans have no particular ceremony for introductions and the exchange of business cards. In Japan, however, there is a proper way to do so. Cards are not offered until after the introduction has been made. Parties will be introduced in order of rank, the most distinguished first. The visiting party should be first to present his card. It should be presented so that the print is right side up and facing the person to whom it is presented. If you wish to express great respect, present your card with two hands. In any case, when a card is presented to you, you should accept it with both hands and take a few moments to read it.

Don't bow unless you understand how and when to bow. Instead, simply shake hands in the Western manner. It is perfectly acceptable to do so.

Bowing is most common in Japan, where it is a gesture of mutual respect. If you are going to bow, you should take a moment to compose yourself into an inward mental state of respect for the person to whom you are bowing. Without a sincere feeling of respect, bowing is an obvious and empty gesture. Who bows first and who bows lower, how many moments elapse between the first party's bow and that of the second, how much lower one party bows than the other; all these things have a subtle significance and place the parties in the proper relationship to one another. It requires an intuitive grasp of the culture that is belied by so simple and short a gesture. Cards are exchanged at the first meeting before bowing. In that way the relative rank of the parties can be established. The junior or lower-ranking party will then decline his head and bow from the waist, hands at his sides. The elder or higher-ranking party will return the bow courteously but not so deeply. The Japanese are alternately offended and amused by Westerners bowing to them Indian-style with hands placed together at the chest in a prayer-like attitude.

Elsewhere in Asia, bowing is not such an important gesture. In China, it is most commonly seen on formal or ceremonial occasions, and among schoolchildren. In social intercourse, a bow is little more than a nod of the head and a slight inclination of the body with the hands held at the sides.

■ THE SEQUENCE OF NAMES

Asian names often puzzle Westerners. The Chinese, Japanese, and Koreans all place the family name first. However, when the name is translated into English, the Japanese, Koreans, Taiwanese, and Hong Kong Chinese most often place the family name last according to Western custom. In China, however, even in translation, the family name remains first. When in doubt, just ask. Asians often have the same difficulty in understanding the order of Western names.

As a form of address, the family name should always be used. The given name is reserved for family members and intimate acquaintances. One notable exception is when an elder of unquestionable superior rank addresses you by your given name as a mark of special favor or affection.

In Japan, you should address Mr. Tanaka as Tanaka San. In China, Taiwan, or Korea, Mr. Lin, Mr. Chen, or Mr. Kim are perfectly acceptable forms of address.

■ THE PRIVILEGES OF RANK

Coming as they do from an essentially classless society, it is difficult for Americans to remember that rank is of utmost importance in Asian society. Especially in Japan, you must overcome your egalitarian sensibilities and give rank its due. You will deeply offend a senior executive if you show the same respect and attention to a young junior executive that you do to him. It is not enough to show him great respect, you must show him more respect than you show to a person of lesser rank.

Age also requires your deference. Pay special attention to the elders. The Japanese especially will judge your character by the way you treat your elders.

■ GIFT-GIVING

The giving of gifts can give rise to problems if one is ignorant of local customs. Remember the example of the American farmer who, unaware that it was the traditional mark of a cuckold, placed a green hat on the head of a visiting Chinese official, right in front of, and very much to the amusement of, his traveling companions.

In February 1989, former U.S. Ambassador to China George Bush returned to China as the President of the United States. He gave a gift to Premier Li, a pair of genuine Texas-made cowboy boots with the flag of the United States worked into the leather of one boot and the flag of China worked into the other. Li was not at all pleased, and the Chinese people were mildly shocked. In Chinese thought, the feet are the lowest and one of the most unclean areas of the body. To suggest that Li Peng might wear either the flag of China or the United States on his feet was in very bad taste.

The Japanese appreciate a beautifully wrapped gift. The Chinese and Koreans don't care that much. Often they laugh about the wrapping being more expensive than the gift.

There are two kinds of gifts. In the first group are items that are selected because they express some connection with you, your company, your home state, or country. They convey your good wishes in a personal manner. They can be items made by yourself or your company, or a product or craft associated with your city or region, or something uniquely American like American Indian art. In the second are status items: a Cartier or Tiffany pen set, a designer belt, wallet, or handbag.

I do not think it is effective to give status items to the mainland Chinese because they do not understand the value of such items. They much prefer something more practical. Good-quality felt-tip pens are ideal for calligraphy. A few of them printed with your company logo amount to only a fraction of the cost of a Cartier desk set. A mainland Chinese person probably does not know how to value a thousand-dollar pen set properly. Unless you leave the price tag on, the generosity of your gift will be lost on him. If he does understand the cost, the effect may not be what you anticipate.

A Chinese associate told me of a doll an American businessman had given to his daughter. When he discovered that the doll had cost $250, he did not feel a sudden burst of goodwill for the man's generosity. He was appalled that money that could have been used to buy something of much more use to him was spent on a child's toy.

Inexpensive digital watches make good gifts in China, but you may have a problem getting a dozen of them through customs. Many Chinese also appreciate foreign cigarettes or liquor. They are status symbols that are widely recognized.

The value of a gift must maintain some relationship to the value of your business relationship. If it is too little, you will offend the recipient. If it is too much, it could look like a bribe.

■ | **TABLE MANNERS**

Few things are more deeply ingrained than our customs at the dinner table. Even the most broadminded person has difficulty suppressing an emotional reaction of strong distaste for someone who violates the particular taboos of his culture. It is important to act well-bred according to local standards in this regard.

Learn to use chopsticks. If you go to Asia at the head of a UN delegation charged with giving money away, you will be able to successfully prosecute your business without being able to use chopsticks. If your business in Asia is anything other than giving money away, you will be severely handicapped unless you can eat with chopsticks.

It is only in China that everyone eats from a common plate. And even in China, at banquets and on more formal occasions, the food will be distributed into individual dishes by a server.

If you wish to serve food to another and there are no special serving tools, turn your chopsticks around and handle the food with the unused end.

The Chinese and Japanese pick up the rice bowl and scoop the rice into the mouth. Koreans leave the rice bowl on the table and lift the food to the mouth with chopsticks or a spoon. Koreans consider it extremely ill-bred to pick up the bowl.

Dropping a chopstick is a lucky omen. It means you will be invited back for another meal.

Asians slurp soup quite noisily and suck in noodles in a way that is disconcerting to well-bred Westerners. Try not to notice.

There are no table manners to speak of in China. To the majority of the Chinese people it has never occurred that there might be a right and wrong way to eat. I have eaten many times with otherwise mannerly and well-bred people who spit chicken bones between their feet.

Do not leave your chopsticks stuck vertically into the food in your bowl in such a way that they resemble sticks of incense. In the ceremony to honor the dead, many Asians offer food to their deceased ancestors by placing incense in the bowl and burning it as a way to carry the food to the other world. It is a common Asian superstition that to place your chopsticks in such a way is bad luck and means that this meal is for the dead rather than the living.

The acceptance of invitations is not as simple as it might seem. A Japanese-American woman I know recently moved to Tokyo when her American husband was transferred there. One morning she met a neighbor woman while they were both carrying trash out to the street. They spoke a few polite words and the neighbor invited her to come in for tea. She accepted. The next day the neighborhood was abuzz with the story of the ill-mannered American woman who had accepted an invitation for tea after she had been asked only once. In Japan, it is considered impolite not to offer an invitation, but it is even more impolite to accept an invitation that has not been extended at least three times.

The protocols involved in seating arrangements are so complex that they are handled most simply by waiting for your host to seat you. Sometimes the order and placement of seating is important, sometimes it is not. Placement varies according to the size and shape of the table, the kind of room it is in, the nature of the occasion.

An important issue whenever you dine out is who picks up the tab. In a banquet situation, it is always very clear who is the host. However, during more casual meals, it is sometimes not so clear. As a general rule, the seller should pay the bill. Among friends, someone who really wants to pay the bill goes quietly to the cashier before the meal is over and simply pays it before anyone has the opportunity to wrestle him for the bill. Those who really don't want to pay the bill fight loudly for the right to pay the bill after the meal is over, each one hoping that the other will prevail.

■ SOCIAL LIFE

When dealing with Asians, you must not segregate your business and social life. Most Asian firms are looking for American firms to do business with over the long term. They are sizing you up as people they would like to play with as well as work with. Play golf, play tennis, and dine with your Asian business associates. Some other company doubtless has a product or service similar to yours, but are they as charming, engaging, and delightful as you?

Asians love to drink, and as a rule they can hold their liquor. But if you do not wish to drink, you may simply tell them so. It will not offend them. You may also just quietly fill your wine glass with tea. That way you do not even have to bring the subject up. If you are caught in your little charade, everyone will have a good laugh and no offense will be taken. You may also plead an allergic reaction to alcohol. Although uncommon among Westerners, it is a relatively common allergy among Asians. Your companies won't think to question it.

Anywhere in Asia except mainland China, you are likely to be taken to a Kara Oke club. This is an innovation of the Japanese that has become popular throughout most of Asia. *Kara* means empty in Japanese. *Oke* means bathtub. The reference is to the universal human propensity to sing in the bathtub. The Japanese simply emptied the tub, electronically provided the instrumental accompaniment for the popular songs of the day, and put the whole thing in the middle of a nightclub where people could come to drink and sing. If you find yourself in such a club, you must not refuse when it comes your turn to sing. You will be thought of as a spoilsport.

■ SPECIAL ETIQUETTE FOR MAINLAND CHINA

Because the People's Republic is a totalitarian, Communist state perched on top of the world's oldest and largest bureaucracy, there are certain considerations about doing business there that apply nowhere else in Asia, or in the world for that matter. Persistence and patience are absolutely necessary virtues for anyone conducting business with the Chinese. It is a slow, grinding process.

Beware of middle management, especially those who are Communist Party members. Quite often they are relics of the Cultural Revolution, old Maoists whose sole purpose in life is to assert their own importance and to keep anything useful from getting done. Don't get bogged down in negotiations with these people. Get to the top men as quickly and directly as you can.

It is easy to assume that the various bureaus and ministries have roughly the same interests in relation to you. They are all on one side of the negotiation and you are on the other. But that is often not the case. Often you will find that you, as the Western expert, will be used to support one side or another in a factional dispute. The Chinese tend to place greater faith in the expertise of Western businessmen than in their own staffs. Anytime that you can enhance your Chinese associate's position in the eyes of his peers, you should do so. He will be very likely to reciprocate by moving your business forward.

In China, there is only one employer, the government. To fall out of favor by having some project that is under your authority go badly is a very serious matter. Fear always accompanies responsibility. Anytime you can lessen your Chinese associate's burden of fear by taking some of the responsibility off his shoulders, he will be in your debt.

The motivating force behind an official in a socialist bureaucracy and the motivation for an entrepreneur in a capitalist economy are entirely different. You must make sure you understand what your Chinese associate wants from you. A Taiwanese entrepreneur wants to make money. A Chinese official may want to conclude an advantageous agreement that will give him prestige and perhaps advancement in the party. But he may simply want four years at Stanford for his oldest son.

When the Chinese talk about joint venture, they don't mean it. What they mean is that they want Western capital and expertise to build, for example, a truck plant. Once it is built, they want the Westerners to go home. Western firms assume, because the Chinese need them to run the plant efficiently, that their interests are protected. But it is an article of faith with the Chinese leadership that an all-Chinese truck plant of questionable efficiency is preferable to a joint-venture truck plant that builds trucks that actually work. David Chen, a consultant who oversees many of their Chinese operations for Nike International, refers to this common misunderstanding between the parties by referring to a Chinese maxim, "Sleeping in the same bed, but dreaming different dreams."

A Western firm undertaking a joint venture in China must be very careful that the opportunity for success is there in the first place, and that it is not later forfeited by giving over control of the project to the Chinese.

Because of their acute lack of capital, the Chinese are very price-conscious. They are always looking for ways to defer expenditures. Often they are willing to trade off price for favorable terms. A Western enterprise that is able to offer long-term financing for its product or service can do very well in China.

In China, time is not money. Time is time; money is money. Shuen Xiao Lieng, a Chinese-American filmmaker who recently returned to the United States after filming in China, remarked that a film that took three months to film in the States would take over a year in China. Time is free, but film has to be paid for. Every scene must be rehearsed until it is perfect, then it is filmed in one take.

In negotiating a project, it is necessary to go to the top. In executing a project, it is necessary to go to the bottom. You must gain the confidence and cooperation of production personnel, supervisors, and low-level management. China is a highly conformist society, but there are many who are eager to be individualistic and creative. If you have an organization employing Chinese in China, look for these kinds of people and encourage them with the proper incentives. You will be amazed at the eagerness and loyalty with which they respond.

17

Paper Tiger or Sleeping Lion?

America is in deep economic trouble. With $200-billion annual budget deficits, she has been borrowing against her own future, and the time of payment is rapidly approaching. Her heavy industries are working with outdated technology, yet there is no capital-formation plan to rebuild and retool the steel industry. Capital instead is used to manipulate paper, to finance takeovers, to speculate in currency fluctuations. Although America is still the center of technological innovation, America's high-tech industries cannot compete either in price or quality with Asian manufacturers.

It does not take an advanced degree in economics or a book full of charts and graphs to figure out what has happened. Blessed with a land of abundance and an intellectual climate that promoted the free exchange of ideas, eager immigrants to this new land created a standard of living never before achieved in the history of this planet. Over the course of two centuries, generations of Americans came to see this ease and luxury as the natural state of things. They forgot the factors that had brought it about: energy, enthusiasm, and hard work. They began to care only for the fruits of this abundance and forgot the process that created it. In short, Americans became lazy and greedy.

At the end of World War II, a half-billion hungry and war-ravaged Asians set about earning the wherewithal to stay alive. Because their need was great, they attended to business with great application and energy. Because the people of each Asian nation had experienced such horror and deprivation together, they developed a strong sense of common purpose. When they rebuilt their shattered industries, they rebuilt them with modern technology.

At the end of World War II, flushed with success and possessed of a sense that they were indomitable, Americans sat down to watch television or went to play a few holes of golf, heedless of the little novelties and trinkets from Asia that were showing up in their daily lives. Meanwhile, Asians began to build the television sets the Americans watched and manufacture the golf clubs they used. Before the Americans knew it, the trickle of Asian goods had grown to a flood. Their own industries had been crippled by the unfair practices of Asian government and industry in collusion to dominate the richest market in the world. They found that they had been borrowing money to pay for the things that they had always taken for granted. They found that they had been borrowing a lot of money.

But Americans are far too willing to concede victory to the emerging Asian economic powers. Although the Japanese boast of their superiority and assert their claim to economic preeminence, a strong undercurrent of uncertainty runs through their boasting. Like most Asians, the Japanese see the United States as a sleeping lion. Their greatest fear is that the lion will awake and assert its awesome strength.

Akio Morita, Sony's CEO, has attributed America's inability to compete to greed and shortsightedness. He implies that America is a culture in decline, without the energy or will to produce, seeking only to manipulate wealth in order to gather more wealth. According to his assessment, it would seem unlikely that the United States could ever regain its position of world leadership.

I believe differently. I believe that the economic problems of the United States with respect to an industrialized Asia result from the open and ingenuous manner with which we have undertaken business relationships with the more subtle and often disingenuous Asians. We have simply given away the store.

I was sitting in a friend's living room recently on a stormy winter evening. She lives in a new home on a new street in a pleasant suburb. A bitter cold wind was howling outside. Inside it was warm and comfortable. Her children were playing on the stairs in their pajamas. The five-year-old was sliding down the banister. The seven-year-old was bumping down the thickly carpeted steps on her bottom. Playing there in comfort and safety, those sweet children had no thought that life could be much different from this. They had never been very hungry, nor had they ever slept in the rain.

I had a sudden moment of clarity. In those children I found the answer to the question I had been pondering. Their childhood was so different from my childhood in Taiwan, so different from the experience of a billion Asian children. How could these happy, trusting children ever grow up to understand the mortal seriousness of success and failure as it is understood in Asia? I saw the answer to the riddle that had puzzled me and puzzles many Asians: Americans are not fools, but why is it so easy to get the better of them in business transactions? The answer is that they pick up their habits of thought in a world where there is enough for everyone. In a land of plenty such as ours, honesty, fair play, and generosity are more highly valued than the skill to wring every advantage out of every transaction. Asians, for the most part, were educated in a school where such ethical luxuries had no place.

Because of their great wealth and strength, Americans often do not feel their national survival threatened. For that reason, they are not always alert to danger. Once attacked, however, they have always responded much like a sleeping lion. They awake to surprise, momentary confusion, and then anger. The Japanese seriously misjudged the Americans once before and found out how terrible that anger can be. The possibility that they might have again underestimated America is very much on their minds.

A career American army officer who had been decorated for heroism during the Vietnam War once told me, "Americans don't want to be soldiers. Even when they are in the military they seem to lack discipline and order. In times of peace, the American military seems completely unprepared to respond to an attack. Once a threat is perceived, however, we have always responded with a surprising effectiveness.

"That is why national defense must focus so strongly on preparation, readiness. In today's world, we can no longer afford to be taken by surprise."

The greatest weakness Americans have in the international marketplace is that they are not aware they are in a war. Because they have never been dominated, they do not perceive the dire consequences of coming under the economic domination of another nation. Asians know that "the marketplace is a battlefield." To the Americans, it is more like a football game.

Each year we spend billions of dollars for military hardware to protect this nation. We are not so naive as to believe that every nation in the world has our best interests at heart. Yet we exhibit no preparation for the economic attacks of other nations. War is a visual, graphic experience. Images of war excite strong emotions. On the other hand, balance of payments, foreign ownership of natural resources, Japanese acquisition of a major media conglom-erate—these are dry subjects. They do not conjure up the same sense of danger as news footage of American sailors leaping from the burning deck of the U.S.S. *Arizona* into the burning sea.

The economic conquest of America is not inevitable. America must simply come to understand the seriousness of the struggle. Pearl Harbor forged a national will and a fierce resolution to do what was necessary to win. But there will be no economic Pearl Harbor to unify and mobilize public opinion. The decisions that must be made are hard ones and politically impossible unless there is a widespread sense of clear and present danger. But, given a national will to victory, America can win the economic war.

The forging of this national will is what the Japanese most fear. Reacting to the increasing sense of American public concern over Japanese inroads into the U.S. domestic economy, in early 1990 the Japanese government hurriedly formulated a plan to disarm that concern. The government very strongly encouraged companies do-ing business in the United States to become "good citizens." The government now provides very attractive tax incentives for Japanese companies to contribute to local charities and civic projects in the American cities in which they are located. This, of course, did not come out of some sudden humanitarian motivation. It is simply a strategy to rock the restless lion back into his dream of ease and abundance.

■ | ## THE POWER FROM WITHIN

> The plan of Heaven is more certain than the plans of men.
>
> —*Chinese proverb*

A little knowledge is a dangerous thing. You have learned something of the Asian mind: how it strategizes, how it calculates its plans. You have noted examples of the many formalized strategies that have been studied in Asia for centuries. But you have not learned enough yet to be adept at the practice of these strategies, especially in negotiations with Asians who have been bred to them. You must proceed with extreme caution in attempting to use what you have learned or your efforts could result in more damage to you than benefit.

The Chinese all say that they study *The 36 Strategies* not to practice deception on others, but to protect themselves from the deceptions of others. It is apparent, however, that someone must be practicing to deceive or there would be no need for protection. But for a Westerner who has learned what he knows about Asian strategizing from this book, a passive posture is perhaps best. Use your new knowledge to recognize the strategies you will encounter. The safest course is to play dumb. If you do not not let it be known that you know such a thing as *The 36 Strategies* exists, your Asian associates will not spend a great deal of time in disguising their strategies. If they suspect your knowledge, they will make their plans more intricate and impenetrable.

In the application of this knowledge, cultivate and trust your intuition. The knowledge of the mind is clumsy and literal. The knowledge that flows from within is subtle and sensitive to the nuances of each individual situation.

> Something existed
> Before the creation of Heaven and Earth.
> In the silence and the void,
> Ever alone and changeless,
> She prevails over all.
> Conceive Her as the mother of the universe.
> I know not Her name,
> And call Her, Tao.
>> —Lao Tzu, *Tao Te Ching*

Index

Jealousy, 195
Joint ventures, 57, 256
Judgmental, Chinese tendency to be, 198
Judgment of right and wrong, 123

K

Kamikaze program, 164
Kanagawa, Treaty of, 88–89
Kao-Zu, 27
Kara Oke club, 254–55
Karma, 114
Keiko, Emperor, 119
Keiretsu, 93
King Wu, 25
Kissinger, Henry, 17, 146
Koito, acquisition of, 93–94
Kojiki (Record of Ancient Matters), 118
Korea
 bureaucratic corruption in, 226
 Chinese territorial claims on, 174
 class system of, 228–29
 culture in, 221
 economy of, 225–26
 industrialization of, 225
 influence of China on, 228–29
 influence of Confucianism on, 229
 influence of Japan in, 230–32
 and loyalty, 245
 opening of Olympic games in, 223
 people of, 227–28
 postwar, 223–24
 sequence of names in, 251
 social and political instability in, 226–27
 table manners in, 253
 urbanization of, 227
Koreans
 animosities between Japanese and, 183–84
 common characteristics of, 232–33
 competitiveness of, 233
 emotionalism of, 232–33
Korean society, influence of China's philosophy on, 181–83
Korean War, 51, 224
Kuan-Xie, 199–200
Kung Min, 13, 59, 71–72
Kunitokotachi, 118

L

Labor-management relations
 in Japan, 95, 122
 in U.S., 24–25
Language
 attempting to learn, 245
 barriers in, 159–61
Lao Tzu, 14, 36, 37, 157, 177, 261
Laxman, Adam, 87
Le, 61
Leadership, 24–25
Lee, S. W., 77
Li, 57
Liabilities, destruction of, 68–69
Liberia, 212
Lin Yu-tang, 156–57
Li Peng, 81–82
Liu Bang, 56, 69
Liu Bei, 13, 79–80
Liu Shaoqi, 207
Li Yuan, 30–31
Local culture, respecting, 245–46
Local guides, use of, 37
Long-term objectives, developing, 243–44
Loyalty
 in Japan, 244–45
 in Korea, 245
 in Taiwan, 245
 of Samurai, 95, 122
Lu Bu, 74–75
Lu Bu Wei, 15

M

MacArthur, Douglas, 224
Macartney, Lord, 165
Made in Japan (Morita) *See also* Morita, Akio, 136
Mao Zedong, 204, 210
 as master of Zheng Ren, 207–8
Marketplace, as battlefield, 12
Medicine, domains of, 80–81
Meetings, host advantages of, in controlling, 62
Meiji, Emperor, 90, 96–97, 104
Meng Tzu, 14
Middle path, 181
Mi Lai massacre, 111
Military strategy, as business practice, 12

About the Author

CHIN-NING CHU is President of Asian Marketing Consultants, Inc. She is an international lecturer and consultant and also hosts a radio talk show, "The Art of Winning."

Ms. Chu was born in Tienjin, near Beijing, and raised in Taiwan after the fall of mainland China to the Communists. She entered a Catholic convent during her high school years in preparation for a a monastic life. At seventeen she was removed from the convent by her father and thrust into the world of higher education.

Chin-ning Chu's career in international marketing began at the age of nineteen, when she juggled a full schedule of college classes with the marketing responsibility for a government-owned pharmaceutical company. After her marketing efforts proved astronomically successful, she was approached by two European pharmaceutical companies to promote their products in Taiwan. Her successes came in the midst of widespread unemployment and in spite of a tradition that prohibited students from holding jobs.

Although Ms. Chu was a student of Catholicism from a very early age, she later expanded her spiritual horizons to include traditional Chinese philosophies, Zen Buddhism, and study of the ancient Hindu scriptures. She has traveled extensively and studied the teachings of sages in India, China, and Europe. Ms. Chu's study of philosophy and psychology has provided her with a powerful tool for examining the complexities of philosophical, sociological, and historical influences on the shaping of the modern Asian mind.